**THE
UNSUSPECTED
REVOLUTION**

Castro talks to his guerrillas in the Sierra Maestra, 1957.

# THE UNSUSPECTED REVOLUTION

## The Birth and Rise of Castroism

## MARIO LLERENA

**CORNELL UNIVERSITY PRESS**
ITHACA AND LONDON

First published 1978 by Cornell University Press.
Published in the United Kingdom by
Cornell University Press Ltd.,
2–4 Brook Street, London W1Y 1AA.

International Standard Book Number 0-8014-1094-0
Library of Congress Catalog Card Number 77-3119
Printed in the United States of America by
Vail-Ballou Press, Inc.
*Librarians: Library of Congress cataloging information appears on the last page of the book.*

**To all Cubans who have died in the pursuit
or the defense of liberty**

# Contents

# Illustrations

# Foreword

The Cuban revolution is in some ways one of the most puzzling events of the Americas in this century. A radical social revolution occurred in a country which was, by most criteria, one of the richest ones of Latin America. A Marxist regime was established largely, it would seem, because of the will of a single man, and he a most untypical Marxist at that. A civil war was won against a large army by a small group of amateurs. A regime which promised a utopia of milk and honey has persisted for many years in material conditions which would have seemed, and have seemed, parlous even in comparison with those of central Europe during the Second World War. The United States, the richest country in the world, has been successfully defied by a small island whose standard of living has, if anything, fallen in the last ten years. A government has been established which for nearly twenty years has based its appeal on spontaneity, improvisation, and experiment—none of which would usually seem to be lasting commodities.

Scholars and observers of this curious phenomenon must welcome any new contribution which helps to throw light on these events. The present memoir written by Mario Llerena is very definitely a major contribution of this sort. For the author was an outstanding member of that generation of Cubans which, coming from the influential Cuban middle class, made immense sacrifices in an attempt to improve the political life of their country in the 1950s.

Llerena, like many others, eventually became associated with Fidel Castro's movement, not without misgivings and not without experiences in other would-be reform groups. For a time he played an important role with this movement, both as its ambassador abroad—a particularly significant position because of the importance of public relations for the movement—and as an ideologue. He left it before its victory, having already begun to see how his own eminently liberal and generous hopes were threatened in so dogmatic an organization. Llerena is therefore a specially effective witness.

I was fortunate enough to read an early version of this book a few years ago, when I was preparing my own study of modern Cuban history (*Cuba: The Pursuit of Freedom*). Dr. Llerena's study struck me then as an exceptionally clear and honest account of these strange events. Though he naturally views what has happened in Cuba from a personal angle, his private interpretation has the advantage of a universal understanding. His portraits of revolutionary leaders—some, like Faustino Pérez, still powerful in Cuba; others, like Enrique Oltusky, of minor significance—are vivid and original. Some of the events described are particularly striking. I especially remember Dr. Llerena's account of his meeting with Castro in Mexico City.

When I had the opportunity of reading this new version of the book, I was delighted to find that my earlier impressions were in no way false. I was pleased, too, to find that the narrative has a compulsively readable character, so that the whole book races along almost like an adventure story. I have no doubt that future historians of Cuba will turn to Mario Llerena's lucid and penetrating account as a first-class source on the revolutionary years of the 1950s. They will find, as I did to my pleasure, that he is not only a good witness but also an admirable writer capable of making events live.

HUGH THOMAS

*London*

# Preface

I joined the organization of Fidel Castro in June 1956 in Cuba and left it in August 1958 in the United States. The story of my experience as the 26 of July Movement's appointed representative abroad during this time, brief as it was, may contribute in some measure to a clearer understanding of the phenomenon known today as the Cuban revolution, and show how it was possible for an originally middle-class reform movement to be transformed by an unprincipled, charismatic leader and a handful of close associates into a full-fledged Marxist-Leninist revolution.

My story will also serve to illustrate, I believe, the unpremeditated yet perhaps decisive role played by nonradical liberals, especially intellectuals, in the formation and development of this radical revolutionary movement, and show how time and accomplished facts awakened them too late to the realities of a revolution quite different from the one they had envisioned.

My disillusionment with the Castro organization began early in 1958. As my dissatisfaction grew, the idea of this book was born. In addition to the events and situations in which I had participated or which I had witnessed, the mass of correspondence with the Cuban leaders and other documents in my possession—I made a practice of keeping everything I received and a copy of everything I wrote—seemed to invite the attempt.

It was not until 1962, however—two years after I

had come back to the United States, once again an exile—that an unexpected stimulus impelled me to set about the actual work. In New York I made the acquaintance of Theodore Draper, then working on his excellent book *Castroism: Theory and Practice* (1965), and let him have access to my papers. Draper's reaction was most favorable: he not only assured me of the documentary value of the material but encouraged me to arrange it in manuscript form and submit it to the Hoover Institution at Stanford University, California, for its reference library. The Hoover Institution was indeed interested and provided the necessary aid for the project. The result was the earlier, unpublished version of the present book, now in the Hoover library, which was later generously cited and quoted by Hugh Thomas in his *Cuba: The Pursuit of Freedom* (1971). For all their help and encouragement then, I have remained deeply grateful to both Theodore Draper and the Hoover Institution.

This new version, of course based on the same material, is essentially much like the first. It differs, however, in a few respects: it not only has been written with a different stylistic approach but contains documents and data that I had not included before—for instance, excerpts from the letters of Hilda Gadea, the first wife of Che Guevara (Chapter 10). I have also cut considerably the quotations from my own letters and reports to Castro and the other leaders of the organization in Cuba and have used theirs more extensively, on the assumption that the reader will be more interested in their words than in mine. Finally, the previous version, conceived primarily for reference rather than for a wide audience, was almost wholly documentary; this one gives more attention to the contexts of the words and events with which I am concerned. The sources for this book are exclusively my own collection of papers and my personal participation in practically all the events and situations recorded. Although I have maintained a narrative sequence in the presentation of views and facts, I have not in any instance knowingly permitted my imagination to slip in and interfere—everything is presented precisely as I recall it. Corroboration and additional relevant information are provided in the notes at the end of the volume.

All documents cited in the text—original letters and communications from Castro and other 26 of July Movement leaders in Cuba, copies of my own communications to them, press releases, and others—are in my possession. When translations from the Spanish have been necessary, I have provided them.

For reading the manuscript and for his kind comments, and of course for writing the Foreword, my deep gratitude goes to Hugh Thomas.

My thanks also to Jaime Suchlicki, of the Department of History at the University of Miami, for valuable suggestions.

M. Ll.

*Miami*

# Chronology of the Cuban Revolution

*The Moderate Phase*

1930–1933     President Gerardo Machado becomes dictatorial, and popular protest erupts: students take to the streets, revolutionary organizations proliferate, terrorist acts and political assassinations are frequent; the 1930 Generation comes into being.

12 August 1933     Influenced by events and popular pressure, the army forces Machado out of office and out of the country. He later dies in exile.

4 September 1933     Sergeant Fulgencio Batista, backed by liberals proclaiming an "authentic" revolution, leads army revolt that topples the provisional government of Carlos Manuel de Céspedes, son of a national hero of the same name.

10 September 1933     The Pentarquía—a five-man revolutionary directorate established after Batista's coup—is dissolved under pressure from Washington, and university professor Ramón Grau San Martín, one of its members, is named provisional president.

16 January 1934     Batista, apparently at the urging of U.S. Ambassador Jefferson Caffery, forces Grau's resignation. Engineer (Annapolis) Carlos Hevia is named in his place but survives in office less than twenty-four hours.

1934–1939     Batista becomes the undisputed center of power and, as head of the armed forces, rules supreme through several successive puppet presidencies. Throughout this period he has the support of the Communists, whom he rewards with political status and government favors.

15 November 1939     Elections for a constituent assembly are finally held and result in a resounding victory for the opposition, especially the Auténtico party. The assembly drafts the liberal 1940 Constitution.

1 June 1940     General elections are held under the new constitution. Batista, who had resigned as chief of the armed forces to become the candidate of a political coalition that included the Communists, is elected president.

1 June 1944     Democracy seems to be functioning. General elections

are held at the conclusion of Batista's term. As re-election is forbidden by the Constitution, the government coalition nominates Batista's friend Carlos Saladrigas. But Grau San Martín, the Auténtico candidate, wins the election. This marks the end of the first Batista era.

1944–1952        The Auténtico era begins. Grau San Martín takes office amid strong popular support and high expectations. Soon, however, the initial enthusiasm gives way to widespread, bitter disappointment. While respectful of democracy and in many ways constructive, the Auténticos, with Grau's obvious blessing, embark on an orgy of unprecedented corruption and scandal.

15 May 1947        Eduardo Chibás, for many years a staunch supporter of Grau, leads the protest within the Auténtico party and founds the Ortodoxo party. The name deliberately implies true representation of the original Auténtico ideals, allegedly betrayed by Grau and his chosen successor, Carlos Prío-Socarrás.

1 June 1948        Prío-Socarrás, the government candidate, is elected president. The evils of the Grau period abate somewhat, but the Ortodoxo opposition continues, more loud and intransigent than ever.

5 August 1951        Following a face-losing public argument with Minister of Education Aureliano Sánchez Arango, Chibás dramatically shoots himself at the end of a radio speech and dies ten days later. His death causes tremendous public commotion.

1951–1952        A heated political campaign for the 1952 general election follows Chibás's death. The Ortodoxos nominate university professor Roberto Agramonte, honest and prestigious intellectual but colorless and uninspiring as a leader. The Auténticos nominate Carlos Hevia, equally honest and colorless. Batista returns from exile in Florida and is nominated by a third political coalition. All public opinion polls give Agramonte a slight edge over Hevia; Batista runs a poor third.

*The Radical Phase*

10 March 1052        Realizing he cannot win the election, Batista conspires with friends in the armed forces and stages his second military coup d'état. The country is taken by surprise and there is almost no open resistance. The second Batista era begins.

1952–1959        Batista's seizure of power starts a period similar in many respects to the post-Machado years of the 1930s: increasing popular discontent, failure of existing political parties, emergence of new revolutionary organizations (Movimiento Nacional Revolucionario, Movimiento de Liberación Radical, Directorio Revolucionario, Organización Auténtica, Castro's 26 of July) issuing manifestos and programs, armed attempts against military posts, political assassinations, terrorism, rigged elections, puppet presidents.

11 April 1953    Rafael García Bárcena makes unsuccessful attempt to take Campamento de Columbia, army headquarters and citadel of Batista's power. The misadventure marks the public decline of both the MNR and García Bárcena.

26 July 1953    Fidel Castro leads a bloody and ultimately unsuccessful attack against the Moncada military barracks in Santiago de Cuba. Castro and others are taken prisoner.

16 October 1953    Castro is sentenced to fifteen years in prison (others receive lesser sentences). During the trial, speaking in his own defense, Castro makes his famous speech "History Will Absolve Me."

13 May 1955    Castro and the other *moncadistas* are released in a special amnesty.

19 July 1955    Castro leaves Cuba for Mexico, vowing that "in 1956 we shall be free or we shall be martyrs."

November 1955    Castro and Che Guevara meet in Mexico; Guevara joins the Castro movement.

25 November 1956    The *Granma* expedition—eighty-two men including Castro—sails for Cuba from Tuxpan, Mexico.

30 November 1956    Frank País, one of Castro's chief lieutenants, leads a nearly successful uprising in Santiago meant to coincide with Castro's landing from Mexico.

2 December 1956    The *Granma* reaches Cuba. The Sierra Maestra guerrilla campaign begins.

24 February 1957    The *New York Times* publishes the first of three articles by correspondent Herbert L. Matthews, who interviewed Castro in the Sierra Maestra. These articles give the Castro revolution immediate international publicity.

13 March 1957    An attack on the presidential palace with intent to kill Bastista is carried out by the Directorio Revolucionario and other organizations (but not the 26 of July); extremely daring and bloody but ultimately unsuccessful.

12 July 1957    Castro issues the Sierra Manifesto, a moderate democratic pledge of political principles and immediate objectives.

July 1957    *Nuestra Razón,* a manifesto written by the author at the request of the Castro organization, is published in Mexico.

5 September 1957    A naval mutiny, secretly supported by the 26 of July Movement, erupts in the port city of Cienfuegos; it fails.

October 1957    A junta of opposition organizations is established in Miami; 26 of July agrees to participate and nominates Judge Manuel Urrutia as provisional president, with the support of the Ortodoxo party. Other organizations favor Felipe Pazos.

30 October 1957      Castro founds the Committee in Exile.

December 1957      In a lengthy angry document Castro denounces the junta's policies and breaks with it.

7–10 March 1958      The Dirección Nacional of the 26 of July Movement meets with Castro for a policy-defining meeting in the Sierra Maestra; a definitely radical course is adopted for the revolution.

April 1958      Judge Urrutia agrees to preside over a future Castro-sponsored revolutionary government.

June 1958      Rebel forces under the command of Raúl Castro seize American properties and abduct American citizens in Oriente Province. The American consul in Santiago enters into negotiations with the rebel command.

July 1958      Communist leader Carlos Rafael Rodríguez meets with Castro in the Sierra Maestra.

October 1958      Rebel forces under the command of Camilo Cienfuegos and Che Guevara reach Las Villas Province, in central Cuba, where the Directorio Revolucionario had also been waging guerrilla warfare.

31 December 1958      Batista flees Cuba.

1 January 1959      A new government headed by Urrutia is established.

16 January 1959      In a speech before Chibás's grave in Havana, Castro denies being a Communist.

17 July 1959      Castro goes on television to denounce President Urrutia after Urrutia repudiates Communists. Urrutia is forced to resign; later seeks diplomatic asylum and goes into exile.

2 December 1961      In a television speech Castro declares himself a Marxist-Leninist.

# Figures of the Castro Movement, 1956–1958

The ages given are approximate, as of the time of the events described in the text.

*Arcos, Gustavo.* Mid-thirties. Apparently left school early and became a shop clerk in Havana. Joined Castro and fought in the Moncada attack in 1953. A wound left him with a permanent limp, which prevented him from accompanying the *Granma* expedition that took Castro from Mexico to Cuba in 1956; was named by Frank País coleader (with Pedro Miret) of the group that remained in Mexico. After Castro's rise to power he was appointed ambassador to Belgium. Seems to have criticized Castro and so fallen into disgrace; has been in a Cuban prison for many years.

*Betancourt, Ernesto.* Early thirties. Holds a degree in business administration. Intelligent, poised, diplomatic. In 1957 became the 26 of July's representative in Washington, apparently with the blessing of the Castro sisters in Mexico; later bowed to the Committee in Exile. Acted as personal adviser to Castro during the latter's visit to Washington in 1959. Cooperated with Felipe Pazos at the National Bank in Havana and is credited with having originated the slogan "Alliance for Progress." When Pazos left the National Bank, Betancourt resigned and later returned to the United States.

*Buch, Luis.* Early forties. A lawyer in Santiago, active in the Civic Resistance Movement and later in the 26 of July in that city. Served as courier between this group and the leaders in exile. Was secretary of the cabinet in the Urrutia government; later fell into disfavor and into obscurity.

*Castro, Emma.* Early twenties. Sister of Fidel. In the late 1950s lived with her half sister Lidia and younger sister Angela at the Gutiérrez home in Mexico City; very active with Lidia in promoting their brother's revolutionary pursuits. It has been said that she did not agree with the radical turn of the revolution. After Fidel came to power she again left Cuba, married abroad, and today leads a totally private life.

*Castro, Fidel.* Born in 1927 in Birán, a village in Oriente Province. Studied law. During his student years belonged to subversive groups and participated in numerous acts of violence; later joined the Ortodoxo party and was a candidate for Congress. In 1948 married Mirta Díaz Balart (they had a son, also named Fidel); the same year went to Colombia and became involved in the bloody *bogotazo.* In 1953 organized the unsuccessful attack against the Moncada barracks in Santiago; was sent to prison but freed in a special amnesty one year later. Divorced in 1954; has not remarried. In 1955 went to Mexico and there organized the *Granma* expedition and subsequent guerrilla campaign of 1956–1958 in the Sierra Maestra. Entered Havana in triumph in January 1959 and has remained the "maximum leader" of the revolution.

*Castro, Lidia.* Late thirties. Fidel's half sister. Took him into her apartment in Havana when he was released from prison in 1955. During 1957–1959 stayed with her half sisters Emma and Angela at the Gutiérrez home in Mexico City; became the leader of a group known as the Pedregal; with Emma traveled frequently to the United States and several Latin American countries to seek support for the Castro movement. Apparently did not agree with the radical course of the revolution; seems to have disappeared into anonymity.

*Castro, Raúl.* Early twenties. Brother of Fidel. Joined the Communist Youth Movement. Took part in the Moncada episode and was a member of the *Granma* expedition. During the guerrilla campaign of 1956–1958 commanded forces in the Sierra Cristal, in northern Oriente Province; in mid-1958 carried out a spectacular seizure of American property and abduction of American citizens. Married guerrilla fighter Vilma Espín. As one of the hard-core Marxists of the movement, arranged for direct talks between leaders of the Communist party and Fidel in mid-1958. Now vice-secretary of the Communist party, vice–prime minister, and minister of the Revolutionary Armed Forces.

*Casuso, Teresa (Teté).* Early forties. Writer, one-time film actress; active in 1930s student movement. Married Pablo de la Torriente, left-wing intellectual who later fought and died in the Spanish Civil War. Self-exiled in Mexico for many years, Casuso became a friend and protector of Castro. At Batista's fall she led a group that took over the Cuban embassy in Mexico City. After doing public relations work for Castro for a while, became disillusioned with the revolution. Wrote a book, *Cuba and Castro,* about her experience. At present is a magazine writer in the United States.

*Chibás, Raúl.* Early forties. Member of executive council of Ortodoxo party (founded by his brother Eduardo); active in Civic Resistance Movement. In 1957 accompanied Felipe Pazos to the Sierra Maestra to see Castro; there the three issued the Sierra Manifesto. Although nominally an Ortodoxo, Chibás was chosen by Castro as financial secretary of the Committee in Exile. Was one of several leaders who converged on the Sierra Maestra in late 1958; there grew a beard and was commissioned a major. During the Urrutia period seems to have declined the post of finance minister. Member of war council in revolutionary trials of *batistianos,* then director of nationalized Cuban railroads. In time he too became disillusioned with Castro and went into exile in the United States.

*Couzeiro, Manolo.* Late thirties. Surrealist painter, involved in underground activities of the 26 of July in Havana. In exile in 1958, acted controversially among 26 of July groups in New York; advocated making contact with Communist labor groups in Washington, D.C. Surfaced in a minor post in the early Castro government.

*Cuesta, Luis de la.* Early twenties. Student of social sciences, director of cultural activities of FEU (Federation of University Students). Never actually joined the 26 of July Movement; most useful as a behind-the-scenes activist. In the Castro government apparently accepted a minor consular post in Spain; has not been heard of publicly in some time.

*Fernández, Marcelo.* Early twenties. Student of engineering. Became a member of the Dirección Nacional of the 26 of July in the Sierra Maestra. Took a radical course early in 1958 and was influential in the movement. Has been ambassador, assistant secretary of the Foreign Ministry, and president of the National Bank; at present is member of the Central Committee of the Communist party and minister of foreign trade.

*Fernández Ceballos, Raúl.* Late forties. Presbyterian pastor. Early in the revolution became involved with the 26 of July underground group in Havana. Has been instrumental in securing the cooperation of the Cuban Protestant denominations with the radical revolution; has been an outspoken propagandist of the Communist regime and has traveled to the Soviet Union and other Communist countries. Still functions as a Presbyterian minister and holds no official position in the government.

*Franqui, Carlos.* Late thirties. Early a militant Communist, he was a proofreader for the Communist organ *Hoy.* Appears to have broken with the Communists in 1947. Around 1954 he joined the Castro movement and became active in underground operations in Havana. Was arrested in 1957, and upon release later that year went into exile. Secretary of organization in the Committee in Exile. In late 1958 went with others to the Sierra Maestra. At Batista's fall was named editor of the daily *Revolución,* official organ of the revolution (later renamed *Granma*). Apparently dissatisfied with the Castro brand of communism, Franqui left Cuba quietly in 1968 and has since been living in Europe.

*Guevara, Ernesto (Che).* Born the same year as Castro, 1927, in Argentina. Studied medicine but never practiced it, choosing instead an adventurous life of international revolution. Took part in 1954 events in Guatemala; escaped to Mexico, where he joined Castro in preparing for expedition to Cuba. A major in the rebel forces, Guevara became second only to Castro during the guerrilla campaign. In the revolutionary government was president of the National Bank and later minister of industries. Apparently incapable of adjusting himself to a normal civilian life, he left Cuba to take the torch of revolution around the world, especially to Latin America. Killed by the Bolivian army in 1967 while attempting to ignite a guerrilla war in that country.

*Guevara, Hilda Gadea de.* Early thirties. First wife of Che. A Peruvian journalist active in the Apra movement. Met Che in Guatemala, where both were political exiles; they married in Mexico in May 1955. She remained in Mexico when Che went to Cuba with the Castro expedition in 1956. Back in Peru, she was named 26 of July representative in Lima by the Committee in Exile. After Castro assumed power she went to Cuba to join her husband, who divorced her a short time later. Presumed to be still living in Cuba.

*Gutiérrez, Alfonso (Fofo).* Mid-thirties. Wealthy Mexican engineer connected with the national oil industry. Became friend and protector of Castro during his stay in Mexico. Welcomed the Castro sisters into his home, which became headquarters for a 26 of July faction in Mexico City. Went to Cuba after Castro came to power and for a time served in some official capacity as an oil expert; soon resigned and returned to Mexico, apparently in disagreement with the radical character of the revolution.

*Hart, Armando.* Mid-twenties. Lawyer. In 1952 became a follower of Rafael García Bárcena, founder of the MNR. Joined the 26 of July and was active in its underground activities. Became secretary of organization of the Dirección Nacional. Married Haydée Santamaría. Was named minister of education in the Urrutia cabinet, a post he kept long after Urrutia's fall. Not originally a Communist, Hart was named secretary of organization of the Communist party. This position is no longer mentioned in Cuba and Hart appears to hold some party post in Oriente Province.

*Llanusa, José.* Late twenties. Former basketball player with no more than secondary education; entered 26 of July Movement via Civic Resistance Movement while an exile in Miami in 1958; the same year, as protégé of Haydée Santamaría, took Franqui's place as secretary of organization in Committee in Exile. Has occupied a number of posts in the revolutionary government, including director general of sports and minister of education. At present he is a member of the Central Committee of the Communist party and director of the Matanzas Genetic Group, National Institute of Agrarian Reform (INRA).

*Miret, Pedro.* Early thirties. Student of engineering from Santiago. Took part in the Moncada attack and was imprisoned with Castro on the Isle of Pines. Was in Mexico during the pre-*Granma* period and remained there when the Castro expedition left late in 1956; was expected to organize a second expedition, which never materialized. Toward the end of 1958 finally succeeded in reaching the Sierra Maestra with some military equipment. Generally considered second only to Castro at the beginning of the movement, but later faded somewhat. Among other posts he has held are undersecretary of defense and minister of agriculture in the Urrutia cabinet. At present is a member of the Central Committee of the Communist party and vice–prime minister for basic industries.

*Oltusky, Enrique.* Mid-twenties. Engineering graduate of the University of Miami, Florida. An early follower of García Bárcena, he then followed Armando Hart into the 26 of July Movement. Became active in underground operations in Havana; was interested in the ideological literature of the movement. At Batista's fall was designated minister of communications in the Urrutia cabinet. When Castro took an open Communist line, Oltusky was left out of the power hierarchy; his loyalty was in question for a time. Has remained a faithful servant of the regime, however, occupying minor bureaucratic posts.

*País, Frank.* Early twenties. Son of a Baptist minister from Santiago; an elementary teacher and engineering student. In Santiago led his own anti-Batista group, Acción Revolucionaria Oriente, which later merged with the 26 of July. Became a member of the Dirección Nacional. Traveled to Mexico and later to the Sierra Maestra to discuss plans with Castro; against his own judgment—for reasons of timing—masterminded the Santiago uprising of 30 November 1956, which nearly succeeded; thereafter had to live perpetually on the run. On 30 July 1957 Batista henchmen killed him in a Santiago street.

*Pazos, Felipe.* Mid-forties. Economist and public figure since the 1930s. In the 1940s worked with the International Monetary Fund; later appointed president of the newly created National Bank by President Prío. Resigned when Batista seized power in 1952 and thereupon became involved in the anti-Batista struggle. Arranged for the visit of *New York Times* correspondent Herbert Matthews to the Sierra Maestra. In July 1957 he himself visited Castro and was one of the signers of the Sierra Manifesto. Shortly afterward went into exile and with Léster Rodríguez represented the 26 of July in the opposition junta in Miami. Resumed presidency of National Bank when Castro took power. After argument with President Osvaldo Dorticós which nearly cost him his life, Pazos went into exile again. At present works as economist in Washington.

*Pazos, Javier.* Early twenties. Son of Felipe. Joined 26 of July as student and became active in underground. Cooperated for some time with the Castro government but eventually became disillusioned and went into exile.

*Pérez, Faustino.* Early thirties. Physician of Protestant background. Engaged in underground activities while practicing medicine. Early follower of García Bárcena. Went to Mexico and joined the *Granma* expedition. Became a member of the Dirección Nacional and took charge of underground activities throughout Cuba. Was named minister of recovery of stolen property at Batista's fall; subsequently has held various government posts, in descending degrees of importance. At present is a member of the Central Committee of the Communist party.

*Pino, Orquídea.* Late twenties. Cuban wife of Alfonso Gutiérrez. Former night-club singer. Became friend and fervent admirer of Castro during the latter's stay in Mexico. Her beauty and personality made her an effective campaigner for the Castro cause. Her brother Onelio Pino, a former captain in the Cuban navy, was the skipper of the *Granma,* the yacht that took Castro and his men to Cuba in November 1956.

*Roa, Raúl.* Late forties. Writer, professor. Became a Communist in the late 1920s; a leader of the Student Left Wing in the 1930s. Unstable in his ideological commitment, he bitterly denounced the Soviet invasion of Hungary in 1956. Refused to talk with Castro in Mexico and referred to him as a "gangster"; as late as 1959 wrote that the Cuban revolution had its own roots and could not be Marxist. Has been foreign minister of the Castro government for many years; is also a member of the Central Committee of the Communist party.

*Roa, Raúl, Jr. (Raulito).* Early twenties. Studied in Havana, Paris, and New York but apparently never graduated. Remained aloof from 26 of July until late 1957, when he offered to cooperate with the Committee in Exile. Has held several posts in the Castro government, including ambassador to Czechoslovakia and to Brazil; now director of Council on Mutual Economic Assistance (COMECON).

*Rodríguez, Léster.* Early thirties. Student of engineering; veteran of the Moncada attack and the November 1956 Santiago uprising. From 1957 on, spent most of his time in Miami or Mexico shopping for military supplies and dealing with leaders of other opposition groups. Persuaded Felipe Pazos to represent the 26 of July in the Miami junta while he himself maneuvered in the background. Nominally in charge of military affairs for the Committee in Exile. Now director of agency called CESETA (Automotive Technical Service Center).

*Santamaría, Haydée (Yeyé).* Late thirties. A founder of the movement and a veteran of its earliest activities, including the Moncada episode (in which her brother Abel and her fiancé, Boris Santa Coloma, were killed); said to be one of the most influential in Castro's inner circle during the guerrilla days. Married the much younger Armando Hart. Has served in a variety of positions in the Castro government; at this writing is director of the Casa de las Américas (the regime's cultural center), secretary general of the Permanent Committee of the Latin American Solidarity Organization (LASO), and a member of the Central Committee of the Communist party.

*Urrutia-Lleó, Manuel.* Late forties. Jurist. On 11 May 1957, while presiding at the trial of one hundred Castroists accused of rebellion, defied the Batista dictatorship with a dissenting vote for acquittal. Named president of the revolutionary government at Batista's fall, but soon his anticommunist views put him in conflict with the Castro clique. In July 1959, after being publicly denounced by Castro, Urrutia resigned and went into exile in the United States.

**THE
UNSUSPECTED
REVOLUTION**

# Introduction

Whenever one speaks of human conduct, context is indispensable. After all, to paraphrase José Ortega y Gasset, man is himself and his circumstance. In any attempt to understand the early stages of the Cuban revolution, therefore, we must have at least a sketchy view of the recent past that bred Fidel Castro. I shall also venture some reflections of my own as to how a Communist regime came to be possible in Cuba, only ninety miles from the U.S. mainland, together with an explanation of the circumstances and idealistic aspirations that ultimately led me to join the young 26 of July Movement.

I feel I must make clear at the outset that I have chosen the first-person account not merely because it is a convenient device to hold my narrative together, or because I happen to have participated in or witnessed most of the events recounted here; I am deliberately using my own experience, and consequently my own person, as the incarnation of a political type, so to speak—the middle-class reformer or "moderate" who inadvertently gets himself involved in and cooperates with an unsuspectedly radical revolution. Because this kind of experience is far from unique, but on the contrary constitutes one of the vehicles on which radical ideas and revolutions travel, I consider it of value to bring it out into the open as a living illustration.

The reader will understand, then, I'm sure, that in writing of my own experiences I have not been moved by any vain pursuit of self-exaltation but rather have taken myself objectively—as a *specimen,* one might even say—as a means of exposing one not-too-well-known aspect of the birth and rise of Castroism—or of any other radical revolution, for that matter.

With these considerations in mind, I believe a word now about my background is not only relevant but indispensable. I reached adulthood in Cuba in the early 1930s, during the dictatorship of Gerardo Machado. Chronologically as well as ideologically, I was a member of the so-called 1930 Generation, the generation that was most actively involved in the struggle for political, social, and economic reforms which characterized the period. I was born and grew up in the town of Placetas in the province of Las Villas, the exact geographical center of the island. My parents could not afford to send me to college in Havana (the university was soon closed by the government, in any case), and I became involved with the local branches of the Students' Directorate (Directorio Estudiantil) and the ABC, then the two most active revolutionary organizations. (The ABC was organized in a series of interlocking cells, each level of cells designated by a letter of the alphabet; hence the name.)

In August 1931 armed revolts against the government erupted in scattered places throughout the island.[1] Having heard of the preparations, I went to a meeting place out in the country and joined one insurgent group. There I was gladly surprised to see several of my fellow students and friends. It was a heterogeneous assembly: there were teenagers like myself and mature and old men, professionals, workers, farmers, unemployed persons, and rich men's sons.

That evening we had a skirmish with an army patrol. Rifle and carbine shots cracked from both sides in the dark, but fortunately nobody was hurt. In the ensuing confusion, however, most of the amateur guerrillas, availing themselves of horses in the rural vicinity, hurriedly left the scene. About a dozen of us who were on foot, fearing that the military might liquidate us there if they came to reconnoiter the place, decided to walk some two miles to the nearest railroad station. That turned out to be an unfortunate decision. The army patrol had already moved into position at the station, and we walked into their hands. We were in prison for four months.

Thus my political thinking began to take shape in a revolutionary climate. Soon I came to be what in contemporary American usage might be described as a left-of-center liberal. My position, however, always remained within the well-defined limits of the democratic concept. I have always hated labels and classifications, political or otherwise, so, for the sake of explaining my participation in the early stages of the Castro revolution, I would say that I viewed it then as a sort of emergency instrument—in emergency circumstances—of my own Judeo-Christian-democratic philosophy.

Let us now take a look at the circumstances. It all began at a time when I had not yet heard of Castro. I was living then outside of Cuba, in Durham, North Carolina, where I had gone in 1948 with my wife and year-old son to be an instructor of Spanish at Duke University. I had received my doctorate at the University of Havana the previous year. As my fourth year in the United States went by, however, an unanticipated urge to return to Cuba began to take hold of me. I myself was the first to be surprised. I had come to the United States seeking a career as a college professor and had found it. I belonged to the faculty of one of the finest universities in the country, where I enjoyed the acquaintance of fine people and distinguished colleagues. The future seemed full of promise for professional advancement and personal reward. Yet one day I discovered that I was not entirely at peace with myself. The tempting possibilities of professional success and material comfort did not completely satisfy me. A vague feeling took hold of me that if one was to achieve some measure of fulfillment, one's life must be closely interrelated with the life of the society of which he or she is a part. This feeling was partly the result of a frustrated Christian vocation. My decision to seek a teaching position at Duke had been reached, after many a sleepless night, when I finally realized, at the end of a year as pastor of a Presbyterian church in a small town southeast of Havana, that I was not really cut out for the ministry. Yet my Christian faith remained intact. If the usual ecclesiastical channels had proved impractical, the original call could perhaps still find expression through other forms of activity. So I began, once again, to contemplate political involvement in Cuba.

My Cuban heritage, for one thing, still spoke strongly deep within me. The United States, because it was such a highly developed society, offered little challenge to an outsider with altruistic preoccupations. Cuba, in contrast, was a young republic still in the process of learning the techniques of democracy and the discipline of constitutional government after the uncertain and turbulent years following the Machado era. Here, no doubt, lay the answer to my quest. I began to take comfort in the idea of active participation in the political campaign then going on in my homeland. The year was 1952.

So I made up my mind and burned my ships. I made all the necessary arrangements for the journey back to Cuba and resigned from my post at the university. We would be leaving in May, at the end of the academic year. It was quite an adventurous decision, since I had no idea how I would be making a living in Cuba.

Then something totally unforeseen happened which radically altered not only my personal plans and expectations but the historic destiny of Cuba as well. It was 10 March 1952. I was at home having lunch before going to the campus for one of my afternoon classes. The radio was on, tuned to a news broadcast. Suddenly one item struck me with the force of a thunderbolt: early that morning the constitutional government of Cuba had collapsed as a result of a bloodless but instantly successful coup d'état. The leader of the conspiracy was an old hand at that kind of affair: Fulgencio Batista, a former president and general of the army, and a candidate for president in the elections scheduled for the first of June under the 1940 Constitution.

Batista's unwarranted seizure of power cut short a heated political campaign in which the paramount issue had been decency in public life. No economic or social or ideological question was seriously debated. The country was enjoying an era of relative prosperity in a climate of unrestricted freedom and civil rights. If anything, liberty had been abused under the two consecutive Auténtico administrations.

Deposed President Carlos Prío Socarrás had come to office in 1948 as the chosen party candidate of outgoing President Ramón Grau San Martín (the Constitution prohibited reelection). As leader of the Partido Revolucionario Cubano, popularly known as the PRC or the Auténticos (that is, the "authentic" revolutionaries), Grau San Martín had won the presidency against Batista in 1944 amid a delirium of popular enthusiasm. The Auténticos' victory in 1944 put an end to Batista's eleven years of uninterrupted dictatorial rule. In addition to being Batista's lifelong adversary, Grau San Martín, a former university professor, had caught the public imagination and become immensely popular with his double slogan of *cubanidad* and *honestidad,* which played on the two most fervent political emotions of the Cubans at that time: an intense nationalism and a craving for integrity in government and public life. The coming to power of the Auténticos, therefore, raised enthusiastic hopes for a new political era, rich in progressive and constructive reforms.

But if President Grau to some extent lived up to the first part of his slogan, he was a disappointment in regard to the second. His administration, although constructive in certain respects and at all times liberal and democratic, permitted and even encouraged such evils as pseudorevolutionary gangsterism, political chicanery, favoritism, graft, and, in a word, corruption on a scale unprecedented in Cuba. All the hopes and optimism created by the Auténticos' promises vanished into disenchantment and frustration.

It was at this point that the perpetually fighting figure of Eduardo (Eddy) Chibás emerged on the Cuban political scene as a decisive psychological factor. Originally an Auténtico himself and a Grau admirer and defender, Chibás polarized the popular discontent under a new slogan, *Vergüenza contra dinero* (honor over money), and readily founded a new party, the Partido del Pueblo Cubano, which became known as the Ortodoxo party.

This brings us to one vital aspect of the Cuban phenomenon that must be kept in mind if Batista's forced intervention in 1952 and the subsequent appearance of *fidelismo* are to be seen in perspective and properly understood. The Cuban people had been conditioned by thirty years of revolutionary rhetoric and ethical political preaching. In the decade before 10 March 1952—the day of Batista's coup—the preaching of ethics in public life, primarily in the campaigns and weekly radio broadcasts of Eddy Chibás, was carried to extremes that led to public fanaticism bordering on hysteria.

The lasting impact of the Chibás style and personality on the political development of the Cuban people in those years cannot be overemphasized. Chibás was an outstanding representative of the 1930 Generation. He had first won notoriety among the university students who opposed the Machado dictatorship. Later, as a leader of the Auténtico party, he attained a political stature second perhaps only to that of Grau San Martín. Chibás's popularity increased tremendously as he gave voice to the general indignation against government corruption. His inflamed oratory and ruthless methods in exposing and attacking those presumed guilty of venality or fraud or any other crime made him a unique figure in

Cuban politics. Although it is difficult to deny many of his allegations or question his motives, Chibás was by any definition a demagogue. He stirred the anger of the citizenry against unscrupulous politicians and scandalous situations without offering any constructive alternative.[2] Thus his endless denunciations of government acts and policies and of persons in public office had in the long run the negative effect of weakening people's faith in the institutions of democracy and, worse, in democracy itself.

Chibás did not seem to be aware of this development. On the contrary, intoxicated by his apparent success, he intensified his verbal lashings, and at last his tactics backfired, with fatal consequences. In 1951, during the Prío administration, Chibás accused Minister of Education Aureliano Sánchez Arango of being involved in certain dubious business in Guatemala. Sánchez Arango challenged Chibás to prove his accusations in a public debate on television. Chibás found himself caught in his own net. Unable to prove his charges and distraught by the loss of face, he gave the most theatrical performance of his career: he shot himself in the stomach at the conclusion of a dramatic speech before a microphone at the CMQ radio station during his regular Sunday-evening broadcast of 5 August 1951. He died ten days later. His death was a profound emotional trauma for the Cuban people.

The question of public ethics continued nevertheless to dominate the 1952 electoral campaign, and was clearly reflected in the choice of candidates of the two major parties, the Ortodoxo and the Auténtico. The Ortodoxos nominated university professor Roberto Agramonte, a prestigious intellectual from an illustrious family (he was a relative of Chibás). The Auténticos' nomination fell to Carlos Hevia, a graduate of Annapolis and an equally prestigious figure in Cuban social and political life. Both of these men were chosen primarily because of their reputations for probity and rectitude, and both were handicapped by rather opaque, colorless personalities. For the first time in Cuban political history, most Cubans appeared to be moved by party loyalty rather than by candidate appeal.

Then there was a third candidate, Fulgencio Batista. The general was surrounded by a number of drifting politicians and a few intellectuals, some of whom had been either casualties or disillusioned participants in the revolutionary wave of the 1930s. These elements found a point of convergence as well as hope for political survival at the side of the "strong man of the fourth of September."[3] But, as everybody knew, it was from the military that Batista drew his basic support. It was a fair assumption, confirmed by all public opinion polls, that the possibilities of victory were about evenly divided between Agramonte and Hevia, with perhaps a slight advantage for Agramonte. Batista did not stand a chance.

The only road that could take the former chief of the army to power, therefore, was the *cuartelazo* (the military coup). And that is the road he took. The 1952 electoral campaign thus came to an abrupt end eighty days before the scheduled election date. Frustration and despair paralyzed the nation. Still under the influence of the unrelenting Ortodoxo attacks on President Prío and his government, portrayed as evil and immoral and now overthrown, most people were confused and did not know how to react. Batista's unwarranted action opened a Pandora's box of political evils. The far-reaching consequences of the "tenth of March" nobody could have imagined then. It not only stopped short the experiment in functional democracy initiated in Cuba with the Constitution of 1940 (that alone could have been of lesser importance), but started the chain of events that was to culminate in the present Communist dictatorship, with its consequent delivery of the island to the imperialistic designs of the Soviet Union.

A dispassionate analysis of the 1952 catastrophe suggests, however, that to place the responsibility for it and all that came afterward exclusively on Batista—or on any other individual or group, for that matter—would be an oversimplification. What was under debate then was not the political system or the organization of society but the ethics of politicians and leaders. A case like Batista's is to be seen as a product of the environment. Leaders and politicians, after all, are part of the society. The interaction of people and circumstances must not be overlooked. Batista was certainly no ordinary man—he had to be specially adapted for the particular role he came to perform in Cuban history—but he could never have attained the power he came to hold if preexisting conditions had not been favorable. It is quite conceivable, for instance, that if Batista had chosen in 1952 to respect the electoral process, Cuba's political system—under which, despite all its shortcomings, a free and prosperous society flourished—would have survived, with every chance of improving itself through the continuous, self-educating exercise of democracy. Yet the fact that that system collapsed so easily at the slight push of a power-thirsty man—and a discredited one, at that—demonstrates that there were many weak spots in the political mentality of the Cuban people. Batista's unpardonable sin was to have willfully deprived his country of the opportunity to overcome its weaknesses and solve its problems through a sustained experience in constitutional government —which is the only alternative to totalitarianism of the right or the left, on the one hand, and to anarchy on the other. With his action, Batista invited certain and violent revolution.

Once the implications of the new power setup were fully realized, the idea of revolution indeed made itself felt in most Cuban minds. Figures of the deposed government, members of the opposition, students, intellectuals, the man in the street . . . everybody thought of revolution one way or another. But what did the Cubans mean by "revolution"? The term was used in such various ways and its meaning was so indefinite that a discussion of the idea would occupy a whole book, and that is not my purpose here. A sketchy exposition will be necessary, however, as the Cuban revolution is in fact the subject of this account.

The term "revolution" had entered the Cuban vocabulary with an aura of prestige during the long struggle for independence from Spain in the second half of the nineteenth century. The organization founded to lead that struggle by José Martí in 1895 was called the Partido Revolucionario Cubano. The idea of revolution, therefore, was from the beginning associated in the public mind with heroic rebellion against illegitimate or excessively authoritarian power, and nothing more. An armed attack against the government by one dissatisfied caudillo—General José M. Gómez, for example, who attacked the government of President Mario García Menocal for alleged irregularities in the election process—was considered a revolution. What was to come after the particular undesirable situation was rectified always remained cloudy in the Cuban mind. Such simple notions as "independence," "freedom," even just "honest government" seemed to suffice.

From the late 1920s on, the word "revolution" began to take on new ideological connotations under the influence of intellectual elites and other groups which until then had usually stayed out of politics. The explosion was triggered by Machado's hard line against his critics. The growing opposition to Machado coincided with the spread of radical ideas from the socialist movements in Europe, which appealed to the younger Cuban generation—the 1930 Generation. In varying degrees, leftist orientation ostensibly characterized all of the diverse militant groups that sprang up in those years. Outstanding among these groups were the ABC, the ABC Radical, and the Organización Celular Radical Revolucionaria (OCRR). During the early days of the first Batista dictatorship the most radical of these organizations, Joven Cuba, was founded by Antonio Guiteras, who had been secretary of the interior in the four-month revolutionary presidency of Grau San Martín (September 1933–January 1934). In this category can also be included the Directorio Estudiantil Universitario (DEU), the official university students' organization. The University of Havana became a center of ideological preaching and political involvement. From its classrooms came such political figures as Julio Antonio Mella, Eddy Chibás, Aureliano Sánchez Arango, Rafael Trejo, Rubén Martínez Villena, Carlos Prío Socarrás, and dozens of others whose names dot the annals of that period. All these student leaders figured prominently in political events, with various, often conflicting, degrees of radicalism.

The return of Batista to power via the cuartelazo in 1952 caused history to repeat itself. The same mushrooming of militant revolutionary organizations can again be seen. Among them were the Movimiento Nacional Revolucionario (MNR), the Movimiento de Liberación Radical (MLR), the Directorio Revolucionario (DR), and also the university students' official organization, this time called the Federación Estudiantil Universitaria (FEU). This second active involvement of the university students in Cuba's political life had its own quota of prominent names: Alvaro Barba, José Antonio Echevarría, Enrique Huertas, Pedro Luis Boitel (he died in 1975 in a Castro prison), Marcelo Fernández, and Fidel Castro, among others, all representing different shades of ideological orientation. There were also minor discussion groups of a doctrinal character, such as the Movimiento Humanista, an offshoot of what was known as the Catholic Left.[4]

Generally such organizations came to life only after the indispensable publication of manifestos, which were regarded as both their raisons d'être and their credentials before public opinion. A notable exception was the 26 of July Movement, which made itself known first through a violent attack against Batista forces without previously having presented anything resembling a manifesto.[5] A published ideological manifesto and program were considered very important requisites. They were believed to serve not only to identify the organization in the public eye but also to bind its leader to its stated principles and objectives. Members of these groups adopted varying and often contrasting shades of the ideological spectrum, but all called themselves revolutionaries and proclaimed the necessity of a revolution for Cuba.

But what kind of revolution? For all the popularity of the term (it appeared even in folk songs), the concept remained cloudy. True, revolutionary phrases permeated the manifestos, press reports, and many intellectual and artistic works. Such expressions as "change of the social structure" became commonplace in campaign speeches and press statements. They may have proved effective in identifying the speaker with popular causes and in stirring the emotions of the crowd, but their full meaning never really reached the hearts and minds of the people who applauded them so warmly. To the great majority, a change in the social structure meant simply a chance for a good education and a good job, and fair treatment by the government.

The popular conception of "revolution" is seen clearly in the content and aspirations of the so-called Authentic Revolution, the political movement that was born under the auspices of the military coup of 4 September 1933, when Batista first appeared on the public scene. Sergio Carbó, one of its civilian leaders and an actively involved journalist, used the expression "authentic revolution" on the front page of his satirical weekly *La Semana,* and the name stuck. What the 1933 revolutionaries meant by this term was that they were geared to go beyond the old political limits of the 1901 constitutional order. In addition to a change in power, they sought to propose and implement important social and economic advances, among them a minimum wage, the eight-hour workday, the right to strike, the requirement that at least 50 percent of each firm's employees must be Cuban nationals, and official regulation of the cost of public utilities. Most of these measures were imposed by decree during the four-month de facto government of Grau San Martín, and practically all of them were later included in principle in the 1940 Constitution. In the context of that period, those progressive changes certainly constituted an authentic revolution. It never occurred to anybody, however, that the revolution might tamper with the basic political philosophy of the democratic system or the constitutional structure of the Cuban republic.

It can be said without hyperbole that the Auténtico movement did satisfactorily fulfill the revolutionary aspirations of the Cuban people at the time and left a positive and constructive balance, despite the individual wrongdoings and frivolous public conduct of many of its leaders. Unfortunately, the excesses of the Auténtico era reached such proportions that at the time it was next to impossible to see the whole picture in true perspective. The two successive administrations of Grau San Martín and Prío Socarrás (1948–1952), particularly the former, indulged openly in an orgy of scandals without precedent in Cuban annals. In addition to rampant graft, peculation, and favoritism, there was large-scale looting of the public treasury and, to top it off, government patronage of armed gangs that operated freely under the guise of "revolutionaries." Members of these groups were popularly known as "gangsters," and their activities were referred to as *gangsterismo.* The gangsters fought each other in ferocious rivalry for leadership and positions in government, or simply for personal jealousy and revenge. Bloody gun battles and assassinations of public figures who would not bow to their demands became frequent occurrences. (One of those who rose to public notoriety in the gangster wars was Fidel Castro, who as a member of the UIR [Unión Insurreccional Revolucionaria], one of the more belligerent gangs, took part in countless violent episodes.)[6]

The impression created by all these excesses prevailed over the positive, long-range accomplishments of the Auténtico program. The sad spectacle of shameless corruption in high places produced a general feeling of anger and frustration, which was aggravated by the Ortodoxos' sanctimonious condemnations. Most people failed to see the deeper and far more important reality of a system that, notwithstanding the deplorable behavior of those in office, still respected individual rights, permitted the economy to function and remain prosperous, and kept open the doors of democracy.

Despite the fact that the tide of scandal had begun to ebb during the Prío administration, too much psychological damage had already been done. The old undefined word "revolution" was once again current in activist and militant circles. Crises were their natural milieu, and they welcomed the opportunity. The 1952 presidential campaign captured the people's attention and for a time seemed like a sure way out of the moral-political quagmire. But Batista, who accepted the democratic process just as long as he was in command, realized that his only chance for public survival was the coup d'état—and the way out was shut off.

Some leaders toyed with the idea—though they would not say so publicly—of a revolutionary dictatorship that would hold power for an indefinite period. One of those who advocated this idea, I later learned, was the poet and philosopher Rafael García Bárcena, founder and leader of the MNR. The standard justification was that only with power unencumbered by constitutional restraints could the accumulation of past evils be eradicated. Grau San Martín's ephemeral revolutionary government was often cited as a historical precedent of positive achievement. It was more or less assumed that the revolutionary government (the word "dictatorship" was carefully avoided) would of its own accord relinquish power to a representative government, through a general election or a constituent assembly, once it had accomplished its mission.

As I have said, revolution was the one objective that all of the anti-Batista groups and movements had in common. How far and how deep the revolution would go, however, none of them ever did spell out. Influences ranging from the far Left to the far Right could be detected. Numerous social and economic clichés were invariably invoked; no respectable revolution could be conceived without them. But all these ideas, whether radical or moderate, originated within the inner circles of the revolutionary elite. They did not arise from any particular condition of social injustice or unrest and certainly did not represent the concerns of the average citizen. Popular demands never went beyond the restoration of constitutional democracy and the subsequent establishment of some form of honest and constructive government. The prevailing sentiment was the traditional rejection of all forms of tyranny. Ever since the days of Machado (1925–1933) and the following Batista era (1933–1944), the specter of strong-man rule was abhorrent to the vast majority of the Cuban people. A second experience with Batista, therefore—especially when his return to power came illegitimately, by way of the cuartelazo—looked too much like a return to a painful past and could not help raising stormy winds of discontent and rebellion. What made Batista's easy success even more unpalatable was that it conveyed the impression that the people of Cuba had proved to be incapable of the continued exercise of democracy and needed a strong man, after all. All during the rest of the 1950s the popular revolutionary appeal therefore focused on the elimination of Batista and his dictatorship. That was "revolution" for most people.

As for me, initially I was satisfied with the popular concept of revolution. I was well aware, of course, that any revolution has far-reaching consequences. But at the time I felt that the restoration of the constitutional order by the overthrow and implicit moral condemnation of Batista was necessary and sufficient for the good of the country. I truly believed that the 1940 Constitution, whatever its faults, was broad enough to allow the institution of the reforms that were necessary. Two separate considerations contributed to my gradual drift toward a more revolutionary position: one was the failure of the politicians and the existing political parties to deal adequately with the Batista situation; the other was the apparent sincerity of the revolutionary groups and their readiness for action. Before long I came to share the widespread delusion that a formal declaration of principles and objectives would serve both to define the nature of the revolution and to commit its leaders to a binding contract.

Still, the imprecise idea of revolution that prevailed among those groups, although a step ahead of the popular concept, was a far cry from any radical rejection of the basic institutions of democracy. In many ways it seemed to be not so much a matter of new ideas as of new people. A rotation of the political leadership of the country was an urgent necessity. The overall revolutionary impetus, notwithstanding the secret hopes of some leaders and activists (who at bottom welcomed the Batista disaster as an opportunity), actually amounted to little more than a middle-class reform movement. And no wonder: it originated in the middle class and drew its main support—emotional and psychological as well as financial—from the middle class. It grew out of disenchantment with the fraud and corruption of previous administrations and reached its climax when the political crisis resulting from the coup d'état shut off the normal outlets of the democratic system.

The word "revolution" became associated in everyone's mind with an ideal yet attainable state. Most people did not realize that the term did not have the same connotations for everyone who used it. For the great majority, as I have said, revolution meant simply getting rid of Batista. For the more concerned minority it meant, besides, a certain program of social, economic, political, and educational reforms. There were doubtless a few who looked upon revolution as a truly radical change in the basic structure of society. But for the time being these few remained unsuspected, blending unobtrusively with the committee members and the rank and file of the more moderate revolutionary groups.

As the anti-Batista struggle progressed, the idea of the programmatic revolution gained in popular acceptance. By early 1958 the

26 of July Movement had emerged as the undisputed leader of the whole process. This fact explains why Castro's later deviation toward Marxism-Leninism caused some people to think of a "betrayed revolution," a notion, by the way, that could lead us into a most interesting and perhaps controversial semantic discussion: What is revolution? Is the fact of revolution per se automatically good? Cannot there be a bad revolution? . . . Such a discussion, however, escapes the chronological limits of this book. Castro's betrayal became manifest from 1960 on, after the revolution was in power.[7] I had made public my separation from the 26 of July Movement long before—on 14 August 1958—as an exile in New York.

# 1 Two Wings for the Revolution

I arrived in Havana at the end of May 1952, less than two months after Batista's coup d'état. My first concern was a job. The University of Havana was practically out of the question; the process of obtaining a teaching position there was too long and complicated. The possibility of teaching in one of the several Havana *institutos* (high schools) vanished with the new political reality. In order to be appointed to any state position (private schools, with very rare exceptions, could afford to pay only very low salaries), it was necessary to have the intercession or the recommendation of some high government official or politician. That closed the doors for me: in Cuba no self-respecting opponent of the current regime would have dreamed of soliciting or accepting anything from those in power—especially when that power had been seized illegitimately. For some time I managed to struggle along as a translator and free-lance contributor to *Bohemia* and *Carteles*, Cuba's most popular weeklies.

One day in June somebody knocked at the door of our small apartment on the Calle Santa Ana, one block from the Avenida Rancho Boyeros. It was Rafael García Bárcena, a brilliant young intellectual—philosopher, poet, journalist, professor—who had recently emerged as a dynamic public figure. A member of the 1930 Generation, García Bárcena had become prominent as an outspoken critic of Batista and his regime. He was the founder and leader of the supposedly clandestine revolutionary organization called the Movimiento Nacional Revolucionario, referred to simply as the MNR. At the time of the March 10 coup, García Bárcena was a professor at the Escuela Superior de Guerra, an institute of advanced studies for officers of the armed forces. Soon after that he was, of course, out of a job.

I was as much surprised as I was flattered by his visit. We had been introduced by a mutual friend, but we were not well acquainted. He explained to me that he had been reading my articles in *Bohemia* and that he was very much in agreement with my views on Cuban problems.[1] But he said that Batista's seizure of power, disgraceful as it was, opened "a new revolutionary cycle in Cuba." These words, as I would in time learn, reflected a favorite theme of García Bárcena's. He used them several times in the course of our conversation. Then came my second big surprise of the day. The main purpose of García Bárcena's visit was to invite me to join the MNR as a member of its national committee (Dirección Nacional). Having just returned to Cuba after an absence of four years, I had had no previous direct contact with political or revolutionary elements, and my ideas about what was going on in the anti-Batista underground were vastly overinflated. To my mind the MNR was a formidable, well-organized revolutionary endeavor, and it never occurred to me that my limited experience and doubtful political maturity would qualify me to be admitted at such a high level. It turned out to be far from what I had imagined. But at the moment I saw García Bárcena's invitation as an unexpected honor and as the desired open door to anti-Batista activity. That was the practical beginning of my involvement in the Cuban political crisis.

García Bárcena had a charming personality: he was kind and soft-spoken, and he lived very modestly. He had an easy, contagious smile. I never saw him angry or irritated. He abhorred terrorism and could not condone political assassination. During the committee meetings and discussions he would listen patiently to all of the various opinions, often conflicting and frequently expressed at inordinate length, and in the end usually managed to lead the discussion to a conclusion acceptable to at least the majority of the group. Most of the meetings of the MNR national committee were held at my apartment on the Calle Santa Ana or at the home of Rubén Darío Rumbaut, a young doctor who lived in La Sierra, a suburb of Havana.

I was a little discouraged by the discovery that the MNR national committee was not exactly homogeneous in its ideological composition. Dr. Rumbaut, for instance, was a devout Christian who read the French philosophers Jacques Maritain and Charles Pierre Péguy and was among the leaders of Acción Católica, a Catholic political organization. A democrat, he approached political problems with a clear and well-organized mind. Rumbaut had been one of the founders of a study group whose members issued manifestos and proposed guidelines of national reform inspired by a philosophy they called "humanism," an idea they seem to have taken from Maritain. (Incidentally, Castro himself used that word sometime during 1959, though it is doubtful that it had the meaning for him that it had for Rumbaut.)

Another unquestionably democratic member of the committee was Amalio Fiallo, also a Catholic leader, a gifted orator with a pleasant gregarious personality. Fiallo was the most politically minded of the group; in the Cuban context, this means that he favored legal, nonviolent action over open revolutionary struggle.

Four other members of the MNR national committee did not feel quite so enthusiastic about the democratic concept. They were Manolo Fernández, a poised, analytical fellow who seemed well read in political matters and was rather cynical about religious and spiritual values;[2] Orestes González Medina, intelligent and practical yet somewhat dense, and an admirer of José Antonio Primo de Rivera, the hero of the Spanish Falange movement; Alberto Guigou, a clever debater with a penetrating knowledge of the whole complex of Cuban politics and also a fervent admirer of Primo de Rivera; and Angela Grau, a young woman with a strong interest in modern artistic trends.

Angela Grau was a close friend of Marta Frayde, a Marxist doctor who had long posed as an Ortodoxo politician and Chibás follower, and of Alicia Alonso, the famed ballerina, whose communistic leanings were then only privately known. Miss Grau, however, began to slacken in her participation after a few meetings and finally faded away altogether. The case of Alberto Guigou is perhaps the most curious. He had been a close friend and associate of the late Eddy Chibás and was still a member of the executive council of the Ortodoxo party. He was also the leader of an organization called Grupos Doctrinales Ortodoxos, a sort of autonomous subgroup of the Ortodoxo party, with branches in Pinar del Río Province. This multiplicity of functions, incidentally, was not uncommon at the beginning of the anti-Batista struggle. García Bárcena himself was also a member of the Ortodoxo executive council, although he showed scant regard for the party or for any of its leaders, including Chibás. Orestes González Medina presented another interesting angle. He had been one of the leaders of a little-known revolutionary organization called Frente Cubano, a group of theoreticians and doctrinaires with apparently fascistic overtones. They cherished the idea of an enlightened, benevolent, yet firm revolutionary dictatorship. It centered around a brother-in-law of García Bárcena, who himself seems to have been involved with the group. With the birth of the MNR the Frente Cubano ceased to be active, but González Medina kept its ideas alive.

It soon became obvious, although they would not explicitly say so, that the majority of the committee members were not particularly interested in a return to the formalities of democracy in Cuba. They appeared to contemplate instead a new revolutionary era, whose true ideological bases were left in a penumbra of vagueness and reticence. They hoped that the MNR, thanks to García Bárcena's growing charisma and secret military connections, would serve to usher in that undefined utopia.

Fiallo, Rumbaut, and I became the democratic wing that counterbalanced the other tendencies in the MNR. To be sure, our friends were all good, decent people, genuinely concerned about the problems of Cuba and in no way guided by any hope of personal gain or thirst for power. Yet they exhibited disdain for what they used to refer to as "the populace" and did not hide their distrust of the rule of the majority. They advocated rather the formation of a revolutionary elite that would take power by any available means in order to impose the kind of government they felt suited the country best. If that meant a radical departure from the historical roots of the Cuban republic, it did not seem to disturb them much—were these not times of change and did not Cuba need a change? By this reasoning, Batista's sudden disruption of the constitutional order had been not a disaster but a most welcome opportunity, since it had opened the door to a new "revolutionary cycle." This was García Bárcena's real position, though he did not make a display of it, and it remained somewhat cloaked, if not embellished, by his gentle, noncontroversial personality. On more than one occasion, after listening to some opinion of mine—I never hesitated to say what I thought—García Bárcena would just smile and say that I had "a very sensitive bent for democracy."

If all these things spoke of potential danger to democracy in

Cuba should this group ever reach power, I did not grasp it at the time. Nor was I struck by any sudden revelation of their true aims: whatever I learned about them came to me piecemeal, in the course of months of clandestine meetings and discussions (in fact, much of it I learned long after the MNR had ceased to exist). Unfortunately, in the atmosphere of constant expectation so typical of revolutionary movements, the significance of loose details and individual ideological nuances is often lost. So no alarm bell rang for me then. On the contrary, the urge to get rid of Batista, coupled with the excitement of being part of a patriotic effort to bring about a new constructive era, overshadowed all other considerations.

To be truthful, the MNR was more a fluid state of mind than a real revolutionary movement. García Bárcena's bold public statements had had a certain popular impact. The MNR had a substantial following among young people, particularly university students, who affectionately used to call García Bárcena *el Profe* (short for "the Professor"). But the movement lacked organized cadres, cells, anything of that sort. Its only structural body, the national committee, did very little beyond holding meeting after meeting, all of which consisted of endless, mostly theoretical discussions that circled mainly around the topic of what should be done in Cuba once Batista was overthrown. As to how this first, indispensable step was to be accomplished, the understanding was that García Bárcena maintained "certain contacts" among high-ranking officers of the armed forces, who at a propitious moment would stage a countercoup—or more precisely a putsch—whereby Batista would be overthrown and a true revolutionary government installed under the "provisional" presidency of García Bárcena. Some of us on the committee would become the members of his cabinet. In time I learned that García Bárcena had been entertaining the idea of a putsch even before Batista erupted on the scene on 10 March 1952.

Curiously enough, no one on the committee seemed to be very happy about this plan or to have much faith in its chances of success. Rumbaut pointed out to me once that, at best, we might end up as the civilian facade of a revolutionary government that, because of its origin, was bound to depend on the military. Yet we stuck there, held by wishful thinking and by the conviction that something must be done to try to get the country out of the mess into which Batista had plunged it. Each of us had been attracted to the MNR by its image as something new and uncontaminated

amid the prevailing political corruption and the failure of the existing political forces, and each hoped that a solution to the crisis and
a new start in the troubled history of the republic might somehow
emerge from the quixotic and disorganized venture. We felt that
such gambling was part of being "revolutionaries."

One evening at the beginning of April 1953 García Bárcena
came to my apartment and confided to me a concrete plan to enter
the Campamento de Columbia—Cuba's military headquarters and
the base of Batista's power—on April 11, which happened to be
Easter Sunday. The essence of the plan was an armed assault
against the camp by a number of students and other underground
activists. The operation was to be carried out in the afternoon
when the guards were changed at the various entrances to the
camp. The assault itself was meant only as a distracting maneuver,
during which García Bárcena's friends among the officers inside
would have an opportunity to take command. Once the Campamento de Columbia was taken, it was assumed, the MNR would
almost automatically be in complete control of power.

García Bárcena asked me what I thought of the idea. I said I was
in complete agreement and encouraged him. My impatience and
enthusiasm had overcome my good judgment. He smiled, obviously pleased. Then he asked me another question that in the
circumstances sounded almost childish. What did I think of the
significance of staging the action on Easter Sunday—might it not
have a negative effect on people? García Bárcena knew that I was
a practicing Christian. I thought I should produce a lapidary answer. Any time, I said, was all right for the conquest of evil and the
defense of liberty.

Two or three days later García Bárcena called an urgent meeting
of the national committee to discuss his plans, or rather to inform
the group that they were already in motion. The meeting was held
at the Colegio Farmacéutico (Pharmacists' Association) on the Malecón, the broad boulevard bordering the harbor. The majority was
aghast at the idea of attempting—and expecting—to take the Campamento de Columbia in that manner; Rumbaut and I were the
only ones to support it. Apparently most of the members of the
committee had never taken García Bárcena's plans seriously. Confronted with the prospect of immediate action, they reacted with
alarm bordering on panic. Guigou, González Medina, and especially Fiallo called the plan just plain crazy. Rumbaut reasoned
mildly against it, but accepted it, he said, as a matter of revolu-

tionary discipline. After all, he reminded the others, wasn't something like this what we had been banking on all along? Listening to Fiallo and Guigou, however, I began to feel that they might be right. But once again my hope that a turn of fate might bring success to an otherwise senseless, even suicidal attempt prevailed, and I said I was in favor of going ahead with the idea. It wouldn't have made much difference if I had argued against it. García Bárcena had not put the matter to a vote; he had merely announced what he was already determined to do. A split in the committee became visible and irreparable. Its rapid disintegration was soon to follow.

When the meeting was over, I took García Bárcena aside and asked him what my assignment was, what he wanted me to do. "Don't worry about that," he said, "I'll have something for you later." Then he added, "Right now we must not put all our eggs in one basket." The following Sunday, April 11, the proposed assault on the Campamento de Columbia was carried out as scheduled. But everything went wrong: the whole plan fizzled miserably. García Bárcena, badly roughed up by the military police, and dozens of his followers landed in jail.

García Bárcena spent some six months in the military prison of La Cabaña, across the Havana harbor. Rumbaut and I visited him there once a week. He continued to enjoy the admiration and loyalty of many friends and followers, but for all practical purposes the Movimiento Nacional Revolucionario had ceased to exist.

Cuba was going through a curious kind of crisis, one that only those Cubans who witnessed it may be able to understand—and probably not all of them. In spite of the political and psychological chaos brought about by the sudden change in power and the collapse of the democratic structure, an appreciable degree of prosperity persisted. The time-fixed image of the "underdeveloped" Latin American country hardly fitted the Cuba of the 1950s. At least, it would have to be carefully qualified. Curiously enough, it was a Communist leader, Aníbal Escalante, who wrote, in the magazine *Verde Olivo* (30 July 1961), "Cuba is one of the countries [of Latin America] where the standard of living of the masses was particularly high." And Hugh Thomas, citing a variety of sources, among them UNESCO's *Basic Facts* and the UN *Statistical Yearbook of 1960–1963*, observes that Cuba had more television sets per capita than any other Latin American country—indeed, more than Italy—and more automobiles per capita than any other Latin American country except oil-rich Venezuela.

There is no question that there was growing tension and rumbling. One could sense that the growing emotional charge was bound to explode sooner or later. But the roots of the discontent were moral as well as political and had little to do with socioeconomic factors. To be sure, some aspects of the organization of Cuban society and the distribution of wealth certainly could have stood improvement. Some Cubans, I among them, were trying to get that message across to public opinion. But the winds of protest, until then fanned only by corruption in government and demagoguery in the opposition, were now whipped to gale force by a no less corrupt dictatorship. And that worsened the situation considerably. If the vices of democracy were hard to put up with, the situation became intolerable when democracy was destroyed and the vices remained.

Sometime after the fading away of the MNR I was invited to join the Movimiento de Liberación Radical, a more recently formed group that was also preoccupied with revolutionary questions and goals. The MLR, however, was presumably a public organization, though it too engaged in clandestine activities. It had been founded by a group of young Catholic leaders, one of whom was Amalio Fiallo. Another was Andrés Valdespino, a lawyer and university professor who had recently gained public attention as a political commentator and contributor to *Bohemia*. Valdespino and Fiallo were, in fact, the two leading figures of the MLR. Both came one day in October 1954 to my new address at Calle Ayestarán 720 to invite me to join the group. After learning about their views and the political philosophy of the movement, and having been given assurances that it was not an instrument of the Catholic church, I accepted their invitation. The usual series of almost daily meetings and discussions followed.

The national committee of the MLR—larger than that of the extinct MNR—was made up almost entirely of professionals, teachers, doctors, bank employees, and other white-collar workers. I was glad to see Leví Marrero, a boyhood friend and later a college classmate, who had made a distinguished career as professor of geography and author of textbooks while doubling as journalist and editor in chief of one of Havana's largest newspapers.[3] Raúl Roa, dean of the School of Social Sciences at the university and a controversial member of the 1930 Generation with a leftist record—he was later to become Castro's foreign minister—who had apparently turned moderate, was also invited. (It was he that had introduced me to García Bárcena.) He told me he was very much interested and liked the MLR people, but after one or two meetings he did not show up again. Roa had let it be known that he thought he was under close surveillance by Batista's secret police.

The MLR secured a place for itself among the opposition with no means but the spoken and written word—and Amalio Fiallo's talent for establishing influential contacts. Despite the word "radical" in its name, there was little politically radical about the movement: it was really moderate. Without necessarily intending to do so, it presented the image of a middle-class intellectual elitist group with revolutionary ideas. The MLR organized rallies (one, in the city of Guanajay, west of Havana, was broken up by soldiers with drawn sabers and dozens of people were beaten and arrested), issued manifestos and press releases, and broadcast a weekly radio hour. It also considered organizing its own insurrectional cadres (surprisingly, Fiallo was in charge of this project) but did not make much progress in that direction. Its main objective was to keep a firm foothold on the national scene through impressing public opinion with fierce denunciations of the Batista regime and a platform of honest politics and, of course, to offer vistas of a programmed revolution. There was not much originality in any of this—it was the usual double formula employed in those pre-Castro days by all new groups seeking to attract popular attention and favor. The MLR's underlying idea—like that of the MNR—seemed to be to prepare itself for the unexpected event that might carry the group on to power or at least put it on the bandwagon. Such an eventuality was not altogether impossible: in the unstable, unpredictable climate resulting from Batista's seizure of power, anything could happen.

Meanwhile unrest was growing day by day in Cuba. The air was always filled with rumors—*bolas*—most of them unfounded but some not. The university students staged almost daily demonstrations, many of which ended in violent clashes with the police. Such insurrectional organizations as the Triple A, led by former Minister of Education Aureliano Sánchez Arango; the Organización Auténtica (OA), formed by followers of deposed President Carlos Prío; and the Directorio Revolucionario (DR), composed mostly of university students, were busy planning, plotting, and carrying on diverse subversive activities. Bombs exploded almost daily in Havana. Caches of arms and explosives were sometimes discovered even in elegant suburban residences. There were martyrs and political assassinations on both sides. Unable to gain public acceptance, the dictatorship began to fill the jails with political prisoners, and police stations doubled as torture chambers.

The ways of violence had already been adopted by young revolutionary Fidel Castro. The bloody assault on the Moncada military barracks in Santiago de Cuba, the capital of Oriente Province at the eastern end of the island, had taken place in July 1953, four months after García Bárcena's pitiful attempt on the Campamento de Columbia near Havana. Although this first major exploit of Castro's was an initial failure that cost many lives and sent Fidel, his brother Raúl, and a group of other survivors to prison (apparently Batista did not feel strong enough to have them summarily executed), its date, 26 of July, was to become a fateful and controversial day in Cuba's historical calendar.

Castro and his companions spent less than two years in the state penitentiary on the Isle of Pines. On 13 May 1955 Batista signed a decree of amnesty that set them free. Castro went to Havana and for some time stayed at the apartment of his half sister Lidia in the Vedado section. Assuming with good judgment that he might still be under the watchful eye of Batista's police, Fidel for a while kept out of the public view.

One evening in June, around ten, I was about to take the bus home after a meeting of the national committee of the MLR when Pedro Trigo, one of the members, offered to drive me home. Trigo, a young manual worker who had lost a brother in the Moncada action, was acquainted with Castro. On the way he asked me if I would mind stopping for a few minutes: he had a message to deliver to Fidel. I said of course I wouldn't mind; I'd be glad to wait. But Trigo wanted me to accompany him; he was quite insistent about it. I declined, however. I didn't know the man and had no interest in meeting him on that particular occasion. "You go on, Pedro," I said. "I'll wait here." Trigo finally gave up and left.

People engaged in anti-Batista activities never parked directly in front of or near a "hot" place—that is, one where revolutionaries lived or met. Castro's sister Lidia lived in the vicinity of Calle 12 and Calle 23, a well-known Vedado intersection. Trigo's car was parked on a short block of Calle 14 that ends at the Calzada de

Zapata. At that point the Calzada de Zapata makes almost a half circle around Havana's monumental Colón Cemetery. The spot where I was to wait for Trigo was half a block from the cemetery itself, and it was dark and deserted at that time of night.

Some ten minutes may have passed when I noticed two shadows approaching. I could see no more than blurred silhouettes against the faint glare of a street light behind them. Then they were at the car and I saw that they were Trigo and Fidel Castro. Trigo did the explaining: when Castro learned that I was waiting there, he insisted on coming to meet me. "Yes, that's true," Castro said, stretching out his hand. There was an exchange of compliments. Though I had not been eager to meet him, I found that I was pleased to meet him now.

Castro had high praise for my political commentaries in the press and asked me if I had read his articles in *La Calle* (a daily recently put out by some Ortodoxos). I assured him that I had. Castro addressed me as "Doctor," and his attitude was that of one who speaks to an intellectual superior. I felt a little embarrassed.

Soon it became evident that Castro had something more in mind than merely making my acquaintance. He again brought up my articles in *Bohemia* and referred to what he called my "ideological position" in regard to Cuba's political crisis, adding that in his opinion it was the "correct" one. Then he mentioned the MLR and said that he had been following our activities with a great deal of interest. He was in complete agreement, he said, with the MLR's pronouncements in the press and at public gatherings. I managed to edge in some words of acknowledgment, and Castro went on. He observed that our respective organizations seemed to concur in their ideological outlook and in their main objectives, and he wondered whether some form of cooperation might be possible. "I've been thinking a lot about that," he said, and waited for my reaction.

The realization that Castro was considering an alliance with the MLR really amazed me. I wondered if Trigo's offer of a ride that evening and then his insistent invitation to go with him to Fidel's apartment had not actually been prearranged at Castro's suggestion. But why should the "hero of the Moncada" desire an alliance between his combat-tested forces and the powerless little MLR? There can be only one explanation (though it came to me only much later). At that time in 1955, just a few weeks after Castro's release from the Isle of Pines penitentiary, the 26 of July Move-

Fidel Castro in the early 1950s.

ment had not yet emerged as a fully developed revolutionary organization. As for the MLR, it was not much more than a public platform from which a handful of young people voiced their opinions and proclaimed their ideas on the rebuilding of the Cuban political structure. But the freshness of their approach together with their intellectual makeup and clean political records gave the MLR an aura of respectability—something that the Castro group lacked. By associating himself and his followers with the MLR, or better yet, by bringing the MLR into his own fold, Castro would be giving his own movement the psychological counterbalance it so badly needed if it was ever to become generally acceptable. At the same time, as an extra bonus, the relationship might help in some measure to erase from the public mind Castro's lingering past as a revolutionary gangster.[4]

None of these thoughts, to be sure, came to my mind on that occasion. Quite the contrary, Castro's suggestion struck me as extremely interesting. It seemed to me that the exclusively vocal MLR would be perfectly complemented by the activist Castro forces. If the two groups joined together, I thought, the revolution would be able to fly properly with its two equally necessary wings: ideology and strategy.

My favorable reaction, even before I had said a word, must have been apparent to Castro. He had an idea, he said. Why didn't I arrange a meeting with the leadership of the MLR to exchange views on the question and "see what comes of it"? He specifically mentioned Valdespino and Fiallo, saying that he would very much like to meet with them. He would bring along a friend or two. I promised to take his suggestion to the other MLR committee members. He surely would understand, I said, that our decisions had to be taken in committee and by majority vote. "That's perfectly all right," he said. "I'll be waiting to hear from you." He added that I could send any message with Trigo.

The following morning I went to see Fiallo and told him about my casual encounter with Castro and of his interest in meeting with representatives of the MLR. Fiallo listened attentively and when I finished said, "What do *you* think?" I was a little taken aback. Fiallo's lukewarm reaction was like a dash of cold water on my enthusiastic hopes of acting on the old theory that a successful revolution requires both the word and the sword. I told him that in my opinion Castro was absolutely right in maintaining that Batista could be dislodged only by force of arms, and that, if only for that reason, it might be worthwhile to listen to what he had in mind. Fiallo brought up Castro's known record as a gangster. I said I didn't know much about that, which was true. The eight years I had spent in the United States (1943–1946, 1948–1952) had created gaps in my knowledge of events in Cuba. I cannot precisely determine today to what extent I may have been influenced by the prevailing tendency in Cuba then to feel that the fact of choosing the "right" political position was like crossing a Jordan that washed away all sins of the past. Fiallo kept saying that Castro's dubious background was a real liability. Even if we were willing to forget, the question now was: Had he changed? After a brief silence Fiallo said, as though talking to himself, "I just don't trust the guy." He nevertheless suggested that we go and talk the matter over with Valdespino.

Valdespino, too, had reservations about Castro. He doubted that any positive results could come of an association with such a controversial figure. "We probably have much to lose and very little to gain," Valdespino said. All the same, he favored going to meet with Castro, "if only to find out what he's up to." If we refused, he said, we might be labeled the snobs of the opposition camp; we already had the reputation of being an elitist group. Anyway, the matter had to be taken to a special meeting of the committee.

A good many committee members voiced opposition to the proposed meeting with Castro. In fact, no one was particularly in favor of the idea. Some came to accept it as a tactical move that we ought not to evade; others did so simply because Valdespino and I spoke in favor of it. After much discussion it was decided by a bare majority that Valdespino, Fiallo, and I would go to the meeting under certain conditions, the first of which was that we were to enter into no agreement with Castro or his group without further consultation with the committee.

Word was sent to Castro through Pedro Trigo: The MLR delegates would see Castro at my apartment on the second floor of Calle Ayestarán 720 at one in the afternoon two days later. Castro came accompanied by four men who gave the impression of acting as his bodyguards. At least two of them carried pistols. Of the four who came with Castro that day I can identify only two: a fellow known as Ñico *el Flaco* (the skinny one) and Pedro Miret, an engineering student who had fought in the Moncada assault on 26 July 1953 and had been in prison with Castro and the others on the Isle of Pines.

Once the handshakes and the customary pleasantries were over, Castro got to the point, although not exactly in a straight line. He began by referring to our conversation of a few days before, and then spoke of the ideals and objectives shared by our respective organizations in the struggle against the Batista regime, and also, Castro emphasized, against the political remnants of "the past." Even if we differed in tactics and in the forms of revolutionary activity, we were still fighting for the same cause. He also elaborated on the necessity of giving ideological content to the armed struggle.

This line of thought caught the interest of everyone in the room. Castro stopped for a moment, interrupted by an outburst of comments and opinions. I used the phrase "the two wings of the revolution," which I had made a kind of pet metaphor. Stressing his point, Castro said that the gap between those who advocated armed action and those engaged merely in the war of ideas was too great, and that "the intellectuals" would never be able to accomplish much unless they joined forces with "the fighters." Fiallo said that the gap did not really exist. We of the MLR, for instance, were not exactly dedicated to doing nothing but signing public statements and issuing programmatic manifestos, just as Castro and his followers had not been occupied exclusively with shooting. He reminded Castro that his speech at his trial after the Moncada events was full of radical suggestions.[5]

Castro replied somewhat defensively that he was well aware of all that, but we had to admit that, for the time being at least, our respective groups had adopted modes of operation that set us miles apart in the public mind. This gap, whether real or imaginary, could and should be conveniently bridged to mutual advantage. We could, for instance, draw up a combined strategy of civil disobedience and insurrectional action. At this point Valdespino expressed his agreement with Castro's approach, "although," he said, "there is nothing new in its theory." But the question now, Valdespino went on, was how to apply that theory to the Cuban reality and, above all, how to arrive at and implement the kind of cooperation Castro was suggesting.

For some unexplained reason, Valdespino's interruption touched off pandemonium. Everyone talked at once and, in typical Cuban fashion, tried to outshout everyone else; the loudest of all was Castro. The shouting caused me no little apprehension: if some angry neighbor should inform the police of this meeting, the outcome would be quite unpleasant. The only ones who remained quiet throughout the entire session were Fidel's bodyguards. They appeared to be attentive only to their assigned duty, ready to act in any critical contingency.

I was careful not to let myself be drawn too deeply into the argument. Much as I personally favored a merging of kindred revolutionary forces, I did not want to appear too eager for an understanding with Fidel Castro, especially after having learned the way Fiallo and Valdespino felt about it. I preferred, therefore, that any agreement come as a spontaneous decision of my two colleagues, who were the founders as well as the leading figures of the MLR. I had been instrumental in bringing that encounter about, but that was as far as I considered I should go.

When the noise subsided somewhat, I could hear Valdespino and Castro engaging in a dialectical debate on the meaning of the term "revolution." Curiously enough, the young law professor and Catholic leader sounded considerably more radical than Castro. Was Castro deliberately concealing his true revolutionary wing-spread, perhaps because he felt the time was not yet ripe? In view of the many radical statements in his defense speech at his trial (with which I was not familiar then), that still seems a reasonable guess. When he explained what he meant by "fighting against the past," Castro's description of revolution struck an almost exclusively negative note. His thinking seemed merely a reflection of the well-known Ortodoxo pattern—and in fact he was still nominally a member of that party. His views on Cuban problems and their possible solutions sounded like a recitation of the familiar slogans of the Chibás period: he was against the unscrupulous politicians, against the scoundrels in government, against the embezzlers, against the military. . . . These anathemas, however, were interspersed with a few others of a somewhat different flavor, not at all reminiscent of Chibás: against the rich, against the landowners, against the big foreign interests, against Yankee imperialism. "Con todo esto hay que acabar" ("We have to do away with all this"). What kind of Cuba was to be built once all those evils were abolished? On this subject Castro would not elaborate.

In the context of Cuba in 1955, however, under the tensions and repressions of a police state, Castro's tested capacity for action and leadership stood out amid the disorganization and vacillation of all the other opposition groups. It was this particular contrast, rather than anything in Castro's imprecise message—or socioeconomic conditions in Cuba, for that matter—that explains the steady increase in popularity of the 26 of July Movement. Many people then, including me, saw in Castro a crude force that could be put to good use if it were properly harnessed and guided. Unfortunately, this is the sort of dangerous delusion from which politically minded intellectuals in particular tend to suffer in prerevolutionary situations: they think they can use the strong leader and end up by being used themselves.

Castro was finally able to deliver himself of everything he had had in mind when he requested a meeting with the leaders of the MLR. He had a strong interest in some kind of alliance, and stressed what an invincible revolutionary force we would make together. He said that conditions were ideal at that moment, but that action must be taken quickly. There were others, he explained, "who are also preparing things." He mentioned specifically the Prío groups. He happened to have information about that, he said. What Castro mysteriously insinuated was hardly a secret: it was well known that people close to Prío were storing up arms in various parts of the city. "They probably won't do a thing except maybe get in our way," Castro said, "but for that very reason we should keep an eye on them."

Castro paused and looked at us as if trying to fathom our thoughts. Then he turned once again to his favorite, almost obsessive theme: a denunciation of the *viejos políticos* (old politicians, in a highly scornful sense), considered by many to be solely responsible for Cuba's ills. Castro left no doubt that for him there was an insurmountable gap between true revolutionaries and politicians, and he reserved his most scathing diatribes and epithets for opposition politicians, in particular Prío and the Auténticos: scoundrels, shameless thieves, spineless lackeys of Yankee imperialism.

The views of the MLR leaders turned out to be not quite so radical on this particular point. Fiallo expressed his disagreement with Castro and said that in a democracy the role of the politician is not only inevitable but necessary. He made a distinction between the conduct of certain men in public life and the theoretical function of the politician. This set off another heated argument. Castro had not expected a difference of opinion on the subject of politicians—not from a group that called itself revolutionary. He was both surprised and chagrined. "Don't tell me you're going to justify those who get rich by sacking the public treasury!" Arguments and counterarguments flew back and forth with typical Cuban ardor. Finally, caught in a position where he might appear to be arguing against democracy, Castro retreated somewhat. He preferred some form of "direct democracy," he said—a democracy in which the active involvement of the people would make obsolete the function of the politician.

A few more exchanges of this sort followed, with all of us joining in. Not exactly made for listening, Castro had always to speak at length regardless of the subject. He diluted his thoughts in a cataract of verbiage that only the magnetism of his personality made tolerable. Finally the essence of his proposition to the MLR leaders that afternoon came out clearly: the fusion of the MLR into his own organization and, naturally, under his personal leadership. For all practical purposes, the MLR would disappear, to become something like the public relations department of the 26 of July Movement—a select team of hired scribes. In return, we were to be the prestigious intelligentsia of the organization.

Castro's proposition was evidently based on the assumption that the MLR did not have much chance of getting anywhere by itself, having already reached the limit of its capabilities (which was not far from the truth). Sensing our unwillingness, Castro tried to put his proposition in a palatable form: the MLR—that is, its national committee—was to become "the voice of the revolution." Fiallo, Valdespino, and I looked at each other. The voice Castro had in mind was bound to be a prerecorded one—his own—and none of us felt inclined to accept the part. We made no immediate comments, however, other than some vague generalities. The meeting had outlasted its reasonable time and we were tired.

I have lingered on the details of this meeting—which I felt at the time was an outstanding event in my life—because I believe they offer an interesting glimpse into the mind of Fidel Castro at this embryonic stage of the Cuban revolution. The real significance of that encounter lay not in its express purpose—discussion of Castro's plan for a merger—but rather in the clash of attitudes and inner motives it brought into the open. It became evident that in order to bargain at the revolutionary table you had to show that you were ready to be something besides an ideological and programmatic discussion group. The idea on which the MLR operated, just to be there in case something turned up, was at best only wishful thinking. The MLR depended entirely on chance, and it proved its profound weakness when confronted with the Castro reality. As for Castro, he had solicited the opportunity and come to the meeting in a most unusual display of humility, but his megalomania and drive for power had soon prevailed. At the same time, paradoxically, Castro seemed to feel unsure of his capabilities as a national leader—as if the suit might turn out to be too big for him. This uncertainty may throw some light on his curious interest in the MLR. The suggestion that he may simply have been trying to associate himself in the public eye with people who projected a respectable image, a group that furthermore had intellectual and even religious overtones, seems reasonable enough. There can be no question that Castro had his course set by then and that he knew where he wanted to go. But he was also aware that in order to reach his destination he had first to cross certain psychological barriers. It is not too farfetched to presume, for instance, that the liability of his dubious, turbulent past was weighing heavily on him. His proposed rapprochement with the MLR responded primarily to a deep feeling of insecurity. There could hardly be any other explanation.

Valdespino reminded Castro that we could reach no decision on the question without consultation with and approval of the MLR's national committee. This was only a half-truth. We had realized at the outset that joining forces with Castro would amount in fact to becoming his satellite, and we saw no useful purpose in sacrificing an independent organization, no matter how small or academic, for that. If anything, the meeting had served to teach us a lesson: that with Fidel Castro equal partnership was impossible.

Instead of telling him how we felt and forgetting about the whole thing then and there, however, we decided to play along with the formalities and put the question to the committee. A second meeting was agreed upon for two days later—also at my apartment—when we would let Castro know the committee's decision and discuss the details if it were positive.

That second meeting was brief. Only Pedro Miret and Ñico el Flaco came with Castro this time. Since, as we had expected, the MLR's committee had unanimously voted against the idea, there remained nothing more to be said. Valdespino diplomatically added that the MLR's committee had based its negative decision on precisely the factor that seemed to make Castro favor an accord: the fact that our respective organizations were indeed cut out for quite different albeit equally necessary roles in the anti-Batista struggle.

And that was that. There was a brief postmortem flare of argument before the final polite handshakes and good wishes, and then Castro headed for the door. Addressing Miret, but obviously intending us to hear, he said with a trace of resentment in his voice, "Well, Pedro, now nobody will be able to say we didn't try. But, you know, maybe it will be better for us to go alone all the way, after all." And they did.

A few days later, July 7, Fidel Castro boarded a plane for Mexico. The SIM (Servicio de Inteligencia Militar), Batista's secret military police—one of several repressive corps—had been keeping a close watch on his movements, and he decided that his preliminary plans could be better implemented in the sanctuary of a neighboring foreign country. The day of his departure Castro sent a dramatic statement to the press vowing to carry on his fight to the end. It contained this sentence: "In 1956 we shall be free or we shall be martyrs."

The Batista dictatorship was paradoxical in ways incomprehensible then to most Cubans, let alone to foreign observers or "experts" in Latin American affairs. Castro, a sworn enemy of the regime with a long record of political violence, not only was set free after having been sentenced to fifteen years in prison for assaulting a military barracks, but was permitted to leave the country unmolested, and his announcement of armed revolution was published in the press. Yet such contradictions did not keep the Cuban situation from growing daily more tense. The FEU, for instance, kept the pot of public activism boiling with constant protests, strikes, and street demonstrations, many of which ended in bloody clashes with the police. Other revolutionary groups added to the student agitation with their own acts of terrorism. Unmindful of the Castro disaster three years before at the Moncada barracks in Santiago, one group attempted to take the Goicuría military barracks in the city of Mantanzas in a practically suicidal commando operation. The attempt failed, and most of the attackers were either killed or imprisoned. There were planned assassinations on both sides. Colonel Antonio Blanco Rico, chief of Batista's SIM, was gunned down at close range as he emerged from an elevator at the Montmartre nightclub in downtown Havana. The killers escaped. Showing total disregard for established diplomatic immunity, the police broke into the Haitian embassy, where a group of young anti-Batista militants had sought asylum, and there shot to death all ten of the unarmed refugees, some of them while they were trying to hide in closets and under beds. The chief of police, General Rafael Salas Cañizares, who personally directed the massacre, was himself hit by a low bullet that pierced his bladder, and he died a few hours later. One version has it that one of the victims, already on the floor seriously wounded, managed to grab a gun accidentally dropped by one of the policemen and fired at Salas Cañizares before the assassins had time to finish him.

Despite the horror of these events and the mounting popular agitation, a number of influential persons still believed in a middle course and advocated a so-called political solution—that is, one that would lead the country peacefully back to at least some semblance of constitutional order without going through the trauma of a national bloodbath. The two most prominent standard-bearers of this position were controversial former president Grau San Martín and Carlos Márquez-Sterling, an untainted figure in Cuban political life who enjoyed general respect for, among other things, having successfully presided over the constituent assembly that drafted the 1940 Constitution. To most Cubans, however, a political understanding with the Batista regime, which would inevitably imply the legal validation of the March 10 coup with all its consequences, smacked of appeasement if not outright treason. The conciliatory endeavors of Grau San Martín and Márquez-Sterling accomplished little except the split of their respective parties, the Auténtico and the Ortodoxo, from which two dissident groups emerged, each assuming the name of its original party. To nobody's surprise, one or two attempts at starting the political machinery failed completely and demonstrated that the problem of Batista could not be solved by the electoral process.

Toward the last half of 1955, the Sociedad de Amigos de la República (Society of Friends of the Republic, or SAR) called for a "civic dialogue" between the dictatorship and the opposition as a desperate means of averting armed conflict. The SAR was headed by Colonel Cosme de la Torriente, an octogenarian veteran of the wars of independence with an honorable record as politician and diplomat; at one time he had served as president of the League of Nations. Don Cosme, as he was called, was indeed one of Cuba's most prestigious figures. The MLR was invited to the discussion table. Fiallo, Segundo Ceballos (an economist formerly with the Auténtico party), and I were its delegates. Most of the opposition parties and organizations responded to the SAR's call. Castro did not, and the Communists were not considered part of the opposition; at that time they were friendly to Batista. The SAR wanted us all to search for a formula that would provide the country with a specific road back to constitutional democracy. For this hoped-for solution, however, some compromise with Batista would have to be worked out.

A series of meetings was held at the SAR offices in the section of the city known as Old Havana. The SAR's secretary, José Miró Cardona, a well-known lawyer and university professor, acted as chairman.[6] But after days of lengthy discussion no formula acceptable to everyone could be found. One obstacle proved to be insurmountable: the opposition was profoundly divided between "politicians" and "revolutionaries"—that is, those inclined toward a political understanding with Batista and those who would be satisfied with nothing short of the complete abdication of the dictator and his government. As for the MLR, it went to the conference primarily for publicity purposes. The occasion presented the movement with a national stage from which to air its views and promote its leaders.

The MLR took the lead in advancing a hard-line position. The Ortodoxo party agreed with us. Personally I felt very strongly on this question, and whenever I rose to speak I did so not only to defend our stand but also to thwart all probes in the other direction.[7] It had become evident that the majority of the delegates were in favor of coming to terms with Batista, but no one dared to say so openly. An agreement with Batista then might conceivably have provided a certain appearance of political normality, but at a high price: the acceptance of a political crime. This was precisely the point—rather than a particular "revolutionary" motivation—that at that time determined my position, and I maintained it not only at the meetings called by the SAR but within the national committee of the MLR, where the same rift began to appear. In fact, I may have become in this respect the most intransigent of all the MLR leaders.

Students of history today may wonder whether a realistic accommodation with Batista at that point could have spared Cuba the catastrophic experience of a revolution that ultimately placed the nation under the yoke of a totalitarian tyranny. On this question, of course, we can only speculate. But to many of us who lived through the events it seems far likelier that appeasement, while perhaps delaying a showdown for a while, would simply have added fuel to the flames, thereby enhancing the image and the chances of Fidel Castro.

In any case, the historical fact is that the "civic dialogue" failed and that, for most, the only course left was armed rebellion. Events soon proved, moreover, that words alone, no matter how rational or eloquent, could not hold public opinion for long. The "liberal" MLR appeared to offer little, even to many of its own leaders, when others were preaching and preparing for large-scale insurrection. One by one most of the members quit, and interest flagged among those who remained. For all practical purposes, the leadership of the movement shrank to Valdespino, Fiallo, and me.

The last important activity of the MLR was its participation in a mass rally organized by the SAR in the Muelle de Luz Plaza in Havana on the evening of 10 November 1955. The rally was called to announce that the search for a compromise formula mutually acceptable to the government and the opposition had been fruitless. The SAR blamed Batista. Colonel Torriente had tried to see him a few times but found the dictator contemptuous of the SAR's endeavors. On his last visit to the presidential palace the old gentleman had been made to wait for a long time and had finally been told that "the president" could not see him that day. It became

The patriotic Sociedad de Amigos de la República (SAR) in late 1956 invited the opposition groups to a roundtable discussion of possible solutions to the constitutional impasse. This is a partial view of one of the meetings. From left: Manuel Bisbé, of the Ortodoxo party; the author, Amalio Fiallo, and Segundo Ceballos, of the Movimiento de Liberación Radical (MLR). (*Carteles* photo.)

clear that the government intended to go ahead with its own electoral plans and had no interest in an accommodation with the opposition. The SAR wanted the people to know what had happened and so absolve itself of responsibility in the matter.

The meeting was attended by almost all the opposition groups, including the university students. The most popular figures in Cuba's political life were there. Neither the Communists nor the Castro followers were officially represented, however. Colonel Torriente presided. The speaker for the MLR was Fiallo. Some 30,000 people gathered in the old colonial plaza by the harbor. During the program, small groups of Castro activists, strategically scattered among the crowd around the high platform, watched for every opportunity to start their rhythmic chant of *"Revolución! Revolución!"* And when José Antonio Echeverría, the FEU leader, stepped before the lectern to speak, an organized Communist group started a commotion apparently aimed at having Salvador García Agüero, a black intellectual who was one of the leaders of the Communist party, invited to the podium. The crowd reacted quickly against the Communists' sabotaging tactics and a melee ensued. Chairs flew in all directions, and from the platform we could see the fist fights and hear the angry shouts of the crowd— "Out with the Communists! Kill the dirty *hijos de puta!*" The Castro supporters stayed aloof from the commotion, but every now and then their chant could be heard. Soon the agitators, badly roughed up, were hustled from the scene, and the rally proceeded with no further interruptions. Batista's police, usually quick to intervene at the slightest sign of public disturbance, stayed in their squad cars nearby and watched impassively as the Communist-created tumult developed.

In spite of that episode, the nonpartisan rally accomplished something very important: it showed that the people were united, despite party differences, against the Batista regime and wanted a return to legal, constitutional, democratic rule. The meeting demonstrated one further point: if some foreign observer had wanted to find out whether the Communists enjoyed wide support in Cuba late in 1955, the spontaneous reaction of that huge gathering would have provided a sufficient and eloquent answer.

Any faint hope of a political solution that may still have been lingering vanished after the public explanation of the SAR. When Colonel Torriente described the disappointing results of his efforts to persuade Batista to submit his de facto power to a real democratic verdict—not just a one-sided, rubber-stamp electoral masquerade—the well-intentioned "civic dialogue" came to an abrupt end. Amid attacks and recriminations, the gap between the established power and the intransigent opposition had now to be recognized as unbridgeable. An acute dilemma opened in very clear terms before the Cuban people: either resign themselves to Batista or take the always risky road of popular rebellion.

In the psychological climate of Cuba under Batista during the 1950s, political grievances combined with undigested revolutionary promises and hurt national pride to carry the conflict created by the unjustified seizure of power and the ensuing constitutional collapse to a point of no return. As days and months went by, the fate of Cuba took an ever more grim and foreboding air.

# 2 A Movement in Search of a Program

**D**uring the first half of 1956 my participation in anti-Batista activities was reduced to occasional attendance at clandestine meetings to which I was invited. Some plan or plot was always afoot in one organization or another. The MLR disintegrated and died quietly soon after the SAR's unsuccessful attempt at a dialogue with Batista. Fiallo and a few others decided to join the Márquez-Sterling Ortodoxo group, thus adopting the political line sponsored by Batista.[1] The rest felt free to go their own ways. The experience of the small, intellectual MLR showed clearly, if nothing else, the ineffectiveness of middle-course positions in times of acute political crises.

I went frequently to the university and became acquainted with a few students, some of whom later became deeply involved in the Castro movement: Juan Nuiry, Luis de la Cuesta, Marcelo Fernández, Germán Amado Blanco, and Lela Sánchez, daughter of the AAA leader Aureliano Sánchez Arango. The university was not only the spiritual headquarters, so to speak, of the anti-Batista movement in Cuba but also a center of underground information and contacts.

Sporadic events kept the political pot boiling but without causing much substantial change in the situation. In April 1956 a military plot to overthrow Batista and restore a democratic form of government was discovered by the SIM, and the officers involved were summarily sentenced to prison for long terms. Only their popularity with the troops saved them from the death penalty. Although the plot failed, it brought to light the fact that the military were not exactly unanimous in their support of Batista. The plot, which aborted when an infiltrated SIM agent notified Batista, was of considerable proportions. Its leader was Colonel Ramón Barquín, a highly qualified officer who had received part of his training on special assignment in the strategic and intelligence branches of the U.S. Army and who at the time of the attempted coup was military attaché at the Cuban embassy in Washington.[2] The chief civilian figure of the junta was Justo Carrillo, former director of the Bank of Agricultural and Industrial Development (BANFAI) and a leader of an anti-Batista organization called Montecristi.

Such incidents would raise a tremendous flurry of excitement and expectation, which dwindled away to frustration when nothing came of them. The much rumored insurrectional plans of the Auténtico groups connected with Prío Socarrás were postponed and postponed again, and never actually materialized.[3] It was known that Fidel Castro was actively engaged in serious revolutionary preparations in Mexico, and had even traveled to the United States, openly campaigning and raising funds for "the Cuban revolution" in New York, Chicago, Los Angeles, Miami, and other major U.S. cities with nuclei of Cuban residents and exiles. The contrast between the Auténticos' indecision and Castro's determination did not pass unnoticed. The Cuban opposition suffered from a lack of capable and aggressive leadership. It is not difficult to understand why many Cubans, accustomed to having some national figure on whom to pin their hopes, began to look to Fidel Castro, even though the "hero of the Moncada" was then a young man with no real political stature, with a long record of dubious episodes in the short span of his turbulent and hitherto purposeless life, and with no claim to public recognition other than an unparalleled audacity.

A frustrating feeling that the Cuban situation had become stagnant overcame me at times. The two organizations I had joined, mainly for reasons of intellectual and ideological affinity, had disappeared one after the other. My working hours were divided between *Carteles*, a popular weekly magazine for which I was staff writer in charge of a section of Latin American news and commentaries called "Nuestra América," and the office of the Cuban branch of the World Committee for Cultural Freedom (with head-quarters in Paris), of which I was secretary.

This Cuban Committee for Cultural Freedom (Congreso Cubano por la Libertad de la Cultura) had succeeded in bringing together a number of intellectuals of varying views on the Batista question. My contacts with that elite group made me realize that the prevailing mood among the Cuban intellectual community was one of accommodation with the status quo, whatever it might be. Yet, because of its very raison d'être, the activities of the committee appeared to have a rather anti-Batista character, if only because they were of an unofficial nature. I was even able to persuade the committee to accept the cooperation of Luis de la Cuesta, the secretary of culture of the FEU.

The president of the committee was José Manuel Cortina, a wealthy politician of the old school and one of Cuba's most talented and respected public figures. Many believed him to be the real drafter of the 1940 Constitution. Although he was a personal friend of Batista, Cortina did not approve of the March 10 coup and maintained a discreet distance from the Batista government.

But the most significant personality in that intellectual coterie was without question the late Jorge Mañach, a Harvard and Sorbonne graduate who taught the history of philosophy at the University of Havana. Mañach was a true liberal. A brilliant author and journalist with a terse and impeccable style, Mañach had a long history of involvement in the political and revolutionary life of Cuba. He had fought against the Machado dictatorship in the 1930s and was one of the founders and leaders of the ABC, a secret and elitist revolutionary organization. When Cuba returned to political normality, at least on the surface, Mañach was elected senator and later was secretary of state and of education during the constitutional Batista administration of 1940–1944.

Now, however, Mañach had turned against Batista. He had even founded his own opposition group, which he called Movimiento de la Nación, a reminder of his old personal conviction that Cuba had not yet reached full nationhood. I had known Mañach personally since the mid-1940s, when I had the honor of exchanging views with him publicly, in a series of articles in *Bohemia* magazine, on the role of the Cuban intelligentsia.[4] On several occasions Mañach invited me to join the Movimiento de la Nación, but I always politely declined. For all my respect for Mañach and for his extraordinary perceptiveness and eloquence in regard to Cuban problems, I considered his approach to the immediate pressing problem of the Batista dictatorship to be inappropriately moderate. Mañach's liberal philosophy, in combination with his characteristic urbanity, made him the typical middle-of-the-roader. And I was convinced, as the SAR experiment seemed to prove, that halfway solutions just would not work.

Meanwhile the Castro movement had been steadily growing. Most people did not realize it then, but Castro's appeal lay largely in the fact that he appeared to be the only leader who was prepared to act decisively against Batista. It was not so much a matter of Castro's personal merits as the fact that he was filling the vacuum created by the failure of the Auténtico and Ortodoxo leadership.

More than a year had passed since the fruitless conversation between Castro and the MLR leaders in my apartment on the Calle Ayestarán. I hadn't heard from Castro or from any of his followers again. The only thing I knew—the only thing anybody knew—was that Castro was in Mexico working on his announced plans to bring armed revolution to Cuba. After the disintegration of the MLR I resigned myself to remaining unattached to any organized group. Perhaps, I thought, I could contribute to the anti-Batista effort just as well as an independent individual, whenever the occasion presented itself. Despite my favorable response when a merger between the MLR and the Castro movement had seemed possible a year before, the idea of joining the Castro group had never actually crossed my mind. I noticed that the number 26 began to appear furtively painted on walls and other places around the city. A friend of mine thought I was joking when I wondered aloud what it meant. Only then did it dawn on me that that was the symbol of the 26 of July Movement—Castro's organization.

One day something happened that, though apparently insignificant in itself, was to affect the course of my life to a degree I could never have imagined. One afternoon, early in the summer of 1956, three young men came to see me at the editorial offices of *Carteles*. Their names were already quite well known in revolutionary circles—and to the Batista police: Armando Hart, Faustino Pérez, and Enrique Oltusky. They were accompanied by Carlos Franqui, a proofreader at *Carteles*. (The four were later to play important roles in the communization of Cuba.)

Armando Hart, the son of a judge of the provincial court of

Havana, was a lawyer in his twenties. A slender fellow who looked much younger than his twenty-odd years, Hart first came to public attention when as a university student he started a turmoil in a live CMQ television panel program conducted by Jorge Mañach in Havana one Sunday afternoon in June 1952. Hart gained further notoriety when he acted as defense attorney in the trial of Rafael García Bárcena after the frustrated attempt of the MNR to take the Campamento de Columbia.

Faustino Pérez, a little older than Hart, came from a lower-middle-class Protestant family from the small town of Cabaiguán in Las Villas Province, some 225 miles east of Havana. He had recently finished his training as a doctor. Because of his Presbyterian background, Pérez was trusted with the direction of the medical dispensary that the First Presbyterian Church of Havana maintained in its Sunday school annex. Pérez decided that he could use the place in connection with his terrorist activities as well as with his medical practice. In the dispensary's cabinets, right next to the children's Sunday school room, he stored dynamite and other materials for the making of bombs. The police, on Pérez's steps, discovered the cache, and Pérez spent several months in jail. After his release he joined the Castro movement.

Enrique Oltusky, also in his twenties, was, as his name suggests, of eastern European ancestry. He had an engineering degree from the University of Miami in Florida and was at the time employed by an American construction firm in Havana.

Carlos Franqui was the oldest of the four; he may have been in his middle thirties. I had first met him when I joined the *Carteles* staff some months before. Franqui was then a thin and sickly-looking fellow, soft-spoken and amiable. Franqui admitted to having been a Communist but claimed that he had broken with the party in disillusionment at its tactics. He had been a proofreader for the daily *Hoy,* the official organ of the Communist party in Cuba, before coming to *Carteles.*

At that time the fact that one had *in the past* been a Communist did not always arouse great antagonism among noncommunists. Many public figures—politicians, labor leaders, intellectuals, and others—at one time or another had looked favorably upon communist or socialist doctrines, but had later recovered from what was popularly referred to as the red *sarampión* (measles). Besides, largely as a consequence of their association with Batista during the decade 1934–1944, the Communists—and with them communism itself—had lost all respect and almost all political significance.

I had known Hart, Pérez, and Oltusky since 1952. They had been admirers and followers of García Bárcena and very active in the MNR. But after the MNR's demise we all had taken different paths, and I seldom saw any of them. The last time such an encounter had taken place, some five or six months before, it ended in a way that was as unexpected as it was alarming. Pérez and Hart had come one evening to my apartment on the Calle Ayestarán, accompanied by a very attractive young woman named Conchita Cheda, who appeared to be very much interested in the underground movement. I had noticed her among the visitors to the radio studio during the first broadcasts of Liberación Radical. Conchita did not stay long; she gave some excuse and left. My friends said they had come to hear my opinion on certain anti-Batista plots involving various groups, and they wanted me to arrange the cooperation of the MLR.

A knock at the door interrupted the conversation. It was past eleven, and my wife and the children were already in bed. I opened the door and saw three members of Batista's dreaded Buró de Investigaciones, carrying submachine guns. They informed me that they had learned that "subversive" meetings were being held in my apartment and that they had come to investigate. I tried to act as innocent as I could. "Subversive meetings here?" I said. "There must be some mistake. You can come in and see for yourselves." The invitation was just a figure of speech: the men were already inside.

"Hey, look who's here," one of the plainclothesmen said half-humorously when he spotted Pérez and Hart in the living room. "What a catch!"

The three detectives, surprisingly, appeared to be in a rather jovial mood. The one who seemed to be in charge took me aside. "Listen, doc," he whispered, "you better watch out. Somebody tipped us off about you." The man smelled strongly of alcohol. While the others searched the place, upsetting everything and frightening my wife and the children, the leader repeated his warning two or three times. Obviously under the influence of alcohol, he seemed to be telling some kind of truth.

The men from the Buró found nothing subversive in my apartment except, of course, Armando Hart and Faustino Pérez, two of the most active conspirators in Cuba at the time. "All right," the leader said, "you fellows have to come with us to headquarters." At least three more detectives, also carrying submachine guns, were outside waiting in two cars. The Buró de Investigaciones was in a gray fortress-like building on the Avenida 23 in the Vedado, near the Almendares River bridge. There were many stories of political detainees' being tortured there. We were told that we would be interrogated by Colonel Orlando Piedra himself, commander of the secret police and one of the key men in Batista's police apparatus. Apparently we were considered important. While the two cars sped along the Avenida Rancho Boyeros I tried to think what I might say or do to get out of this situation.

When we arrived at the Buró I was taken to be photographed and fingerprinted. (Not so Pérez and Hart, whose names had been familiar entries in the police subversive activities files for a long time.) During these procedures I was repeatedly told that "the government" knew all about my "revolutionary" activities and that I had better be prepared to "confess" everything to the colonel. If I failed to do so, the Buró men added with a meaningful smile, I might not fare too well—the colonel had no patience with uncooperative revolutionaries. Then I was taken to a cell where Pérez and Hart were already locked up.

No one came to take me to Colonel Piedra, and the hours passed. It was after three when a detective came and clinked the cell door open. This is it, I thought.

"Come on out," the man ordered sharply.

For an instant we just stood there in the brightly lit corridor waiting for further instructions.

"Don't just stand there," the man said. "Come on, move!"

"Where to?" Pérez asked timidly.

"Out," the man snapped, and then with a sudden smile, "You can go home."

"You mean we are released?" Pérez said incredulously.

"Yes," the man said.

That was all.

Out in the street we decided to go our separate ways. I waited for an early-morning bus right there on the Avenida 23 and went back home. I never did find out who had tipped off the police.

Now, months after that incident, Armando and Faustino came to see me again. This time they were accompanied not by some charming young lady but by two other Castro activists. Faustino explained why they had come. He began by referring to the growing significance of the 26 of July Movement as the only real hope for the Cuban people, in view of the failure or incapacity of the other political and insurrectional forces. He went on to stress the necessity of providing the movement with the appropriate ideological-programmatic revolutionary literature. And this was the matter about which they were now soliciting my cooperation: they wanted me to head a committee (they called it a *comisión técnica*) to prepare and draft such material.

The idea was indeed tempting. What I had always missed in popular discontent in general and in organized opposition in particular, even before Batista unexpectedly seized power in 1952, was a clear definition of both historical explanations and political goals. My friends' request came as a surprise, however, and for a moment I did not know what to say.

Trying to gain time before arriving at a decision, I brought up a matter that would have to be clarified in any case. I said that I enthusiastically endorsed their idea of working on the philosophical and programmatic bases of the revolution, but what about Castro? Would he approve of *my* interpretation of the revolution, *my* personal political thinking and philosophy, which would inevitably be the pattern to which all materials I might be expected to deal with would necessarily conform?

Hart said, "If that's your only concern, there's nothing to worry about." He went on to explain that although the idea of coming to see me was theirs, they would not have made the decision on their own without the knowledge of Fidel, with whom they kept in constant communication. And they knew for a fact that Fidel held me in the highest esteem and that he was quite familiar with my political philosophy. "He reads everything, you know."

Still there were a few more things that I wanted to make clear. I reminded them that the very fact that they were concerned about the appropriate revolutionary literature for the movement was a tacit admission that so far the organization was little more than an insurrectional venture against the Batista regime, with no adequate ideological or programmatic identification. They readily agreed.

This question of a program for the revolution is really at the core of the Castro story. The pamphlet *History Will Absolve Me*, prepared from the speech that Castro delivered in his own defense before the court that tried him for his responsibility in the Moncada episode, contains within its maze of passionate rhetoric ideological and programmatic elements that, according to some commentators, permit it to be considered a revolutionary manifesto.[5] But *History Will Absolve Me,* curiously, was not widely disseminated at that time, and neither Castro nor any of his associates ever made any attempt to present it as a formal declaration of the movement's political basis and aspirations.

As I have indicated, radical and revolutionary statements had become routine. Every political group issued one. All the parties, movements, and so-called revolutionary organizations that appeared in Cuba from 1930 on were invariably intent on displaying an "advanced" position. This had become a sort of ideological fashion during the Machado years and remained so in the years that followed. It was actually Cuba's share of the semantic confusion created in the Western world by the Marxist mutation of values, a dominant effect of the Communist revolution whose most widespread manifestation has been, even to the present day, the glorification of an advanced or "progressive" position. As if to add to the ideological cocktail, among the revolutionary organizations that appeared and disappeared in Cuba during this period there was occasionally one that showed some trace of fascistic leanings. The one characteristic that all these organizations had in common was their intense nationalism, easily understood in Cuba's geopolitical context, especially in light of its relations with the United States.

Now what could be called the intellectual elite of the Castro movement was in turn preoccupied with the old question of an ideological-programmatic manifesto. I pointed out to them that Castro's growing appeal lay not in the undefined area of Castro's ideological pronouncements and eventual political coloring in the future (very few Cubans gave serious thought to this at the time), but rather in his determined stance against the regime imposed by the military coup of 10 March 1952 and against the political corruption that had made it possible.

The situation disturbed me. Look at Eddy Chibás, I said. Chibás had become extremely popular by playing only a negative note. No matter how justified his unrelenting attacks on unscrupulous politicians and corrupt government figures might have been, the overall effect was further to weaken the institutions of democracy until they were powerless to resist the assault of the first unprincipled, power-thirsty demagogue to challenge them. History had shown over and over again that the mass of people was more likely to follow a strong-willed leader than the abstract postulates of a program. And for all my sympathy with Castro's direct approach to Cuba's political crisis, I had no wish to contribute to the rise of just one more strong man or to the substitution of one type of dictatorship for another.

Hart and the others seemed to agree wholeheartedly with my views. Franqui even said that that was precisely why they felt the need to develop appropriate political literature. He spoke with enthusiasm of "the differences between the leader and the chief." The allusion was crystal-clear. The idea of putting in writing the ideological bases and the whole raison d'être of the movement was responsive not only to the established practice but to the danger that the leader, without some specific set of rules, might eventually drift toward the ways of one-man rule. We should, Franqui said, try by all means to forestall such a possibility. The program would be like a bridle with which Castro's impulses could be controlled.

This line of reasoning seems almost childish now, but it played a decisive part in the sum of circumstances that drove me toward the 26 of July Movement. Still, I stated as a condition what I described as "my basic principles": that the Batista crisis presented a tremendous responsibility as well as a great challenge—the responsibility of correcting or improving on all that had been wrong or insufficient in the recent past. Revolution in Cuba must encompass political, social, economic, agrarian, and above all educational reforms, but these reforms must always be carried out *within the framework of representative democracy and constitutional government.* And I reserved the right to end my association with the movement whenever I considered that the organization was becoming merely a vehicle for ordinary power-motivated ambitions.

The four Castro activists seemed satisfied with my views and my comments. At least, they voiced no contrary opinion.

And so I finally promised to cooperate with the Castro movement in the preparation of its fundamental revolutionary literature. At the time I thought it was only a specific, isolated assignment that would end as soon as the task was finished. But a revolution is like a powerful whirlpool: once you let yourself be drawn into its swirling waters, you are inevitably pulled ever more powerfully toward the center until you find yourself completely immersed and caught in its force.

Curiously enough, the idea of my joining the movement itself was never even suggested during the conversation. There was no signing of membership cards or papers, not even any verbal statement to the effect that now I was a member of the organization. Nothing of the sort was necessary. The moment I agreed to participate in that so-called technical committee, I automatically became one more little wheel in the growing revolutionary machinery of the 26 of July Movement.

The committee held its meetings at Oltusky's apartment on the tenth floor of a modern building on the Avenida Menocal, popularly known as Infanta, one block from the Malecón. The meetings turned out to be disorganized and totally unplanned discussions, usually involving only Oltusky and me. Hart came only once. Faustino Pérez never showed up. They were quite busy with other underground activities. Franqui was present on a few occasions. I learned that he was part of a terrorist squad that also used Oltusky's apartment as one of its contact places.

I went to the Oltusky apartment once or twice a week for some time. After a number of largely theoretical discussions that seemed to get nowhere, Oltusky and Franqui placed in my hands a bundle of papers that they had gathered together, a disorderly aggregate of disconnected pieces on various aspects of a prospective revolutionary program which conformed to no discernible pattern. Most of the material was poorly done and of little value. I remember, for instance, an article written by Franqui under the title "Difference between the Caudillo and the Leader," apparently a favorite subject of his. The declared purpose of the article was to demonstrate that although Fidel Castro was the accepted leader of the movement, he would and should never be so in the traditional sense of the caudillo or strong man. Oltusky, too, had concocted a philosophical thesis, extremely abstract and complex, in which, before finally arriving at the problems of Cuba, he discussed the origins of man, evolution, the scientific method, and a few other subjects that were no doubt relevant but of limited immediate application. Hart also contributed several leaflets that had been circulated in Oriente Province.

They suggested that I use this material as a guide or reference in carrying out my special assignment. The proposed document was to deal with the reasons for the revolution and its general objectives. It would be followed by studies on such specific aspects of the movement's program as economic policy, agrarian reform, and education. Because of my experience as a teacher and as a writer on educational matters, they asked me to give particular attention to a plan for the reform of the Cuban educational system.[6] In addition, Franqui asked me to contribute to a clandestine little paper he was putting out, *Aldabonazo,* whose title was later changed to *Revolución.*[7] For this publication I wrote a number of articles and editorials—none of them, of course, signed.

The "technical commission," however, had a very short life. I soon became the sole member, and my visits to the Oltusky apartment were no longer necessary. My contacts with the group were limited to sporadic meetings at various places in the city. Pérez and Hart were engaged full-time in underground activities; Franqui and Oltusky kept their regular jobs and gave their spare time to the movement. Franqui used to drop in occasionally at the office of the Cuban Committee for Cultural Freedom, where I could be found most afternoons.

All of them seemed satisfied with the progress of the manifesto draft. They never even mentioned Castro's speech of three years before, the speech that became known as "History Will Absolve Me"—a literal manifesto.

# 3 Enter the American Press

**B**y summer 1956 the dilemma of the Cuban people had become ever more acute and pressing: either resign themselves to the demise of the 1940 constitutional era, accommodating to the new Batista reality, or prepare for armed rebellion. The latter alternative was the one already chosen and proclaimed by Fidel Castro. From Mexico he had reiterated his slogan: "In 1956 we shall be free or we shall be martyrs." The Castro vow, shrugged off at first by many, began to sound like a new contrasting, indeed promising, reality.

In September 1956 I unexpectedly received an opportunity to go to Mexico. The World Committee for Cultural Freedom organized a conference of Western Hemisphere delegates to be held at Mexico City that month. The Cuban committee appointed three delegates: Pedro Vicente Aja, author and professor of philosophy at a secondary school in Havana; Raúl Roa, dean of the School of Social Sciences at the University of Havana; and me.

Aja and I had been friends for many years. We shared the same religious faith and political philosophy, although Aja was never active in the revolutionary movement. I had become acquainted with Roa only after I returned to Cuba in 1952, but we had developed a cordial relationship. He was one of Cuba's best known intellectuals, though not exactly popular. Roa had emerged in the turbulent 1930s as one of the leaders of the Ala Izquierda Estudiantil (Student Left Wing), and for decades he was generally considered to be a communist. He seemed to have abandoned communism long ago, however. Later that year he even publicly condemned the Soviet repression of the popular uprising in Hungary.

On learning of my proposed trip, Oltusky suggested that I might take a message to Castro, and I agreed at once. Oltusky gave me a sealed envelope and the Mexico City address of someone who would arrange for me to see Castro. I was pleased at the chance of talking with Castro again, especially now, when he seemed to be on the eve of his announced invasion of Cuba. More than a year had passed since the meeting between Castro and the MLR leaders at my apartment.

Early in the evening on the day of my arrival in Mexico City, after checking in at the Hotel Emporio on the Paseo de la Reforma, I took a taxi to the address given me by Oltusky. I found the correct apartment and rang the bell. No one answered. Someone who happened to come out from another apartment informed me that "the lady who used to live there" had moved a few days before.

I felt a little frustrated. For the moment I could think of no way of finding Castro in Mexico, where of necessity, I thought, he must keep his movements unobtrusive. And since I had to return to Cuba, it did not seem advisable for me to start advertising that I was interested in getting in touch with Fidel Castro.

In the morning, however, things began to look more promising. At the opening session of the conference of the Committee for Cultural Freedom I chanced upon Teresa (Teté) Casuso, a Cuban writer and well-known political activist who was attending the conference as an observer. At the noon recess we sat together for a little chat, the main subject of conversation being, of course, the Cuban situation. To my surprise, Teté Casuso was familiar with my political views, and she seemed to be in general agreement with them. She said she was acquainted with Castro, and I understood that she was deeply involved in the movement's activities in Mexico. When I told her of my own activities in Havana and of my interest in seeing Castro, she promised to arrange a meeting. She would let me know the next morning.

Teté Casuso had been active in Cuban revolutionary politics since the early 1930s. She was the widow of Pablo de la Torriente Brau, a young leftist intellectual who was killed while fighting with the Loyalists during the Spanish Civil War. After graduating in humanities from the University of Havana, she had published one or two novels, though without much success. She wrote occasional articles for the Mexican press and had had a minor career as an actress in Mexican films. She had married, then divorced, a Mexican engineer. She had been a resident of Mexico for many years when Castro met her there and asked her to cooperate in his revolutionary endeavors. Teté Casuso proved to be extremely helpful to the movement. She was able to introduce Castro to many influential people, and her rented house in the fashionable Lomas de Chapultepec became a lodging and meeting place for the Cuban revolutionary community. Once, after a police raid, she even landed in jail with some of the Castro men.[1]

At the conclusion of the morning session of the conference the next day, Teté told me that she had talked to Castro and that he had told her he would meet me at her house the following afternoon at about four o'clock.

I arrived at Teté's a little ahead of time. The attractive two-story house and garage, set amid flowering shrubs surrounded by green lawn, looked modest in comparison with the elegant villas of the well-to-do neighborhood.

Castro was late. It was past five when he arrived, driving a battered old car. Teté and I went out to meet him. He was accompanied by four young men and an attractive young woman with the suggestive last name of Amor (love). She traveled constantly between Mexico City and Havana, they told me, serving as a secret courier for the 26 of July Movement. The men were obviously bodyguards; they carried guns. One of them (the only one I remember) was Rafael del Pino, a former student who had been with Castro during the eventful days of the famous *bogotazo,* on the occasion of the Ninth Interamerican Conference of 1948 in Bogotá, Colombia.[2]

Castro greeted me with the characteristic Latin *abrazo,* but I sensed a lack of warmth in his greeting. He turned back to confer briefly with his men, and two of them left, including del Pino. So did Señorita Amor. All this took place outside on the lawn. Then we all went inside.

Once the customary pleasantries were over, I explained my presence in Mexico and told Castro about my recent connections with leaders of the movement in Havana. Then I handed him the envelope Oltusky had given me. Castro opened it, glanced rapidly at the contents, replaced them in the envelope, and put it in his pocket. His expression did not change, and when he spoke, it was about the preparations he was making for his revolution.

It was soon clear that Castro was more interested in talking than in listening. He seemed to be trying to impress me with the seriousness and legitimacy of his ideas and of his movement. He talked insistently and in a thousand ways of the rigorous political and moral preparation that his men (the future guerrillas of the Sierra Maestra) were then receiving in Mexico. Those boys, he said, had to live in Spartan austerity both in and out of the training camps. As if to imprint it well in my mind, Castro told me over and over that, in addition to their military and guerrilla training, the soldiers of the revolution were required to read and discuss a variety of books of historical and political significance, especially, he emphasized, the works of the Cuban liberator José Martí. It was obvious that Castro wanted me to go back to Cuba convinced that he was indeed a sincere, dedicated, and patriotic man.

There was something I could not quite grasp behind Castro's words. It was only after several years and a lot of experience that I realized that Castro's monologue had been a calculated theatrical performance. He knew of my access to the press and that my views were generally well regarded. Being acutely conscious of the importance of popular reaction to his plans, Castro wanted a new, reformed image of himself to replace, or at least overshadow, the unfavorable memories of his turbulent, questionable past.

Teté announced that dinner was ready and invited everybody to the dining room. But Castro said that he had some business to do around town and suggested that instead we all meet there afterward for a late snack. Turning to me, he said, "Why don't you come with us? We'll have a chance to talk, and I'll introduce you to some friends." I said I would be delighted. It was already dark when we left.

Castro took the wheel of the old sedan—a Plymouth, I think it was. I sat next to him. Two of his bodyguards got in the back seat. Castro took me to perhaps three places in different sections of Mexico City, apartments of Cuban families. I came across a few people I knew. We greeted each other in pleasant surprise, rejoicing that we were traveling on the same train. Castro would call some people aside to another room, obviously to talk in private. At one apartment there were women, children, and several guests. It appeared to be some special occasion. They were serving a big

Cuban buffet with plenty of Mexican beer. I thought of Teté's postponed dinner. Castro talked more than he ate. When we left, one of the young fellows who had come with us stayed behind in order to make room in the car for Jesús Montané and Melba Hernández, two well-known veterans of Castro's revolutionary adventures.[3]

The last stop was at the home of Alfonso Gutiérrez, a Mexican civil engineer familiarly known as Fofo. This man was considered to be one of Castro's most generous patrons.[4] He was married to a beautiful Cuban woman, a former nightclub singer by the name of Orquídea Pino. Apparently it was she, an ardent admirer of Castro, who influenced her husband to give aid to the Cuban revolutionary. The Gutiérrezes lived in a modern villa with swimming pool in the Pedregal, a most exclusive suburb of Mexico City. The house, on a small rocky hill, was surrounded by a high stone wall.

The car stopped at the entrance and Castro blew the horn in a way that was obviously a signal. In a minute or two the heavy wooden gate opened and Gutiérrez himself came out. Castro and Montané got out and went to him. They conferred for about ten minutes while the rest of us waited in the car. On rejoining us, Castro said, "All right, folks, what do you say we just head back to Teté's?" The others made murmurs of assent and Castro added, "I really haven't had a chance to talk much with our friend Dr. Llerena, and I'd like to hear his opinion on a few things. . . . But let's get there first. I'm hungry."

I was not familiar, of course, with those surroundings. The car's headlights sliced through pitch-blackness and we were driving through hilly terrain on a narrow, winding dirt road. Trees and telephone poles loomed close to the road. The car went faster and faster. I was in the back seat now with Melba and Montané and I could not see the speedometer, but I was sure we were going more than sixty, faster than I would have wanted to travel on this road on a clear day. We seemed constantly to be heading directly toward a tree or pole, only to swerve toward another as Castro jerked at the steering wheel.

At last I said, "Don't you think we're going a little too fast, Fidel?"

Castro burst into laughter, and the others joined in. When the laughter subsided, Melba said, "Why did you have to speak, Dr. Llerena? We were only testing your nerves as a revolutionary." I learned my lesson.

It was past eleven when we got to Teté's house in the Lomas de Chapultepec. There was hot chocolate in the living room and sandwiches and tacos. The group was composed of some eight or ten people.

We spoke of the situation in Cuba. I gave them my firsthand impression: discontent and protest against the Batista regime were growing, but capable and effective leadership was lacking. While a demoralized government was desperately trying to sell the electoral plan by which it hoped to achieve a semblance of constitutional legitimacy, the opposition forces were disorganized and fragmented, unable to concur on a joint plan of action. Under these circumstances, more and more people were beginning to turn their eyes to the 26 of July Movement as the only remaining hope.

As if on a sudden impulse, Castro rose and invited me to accompany him upstairs, at the same time motioning to Teté Casuso to join us. We went into what looked like a guestroom. Castro's tone became confidential.

"How long do you suppose a revolutionary presence will have to stay alive in Cuba before it can mean real trouble for the Batista government?"

My optimism went far beyond reason. "The way things are right now," I told Castro, "if a revolutionary force can keep itself active there for thirty days, the Batista regime will collapse."

Castro smiled and remained quiet for a moment. Then he said with his characteristic self-assurance, "We are prepared to set up the Hotel Nacional in the mountains and resist six months." The Hotel Nacional was the most luxurious hotel in Havana; Castro clearly expected to be well supplied in his mountain encampment.

It seemed to me that Castro was, if not overconfident, at least lacking in elementary discretion. In mentioning "the mountains" he was revealing not only the kind of operation he had in mind but also the probable geographical areas where he intended to go after landing in Cuba. Even if "taking to the hills" was almost traditional in the history of Cuban revolutions, there was no reason for Castro to be so communicative, especially since I was new in the organization and had nothing to do with military or guerrilla matters.

But Castro did not stop there. Turning around, he said, "Come over here. I want to show you something." He went to a large closet door that was secured with a padlock. Castro searched in his pockets until he found the key. The closet was crammed with au-

tomatic weapons: rifles, carbines, submachine guns, pistols. . . .
Castro was visibly elated, like a child showing off his new toys. I
was not in the least surprised at the spectacle. After all, it was no
secret what business Castro was in—what business we all were in.
I was amazed rather at Castro's unsolicited and reckless display of
confidence.

"Look, what do you think of this?" he said. He had taken out one
of the rifles and was turning it in his hands, fingering the mechanism, almost caressing it. It was Swedish, I think he said, and he
added some other technical details that were beyond my compe-
tence to grasp. The rifle, with a telescopic sight, was exactly like
the one Castro was holding in the photograph taken later by Herbert L. Matthews in the Sierra Maestra and published with his
famous series of articles in the *New York Times,* beginning on 24
February 1957. In fact, that kind of weapon, useful for shooting
from a distance, was to become the characteristic, perhaps even
symbolic, trademark of Fidel Castro.[5]

Teté excused herself and left to join the others downstairs. Castro then turned the conversation to Cuba's immediate political future, and I felt a little disappointed. I thought of myself as a revolutionary, a member of a revolutionary movement, and here was the
leader of that movement talking respectfully about the old parties
and the old figures on Cuba's political scene with a clear sense of
subordination, particularly in regard to the Ortodoxo leaders. Was
it all a pretense to impress me with an image of moderation? In the
eyes of the majority of the Cuban people Fidel Castro was still an
Ortodoxo and the 26 of July Movement was nothing but the party's
shock troops for the proposed attempt to overthrow Batista.

Had Castro not yet outgrown his political allegiances of the past?
The opposite possibility, that he might take a radical course, did
not, of course, occur to me. On the contrary, my fear was that he
might slide down the easy slopes of traditional politics. The pattern
was all too familiar to every Cuban. Were there not enough living
examples from the 1930 Generation around to make such a fear
reasonable?

Castro kept talking with hardly a pause. "Once Batista is out,"
he asked me, "who do you think would be the best candidate for
provisional president?" Before I could answer he went on: "Don
Cosme, Miró Cardona, Raúl Chibás?" Don Cosme, of course, was
Cosme de la Torriente, the old colonel from the war of independence who had tried so valiantly to engage Batista in a civic dia-

logue under the auspices of the SAR. Miró Cardona was still the SAR's secretary. Raúl Chibás was a brother of the late Eddy Chibás and a member of the executive council of the Ortodoxo party. By the time of my conversation with Castro in Mexico, however, it is probable that Chibás was already collaborating with the 26 of July Movement in Havana.[6]

I said that I had not given any thought to the question, but my feeling was that the provisional president should be somebody capable of understanding that Cuba had entered a new era of revolutionary change and development. The 26 of July Movement should cut any ties that still bound it to political organizations of "the past" (I meant specifically the Ortodoxo party, of which Castro was still nominally a member) and try to fly with its own wings. The 26 of July Movement should not be blind to its opportunity—after the failure of so many parties and movements—to become *the* political instrument of a new Cuba.

For the first time Castro listened quietly. He struck an air of deep meditation, his elbows resting on his knees, his fingertips touching, looking downward with half-closed eyes. "We'll come to that, we'll come to that," he muttered. "But for the time being we cannot put every card on the table."

Castro's mood puzzled me, and I wondered again if this man would be only another strong man, one more in the long line of would-be revolutionaries who turned into mere politicians as soon as the revolutionary tide had ebbed.

Perhaps reading my mind, Castro embarked suddenly on a meticulous description of what he called the revolutionary objectives of the 26 of July Movement. He seemed to sense that I needed to be convinced of the real revolutionary character of his movement. In essence, however, what Castro said did not go far beyond the usual list of reforms that had been promised by every politician and written into every platform from right to left for more than a quarter of a century. Castro certainly did not sound any particularly radical note—at most, only that touch of progressive utopianism that was so pleasing to moderate revolutionaries. He achieved a tone of sincerity, and my reservations were somewhat dispelled.

Castro then referred in particular to educational reform, a subject that was very dear to me. In my opinion, I told Castro, educational reform should be given paramount attention by the 26 of July Movement. And I mentioned that, at the request of our friends in Havana, I had started work on one such project.

*"Magnífico!"* Castro said. "Say, why don't you include in it my plan for school-cities?" He described with visible enthusiasm what appeared to be one of his pet ideas. As he explained it, his school-cities were to be educational centers located in strategic rural areas where the students would live as well as study from kindergarten through secondary school. In other words, the children would live apart from their families and be under the guidance and control of the state during the entire period of their formative years.[7]

I tried to hide my distress. His proposal was in direct opposition to my own philosophy of education. The occasion, however, did not seem appropriate for a full-fledged argument, and I merely pointed out some of the practical weaknesses of his plan. For courtesy's sake, I promised that I would give it some study.

We had been talking for more than an hour and it was quite late when Castro said, "Let's go downstairs. I have an economic document they sent me from Cuba recently and I'd like you to see it and tell me what you think of it."

We went downstairs and joined the group in the living room. Castro asked for the "document," and one of his aides searched in a bulky, dilapidated portfolio and handed him a typewritten manuscript. I noticed that everyone seemed eager to attend to Castro's every wish. Teté brought in coffee. The manuscript appeared to consist of about thirty to forty legal-size, double-spaced pages. The corners of the pages were curled; they had been much handled.

"Here," said Castro, handing the manuscript to me, "will you read it aloud, please?" He stretched out on a sofa, puffing on his perennial cigar. Two or three people sat on the floor, leaning against the sofa where Castro lay.

I began to read. As I went along, I noticed that the manuscript bore many handwritten comments, some in pencil, some in ink. The document was a thesis on the economic bases and development of a new Cuba.[8] The fundamental aspects of the economic thesis (that is what it came to be called: *tesis económica*) included control of foreign investments, state interventionism, revision of United States–Cuba treaties, and diversification of industry. A strong note of nationalism ran through it, the same keen nationalism that had developed in Cuba parallel to the revolutionary tide of the 1930s. It was really a sentiment rather than a true political conviction. Cuban nationalism had its roots in the general Latin American view of the United States as a crude, rapacious imperialistic power and was fed by resentment at the Platt Amendment and the visible influence of Washington in domestic affairs.[9] Cuban nationalism moderated considerably through the years, especially as a result of the Good Neighbor Policy of the Roosevelt era, but it remained alive.

I looked at my watch when the reading was finished. It was past 2 A.M. I was tired, and most of the listeners looked tired too. I did not feel like going into a discussion of the whole subject at that late hour. It was evident, on the other hand, that Castro had read and reread that piece of political literature and had his mind already made up about it. He was using the occasion to explore my own thinking on a future economic policy for Cuba.

Sitting up on the sofa and relighting his cigar, Castro said, "Well, what do you think of it?"

I had mixed feelings about the so-called thesis but definitely did not feel like getting into a detailed discussion at that hour. I had to look at it in very broad perspective, in any case, since economics was not my field. But I could not pretend to be enthusiastic, either. I tried to give Castro a noncommittal reply. "I think it's a fine interpretation," I said, "but I have the impression that it goes a bit far in certain respects."

"Yeah," said Castro, "that's the way I feel about it too."

He stood up, and all the others did the same.

"We'll take you to your hotel," Castro said.

He took the driver's seat again while his companions got in the back. The car sped through the deserted streets of the Lomas de Chapultepec and then down the Reforma. They let me off in front of the Emporio. There were good wishes and farewells. That was the last time I talked with Castro face to face.

At the conference the next morning Teté Casuso pulled me aside. "I just can't get over it," she said. "Why Fidel . . . last night . . . . I tell you I never saw him so communicative. Just imagine, showing you that closet! Only two or three of the most responsible people in the movement are supposed to know about it. He doesn't have that much trust in most people." I assured her that I had been no less surprised myself. Then she said, "Where is Roa?" I told her I had not seen him that morning. Evidently he had failed to come to that session. She appeared annoyed and distressed. When Castro heard that Roa was in Mexico, she told me, he said he wanted to talk with him. A meeting between Castro and Roa appeared important to them. "We shouldn't let the opportunity pass," she said. Teté and Raúl Roa had a long acquaintance that dated back to the 1930s and the students' protests against the Machado dictatorship. "Will you tell Raúl when you see him?" I promised her I would.

Roa, Aja, and I, the three Cuban delegates to the conference, were staying at the same hotel, and we usually had dinner together around eight o'clock. That evening, instead of waiting for Roa downstairs, I went up to his room to give him Teté's message in private. I began by telling him about my meeting with Castro. Roa showed no surprise at all. He approved of my involvement and even expressed agreement with the insurrectional position of the Castro movement. But when I told him about my conversation with Teté that morning, that Castro wanted to see him, his face changed. He became visibly nervous. That was a different matter, he said. He was not too sure that, under the circumstances, he should run the risk of a meeting with Castro in Mexico, even a secret meeting.

At that moment the telephone rang. It was Teté Casuso. By listening to Roa's end of the conversation, I got the impression (which Roa confirmed later) that Teté was pleading with him to come to a meeting with Castro. It seemed that Castro was at her house now and was waiting for him. It occurred to me that Castro probably wanted to establish contact with intellectual or public figures who might eventually join the movement and, if nothing else, enhance the organization's prestige and thus contribute to its popularity. I saw nothing wrong with that. What I did not think of then is that perhaps Castro was thinking of using such people as a facade to disguise the undeclared extremism of his plans for the future.

But Roa was not yet ready for Castro's approach. He gave Teté one excuse after another, angry at times at her insistence and finally telling her flatly that he was not interested, that she could tell Castro that he had come down with the flu and had made last-minute arrangements to leave for Havana early in the morning—anything she cared to invent as a reason for his declining the invitation. When he hung up he was in such a state of irritation that he cursed Castro and Teté. He was not going to risk arrest in Cuba, he said, by going to a silly, useless meeting with Castro. Roa forgot that only minutes before he had praised me for having done just that.

Three days later the conference ended and Vicente Aja and I returned to Havana. Roa decided to remain in Mexico for one or two more weeks.

Back in Havana I followed the usual underground routine: secret meetings with students and other anti-Batista elements, contacts with people considered important and sympathetic to the revolution. I spent a good portion of my time working on the *manifiesto-programa*.

On December 2 Castro and his group, eighty-two men in all, landed from the yacht *Granma* in the vicinity of Niquero, Oriente Province, some fifteen miles from the western end of the Sierra Maestra. There they were soon discovered by government forces and were almost annihilated. Castro and about a dozen others scattered and later reached the mountains, forming an active guerrilla nucleus that soon began to grow.

A temporarily successful uprising under Frank País, the leader of the 26 of July Movement in the region, had taken place two days earlier in the capital city of Santiago.[10] This action was meant to coincide with Castro's landing, but the schedule became confused.

The impact of these events obviously affected the course of my own activities in Havana. Most of those in the original Castro group disappeared from circulation. I went to the university almost every day and chatted with Roa at his office in the social sciences building. There I made the acquaintance of a group of university students who were preoccupied with the current critical situation and the future of Cuba. They and other anti-Batista people occasionally came to my office at the Committee for Cultural Freedom.

News of what was happening in Oriente Province, especially in the Sierra Maestra, was vague and conflicting. At first it was said that the Castro group had met with total disaster. United Press International reported that Castro himself had been killed. Also reported dead was Faustino Pérez (I put a $5 bill in a collection box Oltusky passed around for his "widow").

One of the students who came frequently to my office was Luis de la Cuesta, an intelligent and amiable young fellow who was in charge of cultural activities for the FEU. Cuesta, whose gentle manners and weak physical appearance concealed a cool courage in the face of danger, turned out to be deeply involved in the underground revolutionary movement, though he was not committed to any group or party. He seemed to know practically everybody.

Among the people to whom he introduced me were Felipe Pazos and his son Javier, also a student with revolutionary ideas.

Around mid-February 1957 Cuesta brought me word that Felipe Pazos would like to see me as soon as possible. Pazos, an economist who at one time had been president of the National Bank of Cuba, was working then for the Bacardí rum firm, and his office was just three blocks from mine. I walked over and was greeted warmly. Pazos was interested in the 26 of July Movement, and he said he thought Castro was gaining in stature and becoming a great leader. He showed me a copy of a document that he said was an analysis of Cuba's economic ills and a proposal for appropriate remedies. I saw at once that it was the same "economic thesis" that Castro had asked me to read in Mexico. Pazos explained that the document had been prepared by some professors at the Universidad de Oriente, and that he had contributed some of his own ideas to it. But, Pazos said, he had not asked me to come just to talk about the document. He had news: an American friend of his, the *New York Times* correspondent Herbert L. Matthews, had succeeded in traveling secretly to the Sierra Maestra, and had seen and interviewed Fidel Castro.

The fact that an American correspondent had interviewed Castro in the mountains was great news indeed. It could be the much needed breakthrough in the veil of silence imposed by the Batista government. Matthews, Pazos said, was going to write a series of three articles that would appear in the *New York Times* in the next few days. Would I, Pazos asked, be willing to fly to New York at once? Before I had time to react, Pazos explained what he had in mind. He wanted me to get copies of Matthews's articles as soon as they came out, have them reprinted—probably by offset—and airmail them to people in Cuba. I agreed that no better scheme could be devised to circumvent the government's tight censorship. The revelation that Castro was alive and fighting in the Sierra Maestra, coming from a source as reliable as the *New York Times,* would have tremendous psychological impact. Yes, said Pazos, but, simple as it was, an assignment like that could be trusted only to someone of absolute trustworthiness. That was why he had thought of me.

I was grateful for his good opinion of me and told him I was ready to do my best, only . . . I hesitated a moment.

"Only what?" he said. I told him frankly that I could not afford a trip to New York.

"Oh, don't worry about that," he said. "I wouldn't expect you to assume the expenses." Then he took two books from his desk and handed them to me: the telephone directory and the Havana *Social Register*. "Here," he said, "for names and addresses." He also gave me an envelope containing a round-trip ticket and some cash for expenses.

The next day I was on a nonstop flight to New York. Immediately after my arrival I established contact with some local Castro sympathizers, and they introduced me to others. There were several organized groups. All of them were eager to cooperate. Indeed, in no time I had a group of enthusiastic people asking what they could do. I told them. When the three *New York Times* issues were out, I arranged the clippings and pasted them on a large sheet of cardboard for the offset job. Then I divided the work so that some people would be dictating addresses, some typing, and still others stuffing, sealing, and stamping the envelopes. Between three and four thousand copies of Matthews's articles were mailed to Cuba.

While I was in New York I went to see Matthews at the *Times* offices. When he learned that I had just arrived from Havana on a mission for the Castro movement he was delighted to see me. He spoke affectionately of Pazos. He knew Raúl Chibás, too. He told me about his trip to Cuba and how, with the help of the Civic Resistance Movement[11] in Santiago., he had managed to trick the Batista police network in Oriente into believing he was an American businessman and reach Castro's mountain hideout.

It was evident that Herbert L. Matthews was most sympathetic toward the revolutionary cause in Cuba and toward Fidel Castro in particular. He was also willing to help. It would be a good idea, he suggested, for me to go on television—my identity should be disguised, naturally—and speak to the American audience as a secret agent of the Castro underground in Havana. I agreed at once. As a matter of fact, I told Matthews, I had had the opportunity of doing exactly that a few months before in Havana, when, through a *New York Times* representative there, I was approached by some NBC correspondents then visiting Cuba.[12] The interview took place in a room of the St. John Hotel in the Vedado section, and the tape was televised coast to coast the following morning on Dave Garroway's *Today* show. Matthews immediately picked up the phone and called the Columbia Broadcasting System, and eventually was connected with the right person. After hanging up, he wrote on a card the name and office number of one of the directors of CBS News. The man was interested in seeing me the next morning at eleven, if that was convenient.

I had no pressing schedule and was pleased to keep the appointment. At CBS everything seemed to be working out well until I realized that the CBS News director (I have forgotten his name) assumed that Matthews would appear with me before the cameras to conduct the interview. I had received no such impression. When the CBS man called him to clarify the situation, Matthews said he could not do it because he was already too publicly involved with the Castro movement, and a television appearance with me so soon after the publication of his articles might reflect upon his editorial position with the *Times*. The CBS man tried hard to change his mind, but without success. When he hung up he told me he was sorry, but without Matthews there could be no interview. Nevertheless, he hastened to add, CBS News was very much interested in covering the Cuban situation, and he called in two reporters and told them he wanted them to listen to my story. They invited me to lunch. One of them was Robert Taber.[13]

Back in the office, in view of my description of the situation in Cuba and of the activities of the movement, the director said he would be interested in sending a reporter to the island if I could offer some assurance that this man—who would try to pass as a tourist—would be alerted about upcoming revolutionary events and put in contact with key figures of the underground.

I was practically overwhelmed by these unexpected developments. Fully aware of how vital publicity was for a revolutionary enterprise, I told the CBS director that although the final decision did not rest with me, I was sure that everything could be arranged. On this basis, he decided that Taber should leave for Havana in a matter of days (after I had returned and had time to start preparations). Taber would get in touch with me as soon as he arrived. We exchanged addresses and telephone numbers, even code names.

I took a plane back to Havana with a definite sense of accomplishment.

Back in Havana, I resumed work on the manifesto. Changes in editorial policy at *Carteles* resulted in the dropping of my section, "Nuestra América," and I remained as only a contributor of signed articles. I now had much more time to myself, and spent a good part of the day at the office of the Committee for Cultural Freedom.

Luis de la Cuesta and his friends continued to be frequent visitors and we had long discussions on revolutionary ideas and activities. I seemed to enjoy their respect and admiration, although they did not necessarily share my enthusiasm about the 26 of July Movement. Their attitude toward Castro and his organization appeared to be a mixture of disdain and wariness. Among the group were Germán Amado-Blanco, whose father was a Spanish intellectual who had come to Cuba when Franco triumphed in Spain;[14] Marcelo Fernández, who had studied engineering at MIT; and Javier Pazos and Raúl Roa, Jr.

Cuesta, the leader of this little group, appeared unassuming and soft-spoken, even shy, yet he knew and was in touch with important opposition figures, diplomats, and almost everybody in the anti-Batista struggle, and was always well informed about everything that was happening or about to happen in revolutionary circles. Cuesta was liked and respected by all those who knew him, partly no doubt because he never was in anybody's way and was always ready to help any organization or person who actively opposed Batista, regardless of the position such people occupied in the political spectrum. Among Cuesta's specialties was finding refuge for revolutionaries wanted by the police. I once helped him hide a Dominican who had been the pilot of the yacht *Granma,* which had brought Castro from Yucatán to Cuba. Cuesta hid this fellow in two or three homes (many totally unsuspected families cooperated in this way with the revolutionary forces) before obtaining asylum for him at the Mexican embassy. On another occasion, Cuesta persuaded two of his student friends—Germán Amado-Blanco and his brother—to pass on to me fifty pounds of dynamite left over from past terrorist activities; I was to keep it for the 26 of July. I stored the dynamite for about a week in the office of the committee. One evening a meeting of the committee was held there, attended by some twenty persons, among them Jorge Mañach and Raúl Roa. I could hardly keep my mind on the meeting; all I could think of was the dynamite, a few feet away in a cabinet. At my insistence, Cuesta found another place to store the dangerous stuff. He came in a car with Germán Amado-Blanco, and the three of us wrapped the sticks in newspaper and cautiously drove to a house on the Calle Máximo Gómez (popularly called Monte) where another of Cuesta's friends, a surrealist painter by the name of Manuel Couzeiro, lived. It was an old two-story house in an almost entirely commercial district. The dynamite was taken to a small room on the roof. A few days later I helped Carlos Franqui take it away again. He said it was going to be used by 26 of July "action" elements with which he was in contact.

Another member of that group of young revolutionaries was Lela Sánchez, daughter of Aureliano Sánchez Arango. Lela was an unusually intelligent girl endowed with a rare beauty, which she disguised by a sort of offbeat style that seemed a curious anticipation of what is seen today among nonconformist youth groups in the United States. Lela took her revolutionary dedication seriously; she was well informed on political and ideological matters, and she participated not only in student demonstrations and street confrontations with the police but in terrorist activities as well. Cuesta appeared to be Lela's platonic admirer and was her almost constant escort; but she was engaged to Germán Amado-Blanco, whom she later married—and divorced.

The most radical of that group of immature doctrinaires, at least in attitude, was Javier Pazos. He thus made a vivid contrast to Marcelo Fernández, whose boyish face and restrained manners suggested an apprentice philosopher.

Raúl Roa, Jr., was something special. He was a learned young man who could discuss art and literature as well as politics, and was fluent in both English and French. Although he managed to be personable, Raulito (as he was familiarly known) considered himself a cut above the others, and several cuts above Castro and most of the other revolutionary leaders. They were inconsistent and amateurish, he said, and he disdained to involve himself with their activities. Raulito could be described best, perhaps, as a theoretical revolutionary with conservative habits and expensive tastes. He was always impeccably dressed. He was a short young man, and his friends used to refer to him as "the petit bourgeois."

What makes these young people interesting today is the realization that they represented the human material that made the Communist revolution possible in Cuba. They did not come from the "exploited masses"—not from the peasantry, not from the working class, not from any supposedly oppressed minority. They were members of a small elite segment of Cuban society, well educated and affluent. At first they all looked upon Castro and his organization with condescension. Yet in time, as Castro began to emerge as a political presence, all of them drifted to his side and almost overnight became fanatical radicals and active leaders—even Raulito

Roa. At the time I knew them, these budding intellectuals were simply patriotic idealists, discontented with "the system" and willing to do something about it. As long as the anti-Batista struggle confined its just aspirations within the democratic framework, they constituted a positive reserve full of promise for a better Cuba. But once the Castro mystique got hold of their emotions, their very intellectual background and easy life acted, paradoxically, as fertile soil in which the seeds of radicalism soon germinated. I used to think that my personal influence had played no small part in bringing them into the fold of the 26 of July Movement. I no longer believe that. Those young people had within themselves the habits of leisure, the undigested knowledge, and the spiritual vacuum that ultimately determined their ideological conversion.

# 4 A Taste of the Underground

**M**arch came. The draft of the manifesto was practically finished. The guerrilla focus of the Sierra Maestra had come alive—especially after the *New York Times* articles—and seemed to be holding firm and gaining momentum. In the capital, however, the 26 of July was not making much progress. The torch of agitation and subversion was being carried rather by such anti-Batista groups as the FEU and its offshoot the Directorio Revolucionario, the Triple A, and the Organización Auténtica (followers of Prío Socarrás). Many acts of violence and terrorism, including assassinations, were committed. The government responded with arrests, torture, and more assassinations. Military positions were attacked and people died but nothing changed. Rumors of imminent uprisings and coups circulated every day. The country lived in an atmosphere of constant suspense.

For the most part my own activities were limited to meetings and discussions. Occasionally I found myself involved in something of a more hazardous nature. Somebody offered me four Thompson submachine guns for the Sierra Maestra fighters. I called Germán Amado-Blanco, who came in his father's Austin. We drove to the address where the weapons were located, loaded them into the car, and took them to a garage owned by one of my brothers-in-law, Fernando Hernández, who was an active member of the 26 of July.[1] A good mechanic, Hernández specialized in concealing rifles, pistols, and other small weapons in used automobiles. He hid the arms so cleverly that only the most alert expert could discover them. For months Hernández's specially outfitted cars formed one of the supply lines for the Sierra Maestra. Usually two couples pretending to be on a pleasure trip traveled the 600 miles between Havana and Santiago with little or no difficulty at the innumerable checkpoints along the way.

Then Faustino Pérez, not dead after all, showed up in Havana. I saw him several times, always at a different place. Faustino (he was always referred to by his first name alone) had been given the mission of contacting "important" people—professionals, journalists, businessmen, executives—who might be persuaded to join the movement. It occurred to me once again that Castro was trying to dress up the organization with a coat of respectability, so as to avoid or dispel the impression that it was no more than an unprincipled rabble out to destroy society, moved primarily by resentment and hatred and greed. Faustino told me that he would like very much to see Pazos, and I arranged a meeting. Apparently it was successful: a few months later Pazos went to the Sierra Maestra and became one of the cosigners, with Castro and Raúl Chibás, of the so-called Sierra Manifesto of 12 July 1957.[2]

Faustino asked me about my manifesto and, on learning that the first draft was already finished, asked me to let him see it. He read the manuscript, and his reaction was less than enthusiastic. In general he liked it, he said, but he objected to one sentence condemning "communist totalitarianism." Pointing with his finger at the place in the manuscript, he said, "This they are not going to like up there." Faustino was referring, of course, to the guerrilla leaders in the Sierra Maestra, although he did not mention names. He explained somewhat cryptically and apologetically that he did not mean *all* of them but a significant number of those "around Fidel." I realized that Faustino was reluctant to go into the matter much further, and so it was left at that. I also showed the draft to Marcelo Fernández, who by this time had become a full-time activist of the 26 of July Movement. Marcelo's reaction was somewhat like Faustino's. He thought the document should reflect a more radical ideological line, especially in denouncing the evils of capitalism and in its socioeconomic pronouncements in general.

I took both suggestions into account: the direct condemnation of totalitarianism was deleted from the text and the sections dealing with socieoeconomic matters were reworded. I reasoned that, after all, the document was never meant to be my own personal manifesto, and what did a little concession here and there matter when, in the last analysis, the revolution was in no danger of getting out of hand?

At the same time, despite all the editing, the manifesto was in fact my own. For all its revolutionary rhetoric, it remained an essentially democratic declaration of principles, a "liberalized" version, at most, of the traditional philosophy of freedom and human dignity that any schoolboy could find in the works and lives of Thomas Jefferson and José Martí. Its basic ideas, as well as its stated objectives, coincided with those of the Latin American movement known as the Democratic Left, whose main figures are Rómulo Betancourt in Venezuela, José Figueres in Costa Rica, and Luis Muñoz Marín in Puerto Rico. To a lesser degree, similarities existed also with the Apra movement, founded in Peru by Victor Raúl Haya de la Torre in 1924. The same stream of "progressive" democracy ran through the ideas and writings of many Americans of the 1930s, among them John Dos Passos, Waldo Frank, and Carleton Beals.

Faustino's warning remark, however, raises some serious points. It could be taken—especially in the light of subsequent developments—as unmistakable evidence of the active presence of Communists in the highest echelons of the 26 of July Movement. (Which of them were already party members—aside probably from Raúl Castro[3]—has not been clearly determined.) Why did I not recognize the significance of that revelation? The freedom-loving character of the Cuban people, together with the historical and political roots of the young republic and the powerful presence of the United States so close at hand, seemed to guarantee that communism, whether domestic or international, could never be established in Cuba. Moreover, the local Communists were so discredited, especially as a result of their association with Batista in the recent past, that the mere thought of their having any voice or influence in the revolutionary process would have appeared ridiculous to anyone.

I took Faustino's remark as nothing more than an understandable concern for the feelings of some guerrillas whose ideas might perhaps be a little on the radical side. Faustino himself was to me beyond all suspicion of communism or communistic leanings. So I forgot about the incident until much later, when the movement began to show unmistakable signs of heading toward the extreme Left.

I have lingered on these thoughts not in some belated attempt at self-justification—after all, it was Martí who said, *"Todo hombre honrado tiene derecho al error"* (Every honest man has a right to make a mistake)—but because here lies the connecting thread of this book, the painful and costly lesson that the whole experience meant to me: the awesome responsibility and usually irreparable mistake of many sincerely motivated people who, carried away by idealism, join or support the first glamorous revolutionary venture that comes along with convincing and apparently justified claims. Their trust and expectations that the movement will be the long-desired instrument for the eradication of social and political evils and the subsequent opening of a constructive era end too often in bitter disappointment. The new reality turns out to be quite different from what was originally envisioned—and hardly better than the previous one.

Somebody advised me of an important meeting to be held in a house in Santos Suárez, a middle-income residential section south of downtown Havana. Armando Hart, his hair dyed red and wearing dark glasses, had arrived secretly after a long stay in Oriente Province, with frequent visits to Castro in the Sierra Maestra. With him came two Ortodoxo leaders of that province who were actually working for Fidel Castro. Their purpose, Hart explained, was to organize in Havana the Civic Resistance Movement, which was already very active in Oriente.

The CRM was supposed to be an independent, nonpolitical, nonviolent, yet secret organization composed mainly of middle- and upper-class people. Their only common denominator was to be opposition to the Batista regime and a readiness to do something about it. But there was more to the organization, Hart went on, than the canalization of popular discontent. Although appearing to be a totally independent entity, the CRM would in fact be preparing a mass of disciplined activists whose main function was to influence and manage public opinion in a way favorable to the revolution and in particular to the 26 of July Movement. In addition, it would serve to channel contributions to the movement. The CRM, in other words, was to be a typical front organization.

A committee was appointed for the Havana branch before Hart

returned to Oriente. Raúl Chibás and I were to have the leading responsibilities. Chibás was the principal of one of Havana's most exclusive private schools, the Havana Military Academy. A quiet man, the opposite of his famous brother, Chibás had been named a member of the executive council of the Ortodoxo party. He thus became the liaison man between the party and the 26 of July Movement.

The Civic Resistance Movement was to be organized in a pattern of secret cells. I approached a number of friends and acquaintances, mostly professionals, with whose political ideas I was more or less familiar, and found a very favorable response. For some time it looked as if this were going to be my specific area of revolutionary activity. Then Armando Hart returned to Havana with a different mission.

Hart was then acting secretary of organization for the 26 of July Movement. He had married Haydée Santamaría, a woman some years his senior who was one of the founders of the 26 of July and remained a member of the movement's highest echelon. Haydée, known as Yeyé, was a veteran of the Moncada assault, where she had lost a brother and her fiancé. She joined the guerrilla group in the Sierra Maestra shortly after Castro landed from Mexico and stayed there (except for brief excursions such as this clandestine visit to Havana) until almost the end of the campaign. On the two occasions when I saw Hart in Havana, Haydée was with him; it was evident that she exerted a strong influence upon her young husband.

Hart called a meeting of 26 of July leaders at the Colegio Nacional de Farmacéuticos on the Malecón. Six or seven of us were there. Various plans concerning the activities of both the 26 of July and the Civic Resistance Movement were discussed. But the most important subject, and apparently the main reason for this second trip of Hart's, was his announcement that Fidel was about to launch a big guerrilla drive and that he wanted some American newsmen there to cover the events. Whether the drive actually materialized or not, Hart added in a confidential tone, was secondary; what Castro and the Dirección Nacional (National Committee) were primarily interested in was publicity, especially in the United States. He mentioned the tremendous impact of Matthews's articles in the *New York Times*. I suggested that we invite Matthews again. No, Hart said, Fidel preferred to have some other reporters this time. Both Matthews and the *New York Times*, he

Haydée Santamaría
(foreground) and Celia
Sánchez, Castro's personal
secretary, in guerrilla garb
in the Sierra Maestra.

said, could be considered practically in our pockets, so it was better
to keep them in reserve for the future. Good publicity required an
impression of absolute impartiality in the reporting. The question
now was, therefore, whom to contact—and how.

I suggested Robert Taber of CBS. Taber had come down to Cuba
shortly after our meeting in New York in February. After a few
fruitless days in Santiago he returned to Havana, and I took him to
Oltusky's apartment in the Nuevo Vedado section, where he had
moved from the Avenida Menocal. Oltusky, I thought, could arrange an interview with Faustino. The police were aware that
Faustino had come to Havana and the various repressive corps
were after him. He nevertheless managed to move around secretly
from place to place. As it happened, however, Faustino was out of
town at the moment, so Taber could not see him. After a couple of
weeks Taber decided he was wasting his time in Havana and went
back to New York. Considering myself indirectly responsible for
his apparently useless trip to Cuba, I had promised him that I
would advise him by either telegraph or telephone—in a certain

prearranged manner, of course—at the first sign that something was about to develop.

Hart was enthusiastic about the idea—so much so that he rejected the telephone or cable procedure in favor of sending someone to New York personally. I argued that that was not really necessary, but he insisted, and all the others agreed. Only one question remained: Who should go? This did not take them too long to decide either—who else? I knew Taber, I spoke the language, I had a ready visa. Money for the round trip and expenses was produced immediately (the 26 of July leaders always seemed to have substantial amounts of cash at their disposal), and the next day I was once again on a plane to New York.

As soon as I got through customs at Idlewild Airport I called Taber's number. It was early in the evening. Taber was not home, his wife said, and she did not expect him back until ten or ten-thirty. I told her I would call again.

When I finally reached Taber and explained to him briefly the reason for my sudden trip, his enthusiasm was greater than his surprise. "This seems to be it, doesn't it?" he said. He asked me to meet him for breakfast next morning at eight at his apartment in lower Manhattan. We would probably have a full day ahead, he added.

We did. After I explained the plan in detail, Taber called the person at CBS who had handled his previous trip. The man suggested that we come to his office at 2 P.M. It was a long session. There were telephone as well as personal consultations. People from other departments were called in. I assured them that the 26 of July people in Cuba were prepared to take care of Taber and transport him safely to the Sierra Maestra, where he would join the rebel forces of Fidel Castro as a war correspondent. My assurances finally dispelled any doubts they may have had, and it was decided that Taber would go to Havana with complete cinematographic equipment.

Then the CBS News director came up with another idea. "Why do things halfway?" he said. "If we're taking the risk of sending over a cameraman, we might as well send along a sound technician too." The situation was becoming complicated. An extra man with bulky equipment would add considerably to the difficulties of passing through customs and checkpoints. But everybody was optimistic now and the idea was adopted without further ado.

The question of who should go with Taber, however, presented a new problem. Two or three names were mentioned. The one who appeared to qualify best was a fellow by the name of Wendell Hoffmann, who at the moment was on a field assignment in some remote part of Nebraska. They decided to try to reach Hoffmann (there was no telephone at his location) with an urgent message telling him to stop what he was doing and report to New York immediately. If there was no answer from Hoffmann by the next morning, they would look for a substitute, or Taber would go alone as first planned.

But Hoffmann did get the message, got to a phone, and advised that he was coming. He was in New York the following day. Arrangements were made for the three of us to take a National Airlines nonstop flight to Havana scheduled to leave Idlewild at 5 P.M. that same day. The plan called for me to take Taber (and now Hoffmann too) immediately after arrival to the home of a doctor named Martínez Páez in the well-to-do suburb of Miramar, west of Havana.[4]

Everything was going smoothly, yet as we discussed our plans before going to the airport something kept bothering me. The idea of two Americans landing at the Havana airport with all their conspicuous electronic gear, especially when the Batista government was still smarting from the Matthews blow, began to look more and more like a mouse trying to sneak by in front of the cat. I thought of a little trick. Taber and Hoffmann could pretend to be American missionaries on a field tour to inspect and photograph the Presbyterian schools in Cuba. Visits of this kind were relatively frequent. I knew almost all the Americans—not to speak of the Cubans—who were connected with the Presbyterian church on the island.

When I told Taber of my plan, he thought it was a great idea, and I briefed him on names of people and places and other details. Then, leaving nothing to chance, I put in a call to Havana, to the Reverend Raúl Fernández Ceballos, pastor of the First Presbyterian Church and a member of the 26 of July underground. Nearly all overseas calls were tapped by the Batista intelligence apparatus, so I told him that Dr. E. A. Odell (a well-known missionary, for many years director of the West Indies department of the Board of National Missions) had asked me to accompany two missionaries to Havana. I would appreciate it, I said, if he could be at the airport when we arrived. To make sure he would understand what I was trying to tell him, I also asked him to advise Marcelo Fernández about our arrival.

I told Taber and Hoffmann that it would be safer for us to go to the airport separately and appear not to know each other during the flight. At Idlewild our departure was delayed an hour by mechanical difficulties and then another hour because of bad weather, but at last we were on our way.

My message to Fernández Ceballos, unfortunately, had been so well camouflaged that he was not sure whether or not it was to be taken literally. So he decided to play safe: he advised Marcelo, but he also brought along to the airport two other Presbyterian ministers—one of them the Reverend Francisco García, superintendent of Presbyterian churches in Cuba. The result was a double and incompatible reception committee.

Taber and Hoffmann passed through customs without the slightest difficulty. As for me, two of the inspectors knew me personally and they did not even bother to open my suitcase. While waiting there, however, I glanced around and saw a number of familiar faces—Marcelo and a few people of the CRM, including two young women. They appeared stern-faced and mysterious, and instantly I became aware that something strange was going on. They would not come near me or meet my glance. I thought they were overdoing the cloak-and-dagger performance a bit. Then one of the women approached me and started a casual conversation. After a few words she whispered, "The police raided the house. There've been some arrests. Armando was caught. Marcelo will see you outside." She walked away unconcernedly, giving me no time to ask any questions.

I joined the two Americans and the stream of other people moving toward one of the exit gates. Outside I was met by the Presbyterians. I introduced Taber and Hoffmann. When Francisco García—a very timorous man—learned that the Americans were not really Presbyterian missionaries and that he had been embroiled in a conspiratorial scheme of the Castro movement, he was shocked and greatly alarmed, and protested indignantly to Fernández Ceballos and me.

But there was no time to placate the angry clergyman. Standing nearby, half lost in the bustling mass of people greeting relatives and friends, calling porters, loading their baggage into the open trunks of their cars, was Marcelo. I made my way to him. "What happened?" I said.

He gave me a laconic but complete report: The police had broken into Martínez Páez's house in Miramar. They found nothing suspicious, but hauled him and two others off anyway. Hart had been caught in Luyanó, an industrial district southeast of Havana, trying to board a Santiago-bound bus. "We thought," Marcelo said, "the police were acting on a tip and there might be a trap waiting here for you and the Americans. Evidently it's been only a coincidence, but we've had to make new plans for the trip to Oriente." Marcelo paused for a second to glance around and then said, "The Reverend will give you all the details; I've got to go now."

I was about to ask Marcelo something, but he had already turned around and was hurrying away. "Wait a minute!" I said, running after him and grabbing his arm. "When did this happen— the police raid, I mean?"

"A little before nine this evening," he said.

I let him go. I thought of the two-hour delay at Idlewild. If our plane had taken off on schedule, Fernández Ceballos would almost certainly have taken us to Martínez Páez's house before they had time to warn us. We would have run straight into the trap.

It was almost 2 A.M. when Fernández Ceballos' station wagon stopped in front of the Presbyterian church on the Calle Salud in downtown Havana. Waiting there in another car were two other 26 of July militants, armed with pistols and submachine guns. They had been assigned to escort the American reporters to Oriente. Soon another car arrived bringing Taber, Hoffmann, and Marcelo.

Everybody spoke in whispers. Any noise or disturbance at that late hour was bound to attract the attention of the police patrol. With extreme care the equipment and belongings of the Americans were transferred from the station wagon to the cars. When everything was ready, the two cars left for their long journey to Santiago. My part in the mission was over. Fernández Ceballos took me home.

The 26 of July organization succeeded in transporting the two American reporters, with all their paraphernalia, the 600 miles from Havana to Castro's encampment in the Sierra Maestra. Their presence with the guerrillas and their colorful reports—which were broadcast on television and radio throughout the United States and appeared in the pages of *Life* magazine—proved to be another tremendous propaganda boost for Castro.[5]

Hart was in jail. Marcelo had gone to the Sierra Maestra. Oltusky, having been transferred by his employer to Santa Clara, capital of Las Villas Province, had shifted his operations there. Franqui and a few others had fallen into the hands of the police when the place where they printed the little clandestine paper *Revolución* was discovered and raided.[6]

A few days after the raid I received a telephone call from Franqui's wife suggesting that I take precautions for my personal safety. She had the impression that her husband had named his associates in jail under police pressure. (I learned later that he had.) I decided to go into hiding, at least for a few days, and spent a week at my brother-in-law's apartment in the Víbora district. When nothing out of the ordinary happened, I returned home.

Then, early one afternoon in late March, Germán Amado-Blanco called me at the office of the Committee for Cultural Freedom. He said something important had come up and asked if he could come immediately and pick me up. Of course, I said. Some fifteen minutes later he was there.

With the caution of those engaged in underground activities, Germán had parked his car two blocks away. When we reached it I saw two young women waiting inside. As we exchanged greetings I realized by their accent that they were from Oriente. They had arrived that morning with two men on a special mission for the movement. It was an established practice in those days for revolutionaries to travel in mixed couples to give the impression of young men taking a ride with their girl friends.

We were supposed to pick up Javier Pazos at his home, but when we got there he was not home. His mother said he might be at a friend's house nearby and gave Germán the address, but Javier was not there either. Germán grew angry (he was an excitable person) and began to lament in a loud voice that he had ever let himself get mixed up in this kind of business. With their sweet Oriente accent, the girls tried to calm him down. I still had no idea what the business was this time, except that there was some important meeting to be held at a house in the Santos Suárez district. As Germán became more and more nervous, I began for the first time to have an uneasy feeling that something was going to go wrong.

Germán stopped at one more place to look for Javier, but when we still could not find him we decided to go on without him. We drove to Santos Suárez, an old middle-class residential area, and parked on the tree-lined Calle D'Strampes. The house Germán indicated, like most others in the neighborhood, was set amid shrubbery and flowering plants, separated from the sidewalk by a low iron fence. I recognized the place; I had been there before with Armando Hart. It was the home of José Garcerán, a university student who was active in one of the 26 of July student groups.[7] The girls and I got out and Germán drove off; he was not expected to attend the meeting. We climbed five or six concrete steps to the front porch and were admitted to the house. The house, like most old urban dwellings in Cuba, consisted of a series of rooms extending back from the street, with a small rectangular patio at the rear. The living room and master bedroom were at the front; then came another bedroom and a so-called dining room—actually the family living area—and finally the patio, with the kitchen and some other rooms to one side. At the other side and at the end of the patio an eight-foot wooden fence marked the limit of the property.

My first impression was that there were too many people for the occasion. In addition to the Garcerán family—five or six persons—there were three students, the two Castro emissaries, and now the girls and I. Then another man came, a 26 of July militant named René Rodríguez. Rodríguez stayed only a short time, however. He was angry about something and left unceremoniously. According to those who knew him, Rodríguez was a rather contentious person, quick to take offense.[8]

Soon I realized that the only participants in the meeting itself were to be one representative of the Dirección Nacional, Pazos, and myself. Garcerán was to be present only during the discussion of his liaison work with student groups. After the inevitable black coffee in the dining room, Garcerán motioned me to follow him to one of the back rooms by the patio. There I saw Javier, who had come ahead of us without waiting for Germán, and the fellow from Oriente, who evidently did not want to show himself before the others. He was a young man, probably in his late twenties, short and thin but wiry and rugged. His last name was Iglesias, but he was better known by his alias, Nicaragua. He was one of Castro's majors in the mountains. His mission, he said, was to urge the adoption of a joint plan of action by the 26 of July and the Civic Resistance Movement in Havana. The main objectives were to be sabotage, terrorism, infiltration in the government, propaganda, and a fund-raising campaign.

The discussion turned to the organization and functions of various kinds of cells. Garcerán had been making a rough diagram on a piece of paper, but now he had to leave to keep another appointment with a group of students elsewhere. He said he would be back soon.

Shortly after he left, one of the students who had been in the dining room broke in suddenly and whispered, "The Buró is at the door!"

For a few seconds Pazos, Iglesias, and I stared at each other. My mind leaped to my suit coat, which I had taken off when I entered the room—it was a very hot day. Garcerán had gone to hang it up somewhere toward the front of the house. In that coat I had left my billfold, which contained, besides some money and the usual cards, my driver's license with my name and address.

When the police entered a house they usually searched it thoroughly. Should I or should I not try to find and retrieve my coat? I had no idea where Garcerán might have put it, or whether the detectives were already inside the house or still asking questions at the door. But some quick decision was imperative.

It was Pazos' voice that triggered my action. "Let's go!" he said, darting off to the patio and turning toward the back fence. Iglesias and I followed him. It was a tall wooden fence made of wide, unpainted boards nailed vertically to rails that unfortunately were on the other side. It was necessary to jump high in order to reach the top with one's hands and then do some rather difficult and arduous climbing with the help of knees and elbows. Pazos and Iglesias did it in no time. I was the last. I didn't dare look back for fear of seeing the Buró agents coming after me. I jumped with all my might and succeeded in getting hold of the top. The operation cost me a few minor scratches and bruises, but I landed safely in the next yard. A dog barked furiously from behind some other fence. A woman shouted, "What's going on there?" We ran, making our way through clumps of foliage, jumping over hedges, until finally we came to a lane that led to the next street.

Evidently the agents did not see us or even suspect that anyone had run out of the house through the rear. No one came after us and we saw no searching patrol cars. It was a very quiet block. There were no curious passers-by or people staring from windows. Apparently no one but the dog and the woman had noticed any disturbance. Pazos and Iglesias went to the right without a word. I walked in the opposite direction toward the Avenida Acosta, two blocks away.

I tried to put my mind in order and think what I should do next. My first thought was for my family: I must warn them immediately and tell them to get out of the apartment as quickly as possible.

I took a bus and went to Hernández's garage on the Avenida 10 de Octubre, on the opposite side of the city from my apartment on the Calle Ayestarán. I told my brother-in-law what had just happened and then called home. My wife, a nurse at the Anglo-American Hospital, was still on duty—it must have been around four in the afternoon—and our two children were not yet home from school. A nephew of my wife's, a teenage student who was staying with us then, answered the phone. Cautiously (one had always to be wary of tapped telephones) I explained to him the fix I had got myself into. He understood immediately. I asked him to gather together everything I could remember that might be considered subversive—papers and documents of various kinds, and especially a large manila envelope containing the manuscript of the manifesto—and take it all to my brother Eduardo, who was the principal of a Lutheran elementary school in the Reparto Martí, a suburb. I told him to tell my wife that all of them should stay at Eduardo's for the time being. Under no circumstances were they to spend the night at the apartment. I would stay with Hernández for the next few days.

Before the afternoon was over, Hernández was able to learn that the police had taken everyone they found at the Garcerán house to Buró headquarters. As there was hardly any material evidence at the house, it was clear that the police had acted on a tip. Someone in the neighborhood who saw the unusual gathering of strangers? An informer within the 26 of July? I have always been inclined toward the latter possibility. The women, except for the girls from Oriente, were released the following day. The police, according to the newspapers, had found the rough diagram penciled by Garcerán, and announced the discovery of sinister plans of sabotage and terrorism being prepared by the revolutionaries.

The third day after my escape from the Garcerán house, my wife, much against the advice of my brother, went to our apartment to see if it appeared safe to return with the children. After all, she reasoned, the police were interested only in me, and I was not there. She found the lock on the front door broken and the door secured by a padlock.

As she stood there in the hallway, the building manager and some neighbors came to tell her what had happened. About nine that morning, three plainclothesmen, two of them carrying submachine guns, had come to the apartment and, when nobody answered the door, forced their way in. The noise had attracted the

manager. When he realized what was going on, he had coura-
geously insisted on witnessing the search on the grounds that he
was responsible not only for the property but for our belongings as
well. The padlock on the door had been put on by him as a temporary measure after the agents left.

During the last two days the building manager and some of the
neighbors had noticed a couple of suspicious-looking men hanging
around the café across the street. It was apparent that the secret
police had set up a watch to catch me if I came home. When the
quarry failed to appear, they had decided on the search.

The apartment was a mess, although the manager had kindly
picked up clothes and things from the floor and placed them on
beds and tables. We had no valuables, but the police took away everything that could have had any significance in connection with
my activities: a small filing cabinet containing my correspondence,
photos, my passport, and an assortment of other papers.

Two days later the newspapers carried a police report containing
a fantastic accusation against me. The articles were illustrated by
one of the photos seized at my apartment. Curiously enough, the
report made no mention of the incident at the Garcerán house. I
was described as one of the leaders of a terrorist band supposedly
responsible for a number of sabotage attempts at various hotels a
few days earlier. This story, of course, was pure invention; I never
had anything to do with terrorist activities. The police report said
also—I have never understood exactly why—that I had been ap-
prehended and was detained at Military Intelligence headquarters.

The police may have had two motives in issuing this report.
They probably overestimated the role I played in the revolutionary
underground, and by linking my name to terrorist activities, which
were abhorrent to the general public, they probably hoped to discredit all opposition to Batista. My involvement in the 26 of July
Movement was still unknown; but because of my contributions to
the press and other public activities, I was generally regarded as
an active member of the political opposition.

While one of Castro's closest lieutenants had escaped unnoticed
from the raid on the Garcerán house (the people arrested there,
most of them women, had little or no public relevance), I now
found myself presented as a big wheel in the revolutionary machinery. The episode canceled my freedom of movement in Cuba;
it literally put me out of circulation.

The Reverend Fernández Ceballos made arrangements for me to

stay at the home of the García family—members of his church—
who lived on the upper floor of an old two-story house on the Calle
Escobar in downtown Havana. These kind people, despite the
serious risk, kept me at their home for some three weeks. Then,
since the longer a person stayed in one place, the less safe it became, Fernández Ceballos took me to the apartment of Isabel Díaz
de Arce, with whose family I was acquainted, all devout Method-
ists. Two other sisters and a brother lived there, on the second
floor of a house on the Calle Neptuno, two blocks from the university. There I spent two more weeks.

After making a careful analysis of my situation, I decided to
apply for asylum at one of the Latin American embassies. Most of
the embassies were packed with political refugees, and the ambassadors were understandably reluctant to admit new ones except in
extreme cases, but by now I knew I was an extreme case. My
choice narrowed to Mexico, mainly because I believed that from
that country I had the best chance of reaching the United States,
where I had relatives. After receiving a special passport (which the
government sometimes arbitrarily delayed for many weeks), a political refugee was supposed to go directly to the country whose
embassy had granted him asylum.

Meanwhile my family had been able at last to return home. They
had been staying with my wife's relatives in the nearby town of
Güines. The chief of Military Intelligence, Colonel Carlos Cantillo,
had grown up in that town, and he and his brothers had been
boyhood friends of my wife's brothers. Accompanied by Fernández
Ceballos, my wife went to see Colonel Cantillo, partly to seek protection for herself and the children and partly to request that my
passport, illegally retained by the police, be returned to her. I
would need it to enter the United States.

The colonel received them courteously and without delay. He
asked my wife about her brothers and sisters and ordered coffee
brought in. After listening to her requests, however, he said he
was sorry but my passport could not be returned. Mine, he explained somewhat cryptically, was no ordinary case. The colonel
deeply regretted that a person like me should have let himself be
swept up in the iconoclastic revolutionary vogue.

He gave my wife emphatic assurances, however, that she herself
had nothing to fear. She and the children could return to the
apartment with complete confidence. To dispel any worries that
might remain, he gave her his office and home telephone numbers

and told her to call him should any difficulty arise at any time. (A couple of plainclothesmen did knock at the door once and said they had orders to search the place, but when she said she was going to call Colonel Cantillo they begged her pardon and left.)

Since it was not advisable for me to use the telephone in a private home, I had asked Fernández Ceballos to go to see Raúl Roa at the university and tell him about my decision to seek asylum. I knew Roa was a personal friend of the Mexican ambassador, Gilberto Bosques, and hoped their friendship might facilitate my plans. Roa indeed talked to Ambassador Bosques immediately. The ambassador said he was perfectly willing to admit me, but could I wait until at least one of the refugees at the embassy was given his departure permit? All available accommodations were overoccupied now, but he was confident that there would be room in a few days.

So it was. Four or five days later, around eight in the morning, I had an unexpected caller, a young woman by the name of Isabel Martínez Junco. She was a friend of the Díaz de Arce family and also a Methodist. She said she knew me, although I had no recollection of ever having seen her before. I learned that she was the sister of a young doctor whom I had met while both of us were members of the MLR's national committee. Her brother was exiled in Mexico,[9] and now she had come to take me to the Mexican embassy. I had better hurry, she said—police agents and informers were everywhere; we should take no chances. I threw my things in a suitcase as quickly as I could, expressed my gratitude to the Díaz de Arces, and followed Miss Martínez downstairs.

A car was waiting with the engine running. The driver was a young fellow whom I had never seen before. On entering the car I received my second surprise of the day. In the back seat was Marta Frayde, a doctor who was a member of the executive committee of the Ortodoxo party but was known to be a Marxist.[10] What she had to do with my going to the Mexican embassy I have never found out. Perhaps she, too, was a friend of Ambassador Bosques; if so, Roa may well have asked her to add her influence to the case.

At the embassy, which was located in the section called Nuevo Vedado, I had to share a room with four other refugees. One of them had been involved in an unsuccessful attack in March on the presidential palace, aimed primarily at killing Batista. Wives and close relatives were permitted to visit the refugees once a week. When my wife came, I asked her to bring me the envelope containing the manifesto manuscript on her next visit. When she did, the embassy officials intercepted it. I was notified later that the ambassador wanted to talk to me.

Ambassador Bosques informed me that refugees were forbidden to possess or receive political material at the embassy. However, he added diplomatically, in spite of his official position, which he hoped I would understand, he would be willing to ease the rules a bit in my case. But before he could make a decision, he wanted, if I did not mind, to read the document. "Of course, Mr. Ambassador," I said, and he kept the envelope.

Three or four days later I was invited to lunch with the ambassador and his family. This appeared to be a routine courtesy; most of the refugees received similar invitations at one time or another. The ambassador's private quarters occupied the left wing of the building. I lunched informally with the ambassador, his wife, and their only daughter. Ambassador Bosques reminisced about the days when he himself had been an active revolutionary in his native Mexico, but he avoided any comment on the Cuban conflict.

After dessert and coffee, he took me aside to a small studio and told me that he had read the manifesto. "Very interesting," he said in a noncommittal tone, taking the familiar manila envelope from a desk drawer. "And what do you plan to do now?"

I said truthfully, "I really don't know."

He smiled understandingly and handed me the document. "Be careful," he said. "It's a secret that you had that here, eh?"

I gave him my most earnest word, and I thanked him for his personal kindness and for Mexico's hospitality.

"Good luck," the ambassador said, shaking my hand.

It was mid-June when my departure permit arrived. Three other refugees received their permits at the same time. The following day a representative of the foreign minister—according to the established procedure—came to escort us to the airport together with the Mexican consul. There our families were permitted to say good-bye to us. Some twenty minutes later we were flying toward Mexico City.

My immediate future was vague. I knew only that I would try to obtain entry into the United States as soon as possible. I was on my own. I never had been subordinate to anyone in particular within the Castro organization. My specific function for the movement—writing the manifesto—had afforded me a unique degree of independence, without which I would never have agreed to cooperate. Whatever else I had done had been voluntary. None of the leaders got in touch with mé, directly or indirectly, while I was in hiding, although Fernández Ceballos was in frequent contact with them. Marcelo Fernández told him that my asylum was "O.K." Beyond that, I received no instruction, suggestion, or recommendation regarding what I should or should not do. As I flew to Mexico, therefore, I hadn't the slightest idea what my future relationship, if any, with the 26 of July Movement might be.

# 5 The Manifesto That Was Not

After passing through the immigration routine at Mexico City's airport, I called a taxi and asked the driver to take us to the Hotel Emporio, the only one with which I was familiar in the city.

Next morning I went to find Fernández Ceballos, who was then in Mexico attending an interdenominational conference. His address in Mexico City had been given to me in Havana. I went to see him as one goes to an old, helpful friend.

During lunch in the dining room of the school where the conference was being held, he asked me what my plans were now that I was in Mexico and where I was staying. I told him I had no specific plans beyond continuing on to the United States as soon as possible, and that I was staying at the Hotel Emporio. He suggested that perhaps I would be more comfortable at a nice place he knew about, a Mexican home that took in lodgers. A few other Cuban exiles were already living there. Besides, it would be far more economical than a hotel. I agreed immediately, and he took me to the place.

So I became the sixth Cuban roomer in the house with the sonorous address of Pedro Antonio de los Santos 3 in Tacubaya, an old section of Mexico City. The two-story masonry house fronted on the small Plaza de las Flores, so called because flower vendors gathered there in the mornings, setting up their portable stands all around the plaza. On the other side of the plaza stretches the immense, beautiful Bosque de Chapultepec.

The five other Cuban exiles living at the house were Heliodoro Martínez Junco, whose sister Isabel had come to take me to the Mexican embassy in Havana; Juan Nuiry, who had served as acting president of the FEU after its president, José Antonio Echeverría, was killed in the abortive attack on the presidential palace in March;[1] Luis Soto, a student of engineering; Eduardo Bacallao, a traveling salesman; and Aurelio Alvarez, an office worker of some kind. All of them had been involved in acts of violence against the Batista government and had escaped police action by seeking diplomatic asylum in the Mexican embassy, just as I had done.

There is nothing unusual about the Reverend's having known about the house on Pedro Antonio de los Santos. Yet, was it only out of concern for my comfort and finances that he suggested I move there? The seemingly unimportant detail acquired a certain significance in retrospect, after Fernández Ceballos unveiled himself as a communist in 1959 and took the lead in turning the Protestant churches in Cuba into an arm of the Communist regime. (I did not see him again until my return to Havana early in 1959.)

My relations with the other exiles in the house were friendly and cordial. I had known Martínez Junco and Nuiry in Cuba; the others were all new acquaintances. Nuiry had distinguished himself in the student movement; Martínez Junco, Bacallao, and Alvarez were connected with the Organización Auténtica (OA), the insurrectional branch of Prío Socarrás's Auténtico party. I knew little about Soto.

Soon I was spontaneously given detailed information concerning the activities of exile groups in Mexico, especially the Castro followers. A number of them had remained in Mexico when Castro sailed for Cuba in 1956. Most of them had been trained in guerrilla warfare and continued to receive such training under Pedro Miret, one of the founders of the organization and a veteran of the Moncada episode. It was said by others present at the Moncada attack that the weight of the battle had been carried by Miret, while Castro abandoned the field, leaving wounded and exposed men behind.[2] Miret had been among those imprisoned on the Isle of Pines. I had first met him when he accompanied Castro to my apartment for a meeting with the MLR leaders.

Miret was widely considered to be second only to Castro in the movement. Now, however, his standing was being bitterly contested by a segment of the 26 of July colony in Mexico formed around Castro's sisters, Lidia (a half sister) and Emma, who made their headquarters at the home of Alfonso and Orquídea Gutiérrez in the Pedregal, where I had stopped with Castro during my previous visit to Mexico. The anti-Miret faction thus became known among Cuban exiles as "the Pedregal." Miret and his wife were living with Teté Casuso in the Lomas de Chapultepec. The Miret and Pedregal factions bombarded each other with accusations: breach of discipline, nepotism, hypocrisy, even treason.

As I was personally acquainted with most of the leaders of the movement and until recently had been in contact with the underground in Havana, both factions tried to win me to their side. I was invited to the Gutiérrez home and listened to what the Castro sisters and their friends had to say. I also had long talks with Miret, his friend Gustavo Arcos, and Teté Casuso. As it was impossible to avoid taking sides, I reasoned this way: Miret was a founder and a veteran of the organization, an experienced and disciplined militant, while the Castro sisters and their friends were motivated primarily, perhaps solely, by personal ties to Fidel Castro. So, although I tried to remain on equally good terms with all of them, as a matter of revolutionary loyalty and ethics I thought I must recognize Miret as the only official representative of the 26 of July Movement in Mexico. This decision led to my first formal connection with the Castro movement. Until then I had been in the unique position of acting as the writer of a manifesto for an organization to which I did not actually belong.

My decision in Miret's favor apparently gave a great boost to his morale. He was supposed to be preparing a second expedition to Cuba. A project of this nature required vast resources, psychological as well as financial, and the split created by the Pedregal, with the special appeal of the Castro name, was a major hindrance to his plans. Sorely needed support was being diverted to the other side. Miret was not making much progress and he feared that his situation in Mexico might become precarious. He knew he was under police surveillance; so far the police had been tolerant, but that was subject to change without warning. So he began sending reports to the leaders of the organization in Cuba, describing the situation in Mexico and desperately asking for support. He cited me as a witness and proposed that I be designated official spokesman for the 26 of July outside Cuba. This last move was partly intended to curb the influence of the Castro sisters, who had been traveling to various countries, including the United States, granting interviews, issuing declarations, collecting funds, and in general assuming the roles of the movement's representatives. In the opinion of many militants, their activities were not only unauthorized but detrimental to the best interests of the revolution. After all, Miret would say, the 26 of July Movement was never intended to be a family affair.

Miret's efforts were finally rewarded. Two formal communications arrived in Mexico from Santiago, both dated 21 June 1957, handwritten and signed by Frank País "on behalf of the Dirección Nacional of the Revolutionary 26 of July Movement." The first one, addressed "to whom it may concern," stated:

The Dirección Nacional of the Revolutionary 26 of July Movement has considered it proper to declare and clearly establish that comrades Pedro Miret and Gustavo Arcos are the persons chosen by this committee to represent the movement outside of Cuba. Be it also known that this committee, together with the General Revolutionary Staff in the Sierra Maestra, will shortly send abroad a personal delegate with full powers and instructions to get in touch with the above-named comrades and work together with them for the purpose of giving greater unification to the activities of the movement outside of Cuba. . . .

In order to leave no doubt as to its intention, the document stressed its point further: "We want to make it clear that our organization in Cuba maintains no relationship or communication of any kind with any persons other than the above-named comrades." The Pedregal was out—at least on paper.

The second communication was addressed "to Señor Mario Llerena." The main part of its text reads:

The Dirección Nacional of the Revolutionary 26 of July Movement hereby notifies you that you have been named Director of Public Relations for the Movement outside of Cuba.

You are also advised that, for the best functioning, organization, and discipline of our branches outside Cuba, you must work in perfect harmony and coordination with our delegates abroad, comrades Pedro Miret and Gustavo Arcos.

We expect the greatest possible effort from you. These are critical and pressing times.

Finally, we confirm our confidence in your ability and discipline, so many times demonstrated in Cuba.

Those two communications made Pedro Miret very happy. The question of official representation was apparently settled. Frank País enjoyed such prestige that nobody, not even Castro's sisters, thought of openly disavowing a directive bearing his signature. Yet the resolution proved to be more apparent than real. The Pedregal group became less vocal for a while, but it remained alive and active, and never recognized Miret's authority.

The subject of the manifesto (I had brought the manuscript with me) had been discussed and decided upon before Frank País's communications arrived. It came up during my first meeting with Miret, soon after I took lodgings in the house on Pedro Antonio de los Santos. Miret said then that he was very much interested in reading the manuscript, and the next morning he was there again, this time accompanied by Teté Casuso.

I took them to my room upstairs and read the manifesto to them, pausing now and then to elaborate on some point. Their reaction was far more enthusiastic than I had expected. Miret said that we must have it printed as quickly as possible. Teté agreed, but she suggested a more forceful condemnation of "Yankee imperialism." I explained that I was convinced that imperialism was no longer a political reality in the Americas. Some vestiges of it doubtless remained, but they were fading. Imperialism was a thing of the past. There was little sense in making an issue of something that did not exist, I said, and even less sense in playing one of the Communists' favorite tunes. Miret agreed and the manuscript remained as it was.

But might we not be acting too hastily, I suggested, in publishing a manifesto that had not been approved by the Dirección Nacional? The draft had been read and approved (with certain recommendations) by Faustino, Marcelo, Franqui, and Oltusky, but the events leading up to my asylum and exile had prevented me from sending copies to Oriente.

Miret and Teté brushed the question aside. I was too concerned with technicalities, they said. The harsh realities of revolution required one to be more practical. The manifesto belonged not to me but to the movement. For my peace of mind, however, Miret said that he would assume full responsibility for its publication and would write immediately to the Dirección Nacional requesting the formal authorization I was so concerned about.

So, the publication question settled, the manuscript was taken to Manuel Machado, a Cuban long established in Mexico who ran a large printing and binding concern on the Calzada de Tlalpan. A friend and admirer of deposed President Prío, Machado had also

Stgo. de Cuba. 21 de Junio de 1957.

Al señor Mario Llerena:

La Dirección Nacional del Movimiento Revolucionario 26 de Julio le comunica por la presente que ha sido designado Encargado de las Relaciones Públicas del Movimiento fuera de Cuba.

Así mismo le recuerda que para la buena marcha y mejor organización y disciplina de nuestras organizaciones extranjeras es necesario que trabaje en perfecta armonía y sincronización con nuestros Delegados en el extranjero compañeros Pedro Miret y Gustavo Arcos.

Esperamos de usted el mayor esfuerzo ya que los momentos que vivimos son precisos.

Por último le ratificamos nuestra confianza en su capacidad y disciplina tantas veces demostrada en Cuba.

Sin más y deseándole suerte

Por la Dirección Nacional del
Movimiento Revolucionario 26 de Julio
F. País.

P. D. Próximamente irá a visitarlo un Delegado Personal de esta Dirección y del Estado Mayor Rev. de la Sierra con instrucciones precisas para su cargo.

Vale  F. País.

Frank País, on behalf of the Dirección Nacional of the 26 of July Movement, informs the author that he has been named public relations director for the movement outside of Cuba.

known Castro personally in Mexico, sympathized with his aims, and kept in close contact with Miret. He appeared, in fact, to be Miret's most generous financial supporter. He offered the printing of the manifesto as one of his contributions to the cause.

The manifesto came out as a handsome thirty-three-page booklet. I did the proofreading, chose the colors for the cover, and even designed a special style of lettering for the title. With Miret's concurrence, I gave it the title *Nuestra Razón* (Our Cause). I did not write the Foreword until after the decision to print the manifesto was made. This is the only place in the entire document where Castro is mentioned by name, and then only once. I unintentionally caused a little confusion about the date of publication by adding "La Habana, Cuba, Noviembre de 1956" at the end of the text. My intention was to show that the manifesto had been written earlier in Cuba and that Castro's landing on the island in December of that year and the November uprising in Santiago directed by Frank País had therefore not been mere adventurous exploits but had been inspired by a definite revolutionary philosophy. Those who thought November 1956 to be the date of publication overlooked the second paragraph of the Foreword, where reference is made to the presence in the Sierra Maestra of "Fidel Castro, with an outpost of Cuban youth." They also failed to notice the very first sentence of the Foreword: "Este documento se publica en medio del fragor de la lucha" (This document is published in the midst of the battle's roar).

*Nuestra Razón* was off the press and in circulation by the end of June or the beginning of July 1957. I sent copies to journalists and other opinion leaders in almost every country of the hemisphere (I remember handing a copy personally to Don Salvador de Madariaga, whom I chanced upon in the street; he happened to be on a visit to Mexico, and I had known him personally at various conferences of the World Committee for Cultural Freedom). I also mailed a number of copies to Europe. My hope, of course, was that *Nuestra Razón* would give world opinion a positive image of the Castro revolution. A few copies were sent secretly to the movement's leaders in Havana and to a number of intellectuals and other influential people.

At this point someone brought to my attention an article by Carleton Beals which had recently appeared in the American periodical *The Nation,* attacking Castro as an unscrupulous and unprincipled adventurer.[3] The article went into scandalous detail on

Castro's upbringing and family, particularly his father, who was described as, among other things, ·a former cattle thief and now a shady country squire who kept a harem somewhere in the Oriente jungles. In time I learned that, although some details were not strictly accurate, there was a considerable amount of truth in the charges. But at the time the article seemed to me to be a monumental case of irresponsible journalism and malicious fabrication. The statements that struck me the hardest were those referring to the 26 of July Movement. According to Beals, the movement was nothing but a pistol-packing rabble band, devoid of honest political motives and serious ideological content. I wrote Beals a letter in care of *The Nation* and enclosed a copy of the manifesto. I did not comment on anything he had said about Castro personally; my only concern was to show him that the 26 of July Movement did have a political philosophy and that its objectives were legitimate.

A few days later I received from Beals a signed copy of a letter from him to the editor of *The Nation,* bearing a brief handwritten note to me: "Mil gracias, amigo Llerena!" The letter was a tremendously pleasant surprise. Beals reversed his previous stand in regard to the 26 of July Movement and praised the manifesto:

This document covers political, economic and social rights and the problems of education, judicial and penal reform, and international relations, both in general terms and by presenting specific proposals for the recovery of political and economic sovereignty, civil rights, agrarian reform, rights of labor, court reform, inter-Americanism and opposition to totalitarian and dictatorial regimes in the Americas. . . . by and large it is the finest document ever produced in Cuba since the days of independence leader Martí. Here, indeed, is an effective answer to the doubts expressed in my article in *The Nation* regarding the equivocal nature of many elements. . . . This group faces up to all the issues.[4]

Another response to *Nuestra Razón* that I valued especially highly was that of Jorge Mañach, one of Cuba's most brilliant minds. His political moderation made Mañach a frequent target of criticism from the extreme Left, and even I, as I mentioned earlier, had considered his Movimiento de la Nación too moderate to deal effectively with the Cuban crisis. Mañach was now exiled in Spain. I had sent him a copy of the manifesto, and he replied in a letter dated 15 August 1957 at La Coruña. He wrote in part:

You can imagine how avidly I have read a document that, aside from its intrinsic value, means so much as an expression of the ideals for which the most gallant segment of Cuban youth is fighting today, with the intrepid Fidel Castro in the front line. In view of the circumstances in which it has been written and published, as well as the fact that it is inevitably provisional, it is a very accomplished document. . . . Were these times for rejoicing, I would congratulate you on this document, as I seem to detect your hand in its writing, particularly in the repeated references to Jefferson and in some other ideas of which I know you are fond. . . .[5]

While *Nuestra Razón* was being distributed from Mexico, the Sierra Manifesto was issued in Cuba as a magazine article, with authorship attributed to Castro, Felipe Pazos, and Raúl Chibás. It certainly was not intended to be the programmatic document expected from every political party and revolutionary organization competing for public acceptance in Cuba. Rather it was a relatively brief declaration dealing exclusively with the specific situation that existed in the country at the time. But it did set forth a series of premises and propositions that sounded like long-range goals, while presenting Castro and the 26 of July Movement as the champions and restorers of democracy in Cuba.

One of the foremost recommendations of the Sierra Manifesto was the formation of a "Civic-Revolutionary Front" that was to serve as the backbone of the popular struggle against the dictatorship. The "civic" wing of this front would consist of the Civic Institutions, an association made up of representatives of all those nonpolitical organizations—professional, labor, cultural, economic, even religious—that had some degree of public influence or prestige.[6] The front was to take all the necessary steps to bring the country out of the crisis, at the same time ensuring its proper and complete return to constitutional normality. In one of its explanatory paragraphs the Sierra Manifesto said this: "Does anybody think that we, the Sierra Maestra rebels, are not for free elections, a democratic regime, and a constitutional government? We have been fighting ever since the tenth of March precisely because we have been deprived of those rights, and it is because we cherish them more than anyone else that we are here." And its seventh recommendation stated: "It is hereby solemnly declared that the provisional government will within a year hold general elections under the terms of the 1940 Constitution and the 1943 Electoral Law for all the offices of the state, the provinces, and the cities, and will immediately afterward vest its power in the elected officials."

The Sierra Manifesto might have served as a useful supplement to *Nuestra Razón*—a treatment of specific issues of more or less immediate concern to complement my long-range programmatic manifesto. No one within the 26 of July, however, appeared to see any relationship between the two manifestos, or to view *Nuestra Razón* with a fraction of the enthusiasm demonstrated by people outside the movement.

Early in July, for example, three men from the Pedregal group— Alfonso Gutiérrez, René Piccard, and Héctor Aldama—came to see me and demanded that certain points in *Nuestra Razón* be either deleted or radically modified, although the booklet was already in circulation. They specifically objected to any mention of nationalization of public utilities or recovery of subsoil resources. I was astounded until they explained that Rafael Bilbao, a wealthy Cuban businessman long established in Venezuela who was probably Castro's best financial supporter, was distressed by the manifesto and strongly objected to those two points in particular. Unless they were removed from the manifesto, Bilbao would discontinue his financial aid to the movement. The Pedregal emissaries even suggested that I make a special trip to Panama, where Bilbao happened to be at the time, in order to try to placate him.

Bilbao's support of Castro appears something of an enigma. His views were clearly rightist, in sharp contrast to those of the people close to Castro who had complained that the draft of the manifesto was insufficiently radical. A number of people, however, saw in Castro the makings of a fascist dictator.[7]

I refused to negotiate with Bilbao and argued against making changes in the manifesto—not for such reasons, anyway. I was amazed, I said, that friends and supporters of Castro should be upset by an essentially democratic manifesto only because some of its pragmatic recommendations might conflict with their personal interests. I could not understand why people of such conservative bent as Bilbao and Gutiérrez should be at all interested in revolution, anyway. Apparently their close contact with Castro before his departure for Cuba late in 1956 had taught them nothing. The truth is, however, that neither they nor I realized then how blurred and undefined the profile of the Castro revolution actually was at the beginning.

The meeting ended on a sour note. On leaving, Aldama sounded faintly threatening.

My revolutionary standards in those days were comparable to the ethical code of a Puritan. I lacked flexibility. I hadn't yet learned that in all human relations, a degree of diplomacy and a capacity for maneuvering is sometimes necessary in order to avoid useless trouble, and even for the ultimate triumph of the very principles on which one stands. So, without my wishing it, my relations with the Pedregal group became cool, practically nonexistent. Later, however, Bilbao came to Mexico and we had a long discussion on the manifesto. I think I succeeded in dispelling his worries without compromising the document, which remained as it was.

It was November before I received any response from Cuba, and by that time I was in the United States. Communication was difficult and slow, since most confidential materials had to travel by courier, and the people to whom they were addressed were not always easy to locate. My first direct communication from Cuba was a letter from Marcelo Fernández dated 24 June 1957 in Havana. Marcelo informed me that he had just been named propaganda coordinator for the movement inside Cuba, and he commented optimistically on the general situation there. The letter included a brief reference to the manifesto: "The Reverend told me that you were planning to have *Nuestra Razón* published there. Please write and give me all the information you can about this." Then I got a second letter from Marcelo (Havana, 22 July 1957), saying that he now had a printed copy of *Nuestra Razón*. He had shown it to the Harts and Oltusky, and "they liked it, except the text on the cover stating that it is a 'Programmatic Manifesto' of the movement." They wanted me to have the cover changed to read: "*Nuestra Razón*—a doctrinal booklet published by the Propaganda Secretariat of the 26 of July Movement. Mexico, July 1957." "As you know," Marcelo wrote (I did not), "the programmatic manifesto of the movement is at this moment being written in its definitive form in the Sierra, and we wouldn't like to give the impression that there were two programmatic manifestos."

In some consternation I phoned Miret in Mexico City and read him the letter. As far as he was concerned, he told me, *Nuestra Razón* was *the* manifesto. And there was no question then that Miret ranked far above Marcelo in the organization's hierarchy. Besides, now that the booklet had been widely distributed and had been the subject of public comment, Marcelo's suggestion was totally unrealistic, not to say embarrassing. So we did nothing about it.

But I sensed that the manifesto project was turning out to be just short of a sorry waste of time. I stopped trying to promote it. All signs from Cuba pointed to subtle changes in the thinking of the leaders. They appeared to have outgrown their roles as bold adventurers gambling against all odds on the chance of provoking a popular uprising. Much sooner than they had hoped, the movement had become recognized both nationally and internationally. They had successfully resisted and repelled the attacks of Batista's army, thus shattering the myth of his military invincibility. Foreign correspondents swarmed to Cuba and were able to slip undetected into the *territorio libre* of Oriente province. The revolutionary stature of the movement grew until it all but eclipsed the other anti-Batista groups.

On such fertile ground the dormant seeds of a more advanced revolutionary concept quickly took root and sprouted. The original idea of a progressive reform movement working within the framework of constitutional democracy was discreetly abandoned in favor of "all power to the revolution." The reasoned analysis and declaration of principles and objectives embodied in *Nuestra Razón* were brushed impatiently aside.

Another reference to *Nuestra Razón* came in a long letter covering a great variety of subjects and dated 15 October 1957 at Santiago de Cuba. It was addressed to "Léster Rodríguez, Pedro Miret, Gustavo Arcos, and Mario Llerena." Rodríguez, another veteran of the Castro movement, had been one of the organizers of the November 1956 uprising in Santiago. The letter was signed by "Darío" (one of Armando Hart's noms de guerre) on behalf of the Dirección Nacional. *Nuestra Razón* was the sixth of twelve topics discussed. The letter conflicted with Marcelo's assertion that another manifesto was being written in the Sierra Maestra, but it did confirm that one was being contemplated:

The booklet *Nuestra Razón* can be widely distributed. We believe it to be an interpretation of the political thinking of the movement, although, as its authors themselves admit, it needs further elaboration. If there are some small discrepancies here and there, it is probably only a matter of emphasis in the wording. You put it very well when you state that it does not claim to be a final document. We must therefore use it as a basis and write another abroad that perhaps will not be final either, but at least more complete. When I say more complete I mean a pamphlet that will put together *certain aspects of the political thinking of a number of our leaders,* as these aspects have not been treated with the emphasis that Franqui or I, for instance, would have given them. [Italics mine.]

When Franqui and other unspecified "comrades" joined us, bringing together "our ideological leadership," we were to prepare a new pamphlet and send it to the leadership in Cuba "so that Fidel can study it and then have it published under his signature."

This had all the appearances of a compromise solution. *Nuestra Razón* would be used "as a basis" for the proposed new manifesto, which was to be drafted in Mexico without the direct participation of Castro, his brother Raúl, Che Guevara, or any of the other leaders in the mountains.[8] I was to be involved in its writing, but this time as a member of a committee consisting also of Miret, Arcos, Rodríguez, Franqui (expected now in exile after being released from prison), and others—"our ideological leadership." Was Hart not aware of the full significance of the Communist machinations that—as later developments showed—were already in progress within the highest echelons of the organization? Or was this apparent preoccupation with a manifesto just camouflage? One can only wonder.

The last word I received from Cuba on these matters came two months later in a brief handwritten letter from Hart, signed with his real name of Armando and dated 17 December 1957 in the Sierra Maestra. This letter accompanied a lengthy document issued by Castro which was intended to, and did, break the Junta Cubana de Liberación, a joint committee of anti-Batista organizations in Miami (more about this in the next chapter). Toward the end of his letter Hart wrote: "Documents defining our political, social, and economic line, signed by Fidel on behalf of the Dirección Nacional, are going to be published soon. . . . The 26 of July Movement is arriving at a precise and complete definition of its [political] philosophy."

So the 26 of July, which had been waging a guerrilla war to liberate and reform the country since 1953, was at last arriving at a definition of its philosophy. The "documents" Hart mentioned, however, were never published. To the best of my knowledge, they never even existed.

From then on, events outran plans. I found myself caught up in a swirl of exile activities that left me neither the time nor the inclination to work on another manifesto. I had been in the United States since October. In January or February Franqui finally arrived, after having spent some time in Costa Rica. I settled in New York and tried to do my best as director of public relations, the only assignment I had been given. The three or four groups of Castro sympathizers in New York, perpetually quarreling with each other, made the task difficult. The question of new literature for the movement was forgotten.

*Nuestra Razón* circulated among Cuban émigrés in the United States, Mexico, Central America, and particularly Venezuela, where it was reprinted and distributed by the thousands. It never became widely known in Cuba itself, however. Owing partly to the prevailing circumstances but mainly to lack of interest on the part of the leaders, only a limited number of copies reached a few people there. Although officially endorsed, it never was actually accepted by the Dirección Nacional, and Castro remained significantly silent about it. Whatever praise or recognition the manifesto received came from sources other than the 26 of July Movement. There may have been a certain amount of resentment in the leaders' cool reception of the published booklet—I was hardly a member of the inner circle—although that alone could not have been the whole explanation. I remember Léster Rodríguez's response when Miret asked him, just after the manifesto's publication, what he thought of it. Rodríguez shrugged and said indifferently that it was all right. Pressed to elaborate, he said that in his opinion the manifesto of the movement ought to be written by its founders, or by those doing the fighting in Cuba. He didn't care to go into the intrinsic value of the document. The fact that it had been written at the request of responsible leaders, some of them "doing the fighting in Cuba," and printed over my objections at the insistence of Pedro Miret, who was a founder as well as a fighter of the organization, was overlooked.

Rodríguez was not high in the movement—he had been sent to Mexico to help in the organization of supply lines for the guerrilla forces in Cuba—and his remarks would have been soon forgotten if they had not fitted into a pattern of estrangement that gradually developed into open hostility. As for *Nuestra Razón*, it would become again the subject of outside comments and discussion after the revolution was in power.[9] Otherwise, it remained the manifesto that was not.

# 6 Revolution vs. Politics

**T**he crisis precipitated by the Batista coup brought a sharp polarization of public sentiment: some were so taken by the promises of revolution that they came almost to regard it as a God-given instrument for salvation; others clung to traditional politics. Soon, however, the "revolutionaries" outnumbered and outweighed the "politicians." Fidel Castro and the 26 of July Movement gradually became the vortex of a popular frenzy that left behind all sense of discernment, while the traditional politicians became the scapegoats for all the evils and frustrations of Cuba's public life.

For some time, however, the situation was considerably confused by the amorphousness of the prevailing concept of revolution. I myself, from my vantage point only slightly to the left of the center of the political spectrum, became concerned that the 26 of July Movement might not yet be firmly set on the revolutionary path and might be led to change course by supporters who retained ties with traditional political parties. A number of these traditionalists seemed unaware that Castro's course deviated in any significant way from the one they contemplated. Roberto Agramonte, who had been on the way to the presidency in 1952 when Batista took power, and Felipe Pazos came to Mexico while I was there, on their way to exile in Miami, and I talked with each one at length. For Agramonte the 26 of July Movement was still only the youth branch of the Ortodoxo party. He greatly admired Castro and the other leaders, but the idea of a full-grown, independent revolutionary movement seemed to be thousands of miles from his thinking. And Pazos told me that Castro "had never stopped being an Ortodoxo." Such an assertion, coming from one of the cosigners of the Sierra Manifesto, threw me into confusion.

Apparently this ideological dichotomy existed all throughout the 26 of July Movement. It was particularly noticeable among the exile groups. There were actually two overlapping yet separate structures within the organization: the official network of local committees, branches, delegations, and so on, and a parallel unofficial substructure formed by a continuous stream of itinerant personal envoys together with self-appointed local representatives, all of whom boasted (often truthfully) of being in contact with and acting under the direct instructions of Fidel Castro. This dual structure was a constant source of rivalries and bitter conflicts. The Miret-Pedregal conflict had its counterparts in Caracas, New York, Chicago, Miami, Los Angeles, and every other city with a substantial Cuban population. As soon as it became known that I had been designated the Dirección Nacional's delegate abroad, I was flooded with letters, all telling essentially the same story of conflicts and rivalries between "true" and "false" representatives of the 26 of July Movement. The leader of each of these groups asked me to legitimate him on behalf of Castro and excommunicate his rival. All my efforts to explain that I had not been appointed to arbitrate internecine quarrels but to take charge of public relations proved of no avail.

Meanwhile a coalition of other anti-Batista forces had been taking shape in Miami. In Mexico we received reports of meetings among Carlos Prío, Roberto Agramonte, and others, including Antonio de Varona, long-time Auténtico leader and member of Prío's cabinet until 1952; Lincoln Rodón, former congressman; Manuel Bisbé, a former professor of classical Greek who entered politics as an admirer of Eddy Chibás and soon became one of the leaders of the Ortodoxo party; Emilio (Millo) Ochoa, cofounder with Chibás of the Ortodoxo party and a senator at the time of the 1952 coup; Faure Chomón, who emerged from the "gangster" wars of the late 1940s to become one of the founders of the Directorio Revolucionario, the group that organized the unsuccessful attack on the presidential palace in March 1957;[1] Angel Cofiño and Marcos Yrigoyen, labor leaders; José R. Andreu, head of a small party called Demócrata Republicano and minister of health in the last

Prío cabinet; and José M. Gutiérrez, former Ortodoxo senator.[2]

These meetings resulted in the formation of the Junta de Liberación Cubana, whose purpose was to organize and implement armed action against Batista and set up a provisional government that would reestablish democracy in Cuba. Its member organizations were the Partido Revolucionario Cubano (Auténtico), represented by Prío and Varona; the Organización Auténtica, represented by Carlos Maristany, former minister of communications in Prío's cabinet; the Partido del Pueblo Cubano (Ortodoxo), represented by Agramonte and Bisbé; the Federación Estudiantil Universitaria (FEU), represented by Ramón Prendes, Juan Nuiry, and Omar Fernández;[3] the Directorio Revolucionario, represented by Chomón; and the Directorio Obrero Revolucionario, represented by Cofiño and Yrigoyen. The junta aimed to unite most if not all of the sectors of Batistas's opposition, including the 26 of July Movement.

Ernesto Betancourt, an intelligent and able young man who, with the support of the Castro sisters, had assumed the representation of the 26 of July in Washington, informed me that Carlos Prío had requested and been granted an interview with Secretary of State John Foster Dulles. Prío's intention, apparently, was both to keep Washington informed about the junta's business and, above all, to obtain American government sanction of its plans.

In Mexico we viewed all these activities with great concern. If the old political parties and organizations succeeded in grabbing the leadership of the anti-Batista struggle from the 26 of July, the result would be not simply the eclipse of Castro but, worse yet, the loss of a unique historical opportunity for a true revolution to become a reality—the kind of revolution proclaimed in *Nuestra Razón*.

Rodón and Bisbé were in frequent telephone communication with Pazos, urging him to come to Miami. Pazos' public prestige and somewhat apolitical image would unquestionably be an asset for the junta and would make him an ideal prospect for the future provisional presidency. Miret, Arcos, and I discussed the situation with Pazos and learned that he was only waiting for his visa before leaving for Miami. He said he was not bound by any specific commitment to the 26 of July Movement, and he therefore felt free to participate in the junta discussions. He did not rule out the possibility that he might accept a high position in the provisional government if it were offered to him.

Pazos's attitude came as something of a shock. In view of his interest and collaboration in the past, his trips to guerrilla territory, and, above all, his signature next to Castro's on the Sierra Manifesto, we had all been under the impression that Pazos was committed to a revolutionary course. I had even suggested his name as representative of the movement in the United States. The only member of our group in Mexico who sided with Pazos was, surprisingly, Léster Rodríguez. Two days after Pazos arrived in Miami, he called Rodríguez. Obviously as a result of this conversation, Rodríguez informed Miret that he too would be leaving for Miami shortly.

As a delegate of the Dirección Nacional, I considered it of the utmost importance to get the leaders' views on these developments. Nothing seemed certain; perhaps Pazos was right, and Castro was still an Ortodoxo at heart. I therefore prepared a lengthy memorandum succinctly itemizing a number of questions. This memorandum was, in essence, a demand for a definition of principles: would the 26 of July Movement continue to be an independent revolutionary organization or would it instead follow the beaten path of the other opposition forces? I outlined what was going on in Miami and ended my communication with this paragraph: "Whatever way you look at it, you can be sure of one thing: for the 26 of July Movement it is very important and very urgent to have a clear and concrete answer to each of the questions listed above as soon as possible. My own . . . readiness to serve in the future will very much depend on the reply I receive from you." I sent this memorandum to the Sierra Maestra from Mexico on 5 October 1957.

The Dirección Nacional's replied in a letter signed by Armando Hart as secretary and addressed to the 26 of July leaders in Mexico. By the time it arrived I had received my visa and had left Mexico. It came to Léster Rodríguez in Miami, and I read it there. The committee responded to my queries this way:

The 26 of July Revolutionary Movement is an organization that has come of age. It cannot, therefore, be taken as a part or branch of any other political group in the country. The fact that some of our leaders, Fidel Castro in particular, have come from the Ortodoxo party does not mean that the 26 is to be considered a branch of that party. By that reasoning, the Ortodoxo party could itself be considered a branch of the Auténtico party simply because Eduardo Chibás used to belong to that party. The 26 of July is and intends to remain the revolutionary instrument of a generation that suffered the consequences of the 10 of March [coup d'état] and which practically alone (we have had very few guides) is trying to find the solution to a crisis brought about by the irresponsible behavior of the political parties of 9 March.[4] It might not be tactically advisable to speak now of the way in which no political party measured up to the historical circumstances then. But that does not mean that publicly we have to overlook what today is our first responsibility, namely, to create the revolutionary organization capable of coming to terms not only with the 10 of March but above all with the series of political, economic, social, and even moral conditions that made it possible for Batista to seize power that tragic morning. . . .

For a delegate who fancied himself a defender of the purity of the revolution, this reply was most gratifying. The line of demarcation between revolution and politics had been clearly defined. The 26 of July Movement was, after all, what *Nuestra Razón* proclaimed it was.

Or so I thought. For the time being, however, this stated position did not seem to have much impact on Rodríguez, who went on negotiating with Prío and the junta. And it never registered with the great mass of Cuban émigrés and Castro admirers, whose eyes and ears were fixed only on their hero.

I had flown from Mexico City to Miami on October 22. Miret had given me Léster Rodríguez's address in Miami Beach and urged me to get in touch with him. Perhaps I might be able to persuade him to come back to the right path. I was interested in seeing Rodríguez in any case. As his job was to establish new lines of arms supply for the guerrillas, he received all the courier-carried communications from Castro headquarters on the island; and I was awaiting replies to the letters and reports I had sent from Mexico.

I got in touch with Rodríguez immediately, but it was soon clear that, though he seemed friendly and cooperative, he was not receptive to any suggestion of mine. He lost no opportunity to remind me of his seniority within the movement. The junta business would certainly go on. Moreover, he had persuaded Pazos—who had disclaimed any commitment to the 26 of July—to represent the movement in the junta, while he himself remained in the background as the power behind the throne. As he was supposed to be acquiring arms for the guerrillas—an illegal activity—he could not assume a public posture.

As a result of these maneuvers, Rodríguez was the object of special attention from the opposition leaders. They were understandably eager to keep Castro and the 26 of July Movement in the junta's fold. Since the 26 of July was the only revolutionary organization that had succeeded in creating a sustained state of rebellion within Cuba, a revolutionary junta in exile would amount to little without its presence. This fact placed Rodríguez in a position to deal on an equal, perhaps even superior, footing with former presidents, party leaders, and other public figures. It became quite obvious that the unexpected role had gone to his head, and for a time he seemed to forget all about the revolution. The ways of the politicians seemed far more realistic and promising.

Meetings and caucuses were constantly being held. Some hangers-on, with typical Cuban cunning, engaged in petty backstage maneuvering. The Cuban community in Miami seethed with rumors of Batista's imminent fall.

The main political force in the junta was, visibly, Carlos Prío. He was the only one in a position to be the financial power behind the revolution. Prío controlled not only the PRC and the OA, but the Directorio Obrero Revolucionario as well—and, somewhat indirectly, even the FEU. Most of the leaders of these organizations subsisted in exile under Prío's financial umbrella.

To all appearances, the decision for the 26 of July Movement to join the Miami junta had been made by Léter Rodríguez alone, without consultation with the leaders in Cuba; Pazos was simply persuaded to go along. The other delegations were unaware of anything irregular about Pazos's position as delegate of the 26 of July. I learned that a secret subcommittee had been appointed to deal with the military aspects of the junta's plans. The 26 of July's representative on this subcommittee was Jesús Yáñez Pelletier, a former army officer who had saved Castro's life after the Moncada attack, when other Batista followers wanted to kill him. Yáñez's action had cost him his commission.[5]

Rodríguez suggested that I attend the junta meetings as part of the 26 of July delegation. I refused. In principle I had always favored joint action, but the time for that seemed past now. The 26 of July Movement had unquestionably emerged as the leading national force against the Batista dictatorship, so far ahead of the other opposition groups that I felt an alliance with them now would only weaken its revolutionary momentum. I communicated these views to the leaders in Cuba, but I decided not to argue the

point further with Rodríguez. I simply explained to him that I had
to get to New York to set up a public relations office for the movement. This was true enough, of course, but at the moment I welcomed the excuse to detach myself from the junta's activities.
After a few more days I took a plane to New York and settled in at
my brother-in-law's apartment at 170 Eighth Avenue, which became the official address of the 26 of July delegation in the United
States.

Not many days had passed before I got an urgent call from
Léster Rodríguez in Miami. He wanted me to take the next flight
back. He had received some communications from Cuba—he
would not elaborate—and my presence there was absolutely essential. The next morning I flew back to Miami.

A number of important communications had indeed been received, among them one addressed to Pazos and Rodríguez dated
26 October 1957 at Santiago de Cuba. It appeared that Castro and
the other leaders had learned a little too late about the activities of
their "delegates" in Miami. The message was a rebuke, but it was
couched in courteous terms, no doubt out of respect for Pazos. The
first paragraph, after explaining at length that revolutionary discipline must prevail over personal or emotional considerations,
said:

There can be no justification for the publication of the final principles of
unity [of the opposition groups] in the *New York Times* before the
members of this Dirección Nacional had a chance to approve or disapprove them. In his letter of 20 October Dr. Pazos says that your decision
for or against the principles was always subject to the ratification of this
Dirección Nacional. But the truth is that it has been presented to us as an
accomplished fact—one that, moreover, has been widely publicized and
discussed. . . .

The Dirección Nacional, however, not only accepted the accomplished fact but confirmed Pazos and Rodríguez as delegates,
and detailed the conditions under which they were to continue to
cooperate with the junta. There followed a prolix discussion aimed
at explaining to Pazos and Rodríguez (at that stage of developments!) the political philosophy and the revolutionary strategy of
the 26 of July Movement. Some of its passages make interesting
reading today. One, for instance, said:

We must make it clear—and so we point it out to you—that to us the principles of unity look like the clever political trickery of certain discredited

opposition leaders who are simply trying, on the one hand, to mystify the revolutionary forces and, on the other hand, to stem the growing strength that is being shown by the civic and representative groups of the country. It so happens, however, that it is of very special interest to the new generation that those civic and representative groups gain in influence and importance. They represent *legitimate areas of middle and conservative public opinion with which the Revolution may have to establish a balance of power in the future.* Bear in mind that the 26 of July does not share the ideological orientation of the Civic Institutions; but *because of its democratic spirit, the 26 of July Movement wants every ideological position truly representative of the Cuban people to appear in our political scene. . . .*

. . . we are primarily interested in influencing three areas: international public opinion, the military, and the conservative classes. [Italics mine.]

As for the instructions given to Pazos and Rodríguez, they were three: (1) that no executive of the proposed provisional government was to be a candidate in the ensuing elections; (2) that the junta should proceed forthwith to the formation of a government in exile, and to that end should ask the Civic Institutions to designate persons to assume the various offices in such a government; and (3) that they make it abundantly clear that the 26 of July Movement would not participate directly in the government in exile.

Rodríguez and Pazos, however, decided not to commit themselves to these instructions. Instead, Rodríguez tried to throw the whole problem squarely in my lap. That was the main reason for his urgent call to me in New York. He saw his opportunity in another of the documents he had received from Cuba: a handwritten letter from Castro to me. Writing on behalf of the Dirección Nacional and for himself personally, Castro not only confirmed my designation as director of public relations for the 26 of July Movement outside of Cuba but announced the creation of a so-called Committee in Exile, of which I was thereby appointed chairman. Here is the letter:

Sierra Maestra, 30 October 1957

Dear Mario:

With Daniel[6] here, who has paid us a visit for a full discussion of the affairs of the Movement, I am writing you these lines, brief though they have to be—because these days there is hardly time for anything around here—to let you know that we have read and considered your document of October 5 and that I am in complete agreement with the Dirección Nacional's reply to it of October 15.

We have heard from Daniel that Raúl Chibás has been released and has gone into exile.[7] As we see it, that solves the problem of who should take charge of finances. All of us in the Dirección Nacional agree that he should have this job. On our behalf, please ask him to accept. I know he will do everything he can to help us.

The Committee [in Exile] would then be composed as follows:

Propaganda and Public Relations: Mario Llerena
Organization: Carlos Franqui
Military Affairs: Léster Rodríguez
Finances: Raúl Chibás

Although, naturally, the Committee should elect its own chairman, we propose that they nominate you, so that you may represent the Committee in any activity or meeting with a full vote of confidence. That would facilitate its work considerably.

The thing that has prompted us to propose you [as chairman] is the clarity with which you have expressed the position that, as all of us see it, the 26 of July Movement should maintain amidst the chaotic confusion of the political parties. I in particular, for I have great faith in your ability and integrity.

You will have a wonderful fellow worker in Raúl Chibás, for he is the most unselfish and noble person I have ever known. Unlike others, he has no political ambitions, and it's a constant struggle to get him to accept the positions that his name and prestige bring to him. Political chicanery has done much harm in Cuba and will try to do the same outside of Cuba. But we have succeeded in having political chicanery exiled, and that is at least one step forward.

Don't let anything discourage you. The 26 of July Movement is now very strong. Act in the complete assurance that you represent an undisputed majority of the Cuban people.

Daniel has received a strong impression of all that we have accomplished in the Sierra. The whole territory is under our control. A *hundred percent* of the population is actively behind us, and we are getting ready to repel what may be the last push of the Dictatorship.

All of you do your best to see that some aid gets to us from abroad, for it would help to consolidate our position and we need it for the last and hardest battles.

We will be glad to hear from all of you and know that everything is going well up there.

Here we are still full of hope, with that same faith you saw in us on that trip of yours to Mexico, which looks so distant now that our dreams are coming beautifully true.

A big *abrazo* to all of you from all our soldiers.

FIDEL CASTRO R.

Here is the Castro that we wanted to believe in: kind, modest, understanding, confident, courageous. To Rodríguez, however,

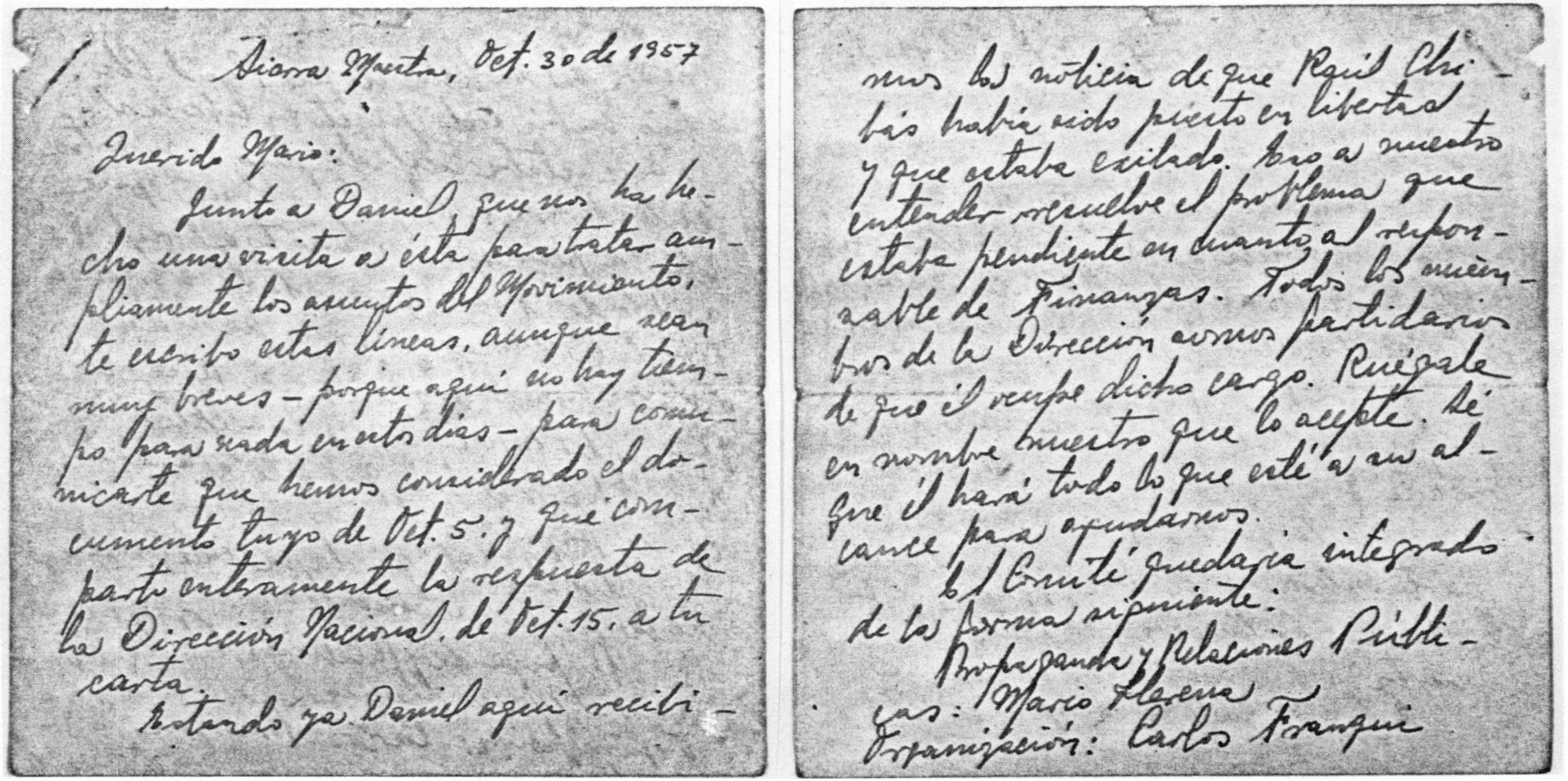

Sierra Maestra, Oct. 30 de 1957

Querido Mario:

Junto a Daniel, que nos ha hecho una visita a ésta para tratar ampliamente los asuntos del Movimiento, te escribo estas líneas, aunque sean muy breves —porque aquí no hay tiempo para nada en estos días— para comunicarte que hemos considerado el documento tuyo de Oct. 5, y que comparto enteramente la respuesta de la Dirección Nacional de Oct. 15, a tu carta.

Estando ya Daniel aquí recibimos la noticia de que Raúl Chibás había sido puesto en libertad y que estaba exilado. Eso a nuestro entender resuelve el problema que estaba pendiente en cuanto al responsable de Finanzas. Todos los miembros de la Dirección somos partidarios de que él ocupe dicho cargo. Ruégale en nombre nuestro que lo acepte. Sé que él hará todo lo que esté a su alcance para ayudarnos.

El Comité quedaría integrado de la forma siguiente:

Propaganda y Relaciones Públicas: Mario Llerena
Organización: Carlos Franqui

Letter of Fidel Castro establishing the Committee in Exile and designating the author as its chairman.

la estricta confianza de los Parti-
dos Políticos. Particularmente, yo,
por la gran confianza que tengo en
tu serenidad e integridad.

En Raúl Chibás tendía un magnífico compañero porque en él tendía
más dentralizado y todo que he creo-
ido. Plácido de tino, no experimenta un
dar, y hoy que está luchando siempre
en y para su nuevo lo largo por
su histórico representar y llamada
su pública pantera. He hecho mucho de-
río en Cuba y tratare de hacerlo hoy.
Bien firme de lucha. Pero que tenerlo
Siempre que la política la crude...
y uno al menos es un avance.

'Asunto Político: Felipe Rodríguez
Finanzas: Raúl Chibás

Aunque naturalmente, al Comité debe elegir su presidente de su
propio seno, proponemos que se
te designe a ti, hasta que se cue-
tre testigo o relación pudre esta
ta el Comité en un empleo
unidad la resistencia civica —
de Confianza, aro faculta-
cho el trabajo del interior
—

La razón que nos mueve a propo-
nerte en la claridad con que tan impo-
ando los hechos ff... mantener el
criterio del todos del Julio en cuadros de
Movimiento 26 de Julio en cuadros de

who now found himself technically subordinate to me, it was the last straw. On receiving the Dirección Nacional's reprimand, he and Pazos decided not to continue as 26 of July delegates to the junta, even though the leadership had accepted their participation. In urging me to come to Miami, Rodríguez intended to switch the responsibility for relations with the junta to me. Castro's announcement of the Committee in Exile gave him a perfect excuse. He quoted Castro's letter to me: as chairman of the Committee in Exile, I was to "represent the Committee in any activity or meeting." That certainly included the junta, didn't it?

Rodríguez was technically right, but at the same time, the leadership had specifically confirmed him and Pazos as delegates to the junta. I would therefore assume their responsibilities only if the leadership instructed me to do so. So they asked Lucas Morán, a lawyer from Santiago and 26 of July sympathizer, to act as provisional delegate. I returned to New York and wrote to the Dirección Nacional for instructions.

In New York the Committee in Exile ran into its first test of authority—and failed. Arnaldo Barrón, a friend of Castro's and head of an old Ortodoxo group, continued to act as though the Ortodoxo party and the 26 of July Movement were two sides of the same coin. He claimed to be in direct communication with Castro and insisted that he was the only true representative of the 26 of July in New York. The Barrón group never recognized the Committee in Exile, despite all the formal authorizations sent by the DN and by Castro himself. On the contrary, they maintained a hostile attitude, and even resorted to defamatory tactics.

Late in October Chuck Ryan, one of three young American navy men who had joined the rebel forces in the Sierra Maestra during the summer,[8] was scheduled to come to the United States, apparently to make a propaganda tour for the Castro cause. His return was arranged through the American naval base at Guantánamo. Before Ryan left the mountains, Castro personally gave him a letter addressed to Barrón.

When Ryan arrived in New York he sought out Barrón in order to deliver Castro's message. The Barrón people felt as though they had found a treasure: here was an opportunity to demonstrate their direct recognition by Castro, independently of the Committee in Exile. They took charge of Ryan and kept him practically incommunicado in a hotel room for three days while they publicized a rally to be held at the same hotel, at which they would present a big surprise.

On the day of the rally, I was in the audience. After keeping us in suspense with speeches and announcements, Barrón finally produced Ryan and triumphantly introduced him as Castro's personal envoy to him. Ryan then ceremoniously handed Barrón the letter amidst clamorous applause, and parts of it were read. Some portions, he explained, were strictly confidential. The letter was little more than a courteous acknowledgment of the group's financial contributions to the movement, with exhortations to keep up the good work.

At the close of the rally I made my way to Ryan and introduced myself. Ryan said he knew who I was but had no messages for me. He brushed aside my suggestion that we meet for a talk the next day. He was deliberately cool, and I realized that the Barrón people had succeeded in turning him against the Committee in Exile.

Ryan received considerable publicity in the American and international news media, all of which gave a tremendous psychological boost to Barrón's undisciplined and vociferous group at the expense of the newly born Committee in Exile, one of whose supposed functions was the handling of precisely that kind of affair. Castro's operations required a constant flow of money, most of which was expected to come from the United States. Favorable publicity was essential. It was for this purpose that the Committee in Exile had been created. The Ryan mission was to have been carried out through the committee. Unfortunately, Castro, unaware of the special complexities of the émigré groups and happy to reward a regular contributor with a cordial letter, caused the whole plan to abort.

I of course complained immediately to the Dirección Nacional in Cuba. Replying in its name, Hart explained that the American consul in Santiago had whisked Ryan away before they had a chance to give him the papers they had prepared for me. "Fidel's letter to Barrón," Hart wrote, "must have caused you many problems. Fidel had no knowledge of the committee's reports on the Barrón case. Daniel tells us that he [Castro] put his hands to his head when he realized the possible consequences of his action. In any event, if after your credentials arrive Barrón does not submit to your authority, let us know about it immediately and we will issue a letter of expulsion from the Movement to be published abroad. . . ."

A new letter was then sent (with duplicate in English for Ryan's benefit) informing me that Ryan was instructed to work closely with me in organizing a publicity campaign. Apparently Ryan had also received some communication from Cuba, for a few days after the rally he phoned me to apologize for his earlier abruptness and offered to cooperate with the Committee in Exile. By that time, however, I wanted nothing to do with Ryan and told him to forget it.

The "credentials" mentioned by Hart came to me a few weeks later directly from Castro. They consisted of another handwritten document, dated 9 January 1958 in the Sierra Maestra, intended to be circulated among "Cuban exiles and émigrés." This was Castro's specific response to my reports on the disorganization and lack of discipline I had found in the 26 of July groups everywhere, and especially in New York:

Once again, the role of the Cuban exiles and émigrés in this struggle is to be understood this way: financial contributions, public denunciation of the crimes our country is suffering, and a campaign to promote the Cuban cause directed toward American democratic opinion.

But if the exiles and émigrés really want to help us, they must immediately put an end to all the rivalries and feuding that have been frustrating the aid so badly needed by our fighters. . . .

Some months ago, in order to make really effective the cooperation of those Cubans living abroad, the Dirección Nacional created the Committee in Exile. This committee, based in New York, has been given full authority to organize and direct all these endeavors, as well as to name its own delegates in all the groups or centers of Cuban population. All activities and financial contributions of the movement outside Cuba are to be carried out solely through these delegates. . . .

Cuban exiles and émigrés are hereby informed that the chairman of the Committee in Exile is Dr. Mario Llerena. The secretary in charge of finances is Dr. Raúl Chibás.

The Committee in Exile has also been instructed to publish a newspaper under the title *Nuestra Razón* [I had suggested this name, but later changed it to *Sierra Maestra*], which is to be our official organ abroad.

This document—which also included authorization to expel from the organization anyone not willing to abide by its norms—was photocopied and circulated widely among all the groups, but the situation it aimed to correct changed not at all.

I had been in New York scarcely two weeks after my last return from Miami when I received a call from a man who identified himself as Herrera. I recognized the nom de guerre of Santos Buch, a friend of Armando Hart and the national leader of the Civic Resistance Movement. I had not met him personally but I knew who he was. Buch explained that he had just arrived in Miami with important instructions that made my presence there imperative. I of course made arrangements to leave immediately.

In Miami Santos Buch, an amiable white-haired old gentleman, took me to the apartment of Raúl Chibás, who had also just arrived from Mexico with his wife. Buch was the bearer of yet another communication from the Dirección Nacional for me, signed and stamped by Hart as secretary of organization for the 26 of July Movement. Its central message was my designation as delegate of the movement to the Junta de Liberación Cubana.

As usual, the document dealt at length with a variety of subjects. Its tone was cordial, even affectionate. Hart discussed a number of topics before he finally came to the question of the Junta de Liberación Cubana in Miami: ". . . the Junta de Liberación must disappear and its place be taken by a nonpartisan junta supported, if possible, by the Civic Institutions, as suggested in the Sierra Manifesto. . . ."[9]

Castro and the Dirección Nacional seemed to be determined to follow a moderate line. From my vantage point in exile, I could see clearly the complete inability of the old political forces to cope with the critical situation created by the constitutional collapse in Cuba, and I had therefore urged the movement to assume the sole leadership of the democratic revolution in which I assumed it was engaged. But the movement's leaders appeared not to be ready for an independent course, even not too sure of the decisive role they were already playing in the revolutionary transformation of Cuba. It was the old semantic paradox: apparently I was the impatient revolutionary, they were the moderates bent on drawing the political, social, and economic elements of the pre-1952 status quo into their sphere. Notice, for instance, this passage:

Who is going to succeed Batista? That can be answered only by the organization of the masses—which is what we have been doing here in Cuba—and by involving certain figures who represent interests that must be persuaded to support decisive action at the moment they ask themselves that question. Such interests are: the military, the banks, big business, the sugar-mill owners, the big sugar-cane planters, etc. They are the very social elements on whom we want to make an impression with a government free of political partisanship. . . .

Then the communication assumed a more personal tone as it moved on to the subject of my taking over the representation of the movement in the junta: "I wish the Revolution did not have to use you in an assignment so unrewarding that perhaps it might have been better to let those who have been doing it so far continue with it. But as the days pass and nothing definite comes in response to all our suggestions, we thought it indispensable that, with our total support, you assume the political direction of the matter. . . ."

The deep ideological gap between the 26 of July revolutionaries in Cuba and the opposition leaders in Miami was becoming increasingly evident. This letter, however, amounted to the "specific instructions" I had required as the condition for my acceptance of the post of delegate to the junta. Now I had no alternative. Chibás and Buch were of the same opinion. As if hoping that flattering my ego a bit might help to convince me, Hart added: "The reason we have picked you for this is that nobody has expressed so clearly and accurately as you have the revolutionary thought of the movement."

On November 26 I sent the Dirección Nacional a long letter acknowledging the assignment but repeating my views on the Miami situation. I regretted that the time devoted to junta affairs could not be spent on public relations, which to me was at the moment far more important. To stress my point, I told the leadership about a publicity problem in which I had recently been involved.

The 26 of July group in Costa Rica was publishing a magazine called *Cuba Libre*. In its August 1957 issue it had carried an article, attributed to Fidel Castro, which had actually been composed of out-of-context passages from Castro's 1953 speech "History Will Absolve Me."[10] The overall impression created by the article was one of extreme radicalism. A copy of *Cuba Libre* fell into the hands of a Princeton graduate student, P. W. Murphy, who translated the article into English and sent it to *The Nation*. It appeared in the November 30 issue under the title "What Cuba's Rebels Want." I told the DN that this article, "by Fidel Castro," appeared to support accusations that the 26 of July Movement was Communist. When *The Nation* announced the publication of the Castro article, I began to get excited calls in Miami from the *New York Times* and United Press International, asking my opinion of the views expressed in the article and if I would confirm Castro's authorship. I issued statements emphatically denying that *Cuba Libre* had official authority to speak on behalf of the 26 of July Movement and explaining the (to me) democratic philosophy of the movement.

The *New York Times* published my interview on November 24, and UPI also circulated it. I had firm ground to stand on. At that moment I had in my possession an advance copy of an interview recently granted by Castro to correspondent Andrew St. George, who had given it to me just before I left for Miami. The interview was published by *Look* magazine in the issue of 4 February 1958. It contained the following question and answer:

*Charges have been made that your movement is Communist-inspired. What about this?*
This is absolutely false. Every American newsman who has come here at great personal peril—Herbert Matthews of the *New York Times,* two CBS reporters and yourself—has said this is false. Our Cuban support comes from all classes of society. The middle class is strongly united in its support of our movement. We even have many wealthy sympathizers. Merchants, industrial executives, young people, workers are sick of the gangsterism that rules Cuba. Actually, the Cuban Communists, as your journalist John Gunther once reported, have never opposed Batista, for whom they have seemed to feel a close kinship.

After bringing all these things to the DN's attention, I moved on to the junta. The idea of replacing the political junta with a nonpartisan one was totally unrealistic, I said.

I discussed the matter in private with Ortodoxo leaders Bisbé and Agramonte, and they are of the opinion that the idea does not stand the slightest chance of passing. On the contrary, they say that insisting on the point might bring about the collapse of the junta—which is to say of the unity of the opposition. . . . In view of this situation, the 26 of July has no choice but either to risk disrupting political unity—with all the consequences that would bring—or to try to make the best of the situation and cooperate in the designation of an acceptable figurehead for the provisional government. . . . This latter alternative could very well be the psychological culmination of the idea of opposition unity. . . .

I said that it appeared to me that the 26 of July Movement was not yet mature enough to assume the full "responsibility of revolutionary power." I still urged a full "revolutionary course," but for the time being, inasmuch as the movement had publicly entered into the junta discussions, I felt it wiser to stay and try to influence developments from the inside.

As things stand at the junta at the present moment, it might not be too difficult to have certain conditions accepted, for instance, not to use power for political ambitions, absolute neutrality concerning both ideological and programmatic matters, etc. . . . . All this brings me to the point—which I hereby submit to you—that we must adopt a position of flexibility that will allow me to maneuver in the direction of a provisional government as soon as possible and, of course, in the naming of its presiding figure. This is what appears to be all-important now.

I think, incidentally, that the Civic Institutions have accepted the part of naming the provisional president from a list of names presented to them by the junta. . . . Speaking of names likely to be considered for the position of provisional president, let me say that of all those I have seen, the one that seems most acceptable to me is that of Judge Urrutia-Lleó. . . . The most probable, however, is Dr. Felipe Pazos.

On November 29 I attended my first meeting of the junta. The debate started when Tony Varona, speaking for the Auténticos, proposed that each member organization designate a delegate in Cuba for the purpose of forming a Havana junta that would take over the direction of the war on the island. Any such body, of course, would automatically assume authority over the Sierra Maestra forces. That was the second suggestion I had heard that day about a counterpart junta in Cuba. Carlos Maristany, the OA delegate, had talked to me earlier about naming another delegate for each organization in order to form a committee in Cuba "to raise funds for the revolution."

I contested Varona's proposition—which had the support of all the other delegates—arguing that it was neither necessary nor advisable to create in Cuba a replica of a strictly political group that had reason to exist only outside Cuba.

My point raised a great commotion. All the delegates tried to speak at once. When the meeting was finally brought to order, Varona insisted that the raison d'être of the junta was "to organize and direct the revolution in Cuba," and that this concept had been agreed to by Léster Rodríguez and Felipe Pazos. I replied that I was unaware of any such agreement, and that, on the contrary, according to the instructions I had received from the 26 of July Dirección Nacional, the movement's own concept of the junta differed substantially from that expressed by Varona. Someone asked me to explain what I meant by that, and I replied that the junta was neither a coalition nor a fusion, with authority to direct the policies and activities of its member organizations, but simply an assembly through which delegates of the member organizations tried primarily to reach an agreement on the nature and the manner of designating the provisional government. Further, since this

political assembly was supposedly complemented by a secret sub-
organization in charge of coordinating military action, it was only
through this subagency that all matters concerning armed activities in Cuba were to be channeled.

My words had the effect of a bomb—and understandably so. The
truth is that the 26 of July's involvement with the junta had been
inconsistent from the beginning. In view of what it had already accomplished independently, the 26 of July Movement should have
declined to join the junta. But once it had acquiesced in the negotiations initiated *motu proprio* by Rodríguez and Pazos, then it
should have joined fully in the unity maintained by the other organizations. My personal position, therefore, could not have been
more uncomfortable. I went to the junta against my own will and
judgment, yielding to an excessively acute sense of group loyalty
and discipline. I was expected to justify an attempt to downgrade
the unity on which the junta was based in favor of an actual su-
premacy of the 26 of July Movement. How could the Sierra Maestra boys imagine that the experienced politicians in Miami would
accept that?

For a second or two there was stony silence. The delegates
looked at each other as if to make sure they had heard correctly.
Then somebody said that that "confronted the junta with a crisis,"
and everyone demanded a turn to speak in what threatened to be a
very long and probably heated debate. Knowing that a debate at
that point would take us nowhere, I proposed a temporary recess.
My instructions from the Dirección Nacional, I said, were even
stiffer than I had suggested. I was requesting a more flexible approach so that the 26 of July could better contribute to an agreement on the designation of the provisional government, but until I
received specific advice from the movement's committee, there
was very little that I could do. I therefore proposed that we recess
until Friday, December 6. The motion was carried.

A few days after my request for new instructions, a special envoy
of the Dirección Nacional arrived in Miami. This was Luis Buch (a
distant relative of Santos Buch), a lawyer from Santiago whose revolutionary leanings were not yet publicly known and who could
therefore serve as a courier without arousing suspicion. Buch
handed me credentials signed by Faustino Pérez, but his instructions were verbal. If they were authentic—and Faustino's letter left
little doubt that they were—the leaders in Cuba seemed to have

done an about-face. The new instructions amounted to almost a duplication of the position maintained throughout by the other organizations. The only distinction, if any, was the 26 of July's emphasis on having the Civic Institutions in Cuba select the head of the provisional government as well as the members of the cabinet, and propose the bases on which the future provisional government was to function.

Buch suggested that we have an informal meeting with the junta delegates. I got in touch with all I could, and we agreed to cancel the continuation of the debate previously scheduled for Friday the sixth and advance the date to Tuesday the third at 5:00 P.M. The main business now was to discuss the 26 of July's proposal that a list of five names be sent to the Civic Institutions, which would select one as provisional president. A suggestion by Buch that the five persons named by the junta should constitute a kind of executive council or government in exile was not favorably received by the others.

Buch had brought a list of five names representing the movement's own choices. In order of preference, they were:

1. Manuel Urrutia-Lleó, a judge of the provincial court in Santiago who had voted to acquit the *Granma* defendants in May 1957, on the grounds that they had a constitutional right to rebel against an oppressive government. The two other judges on the tribunal voted to convict the defendants and they were sentenced to terms of up to eight years, but Urrutia's courageous stand had won him wide acclaim.
2. Felipe Pazos, economist and former president of the National Bank of Cuba.
3. Dr. Raúl de Velasco, president of the Cuban Medical Association and chairman of the Civic Institutions.
4. Justo Carrillo, former president of the Bank of Agricultural and Industrial Development and active in a number of opposition organizations and attempted revolts.
5. José Miró Cardona, lawyer and university professor.

(I included the following paragraph in a communication sent to the Dirección Nacional on December 3: ". . . the best of the names suggested is without question that of Judge Urrutia-Lleó. I have talked with some of the other delegates, trying to influence them in his favor. I believe the suggestion has been well received.

If the DN agrees, it would be good to let the leaders of the Civic Institutions in Cuba know about our interest in Judge Urrutia.")

But all that came of the Tuesday meeting of the junta was an agreement to send a communication to the Civic Institutions in Cuba requesting (*a*) their consent to include some of their own leaders in the list of presidential prospects and (*b*) the withdrawal of their condition of having a constitutional statute before proceeding to select a name. The junta then declared itself in recess until December 17 in order to await a reply from the CI. Buch left to inform the leaders in Cuba.

# 7 The Turning Point

From the Miami viewpoint, the anti-Batista struggle had finally taken a regular course. Cubans were now tackling their national crisis in very much the same way they had successfully tackled similar crises in the past.

Personally I was rather confused. What was really going on within the leadership of the movement in Cuba? Had they actually decided suddenly to shift gears and steer the revolution toward the easier paths of traditional politics? Or were they perhaps only playing for time? Did Buch's mission truly represent the thought of the Dirección Nacional, or was it just a bold move of the Santiago group behind the Sierra Maestra's back?

With the perspective of time it is obvious today that no one in Miami had a clear picture of what was really going on. History was running at a much faster pace in Cuba than in the limited world of the émigrés. Both in capacity for action and psychologically, the revolution had progressed to a degree far beyond the revolutionaries' own expectations. The initial preoccupation with a printed manifesto and other literature that would present the movement's objectives in a favorable light had been all but forgotten. Rhetorical justifications were no longer necessary. The vacuum of leadership left by the existing political forces as a result of their monumental failure to cope with the Batista challenge was being filled by the youthful and aggressive 26 of July, and the people had found a new dashing hero to take the place of

Eddy Chibás. A military victory by the rebel forces might still look far away, but the signs of weakening and demoralization in the government ranks were unmistakable. The guerrillas' nostrils were already filled with the smell of power.

Why, then, the Miami involvement—the inconsistent denunciation of the Pazos-Rodríguez negotiations while in the same breath the leadership accepted the fait accompli and confirmed them as delegates; the later insistence on my own participation in the junta despite my reluctance; and finally the unannounced appearance of Buch with instructions that amounted to a complete reversal of the position I had been previously asked to maintain?

I learned in time that my new instructions had nothing to do with a turn toward traditional politics; they represented an underhanded maneuver aimed at swindling Prío. It may even be that Rodríguez had not been acting on his own, after all. I still had a lot to learn.

On the whole the junta did not appear to be in a great hurry to get on with its business. Most of the other delegations (with the possible exceptions of the Ortodoxo party and the Directorio Revolucionario) moved in an orbit around Prío. Although he never personally attended any meetings, Prío was the *éminence grise* behind the junta. Most of the delegates were primarily interested in promoting the importance of the junta as a political force in itself—which was tantamount, of course, to ensuring that Prío would be the deciding factor in any development. They urged the organization of juntas in other cities of the United States, and of junta-sponsored public rallies as well as a fund-raising campaign inside Cuba.

The junta's military activities appeared to be at a standstill, and Varona blamed the 26 of July. Léster Rodríguez and the other 26 of July military delegates, he said, had stopped attending the meetings of the military subcommittee.

The Ortodoxos (the only other pro-Castro delegation) were not happy about the way things were going. Bisbé confided to me that he was worried about the "secret aid" Prío was supposed to give. According to Bisbé, the Ortodoxos had been led to understand that Prío's aid—either in money or in equipment—to the revolution, especially to the Sierra Maestra guerrillas, was a fundamental condition for the joining together of the opposition parties in the junta. Bisbé said that Léster Rodríguez had assured him at the beginning of the exploratory talks that that was one of the secret articles of the "Miami pact," and that the Ortodoxos had agreed, "making a moral sacrifice" (the Ortodoxo party, after all, had been founded to combat corruption in Auténtico administrations, including Prío's), only in order to follow what they were told was the 26 of July's line. If that aid did not materialize soon, Bisbé said, the so-called unity was "just one more of Prío's deceitful schemes."

All this was totally new to me. As chairman of the Committee in Exile, I thought I ought to have a talk with Rodríguez about Bisbé's revelations, despite the fact that Rodríguez had always been uncommunicative and took his membership in the Committee in Exile lightly. Rodríguez came to see me accompanied by Jorge Sotús, a captain of the Sierra Maestra guerrillas who had surfaced in Maimi on one of Castro's "special missions."[1] When I asked just what the situation was in regard to Prío's much-talked-about aid, Rodríguez said that Prío was blackmailing the 26 of July: he was withholding all aid until he was sure who the designated president would be. It was no secret that Prío and his allies strongly favored Felipe Pazos for the presidency. It became abundantly obvious now that, in urging Pazos to act as a 26 of July delegate earlier, Rodríguez had been playing a little game of his own.

Rodríguez said that he had thought of attending the junta sessions again to see if he could "persuade Prío to give something" (he apparently thought he could be a delegate or not, at his convenience), but then he changed his mind and decided that perhaps he should first consult the Dirección Nacional. His idea, he said, was to try to get all he could from Prío by pretending to go along with his scheme in the junta. At any rate, he would let me know.

At the time I thought that all this dubious diplomacy originated with Rodríguez. My perception was clouded by the abundant correspondence from the DN in my possession proclaiming entirely different views. Only when more pieces of the puzzle came together did I realize that little Léster could not possibly have been acting independently.

Two days later Rodríguez showed up again with Sotús and said he had good news. He wanted to talk to the Ortodoxos also, so we all went to see Bisbé and Agramonte at Bisbé's rented house in Coral Gables. Rodríguez explained that there was a military plan whose approximate cost was $90,000. Prío was willing to contribute two-thirds of that amount if the 26 of July signed on for the rest *and if the junta's decisions were agreeable to him*. Rodríguez said it was to our advantage to accept this plan. The important thing was to obtain the financial aid the revolution so badly needed. Playing an apparently political role at the junta, he said, was just a tactical step that would soon be forgotten once the revolution was in power. He wanted the Ortodoxos' cooperation in carrying out this plan. Sotús added his own urging to Rodríguez's.

Bisbé and Agramonte looked at me with question marks in their eyes, waiting for my reaction. After all, I was the official representative of the 26 of July; I was supposed to be in a position to say the last word. I was repelled by the notion of pretending to dance to Prío's tune only in order to wheedle him into parting with his money, but the full Machiavellian duplicity of the mind behind that scheme was not yet apparent to me. I still thought I was dealing with a little man who, dazzled by his association with men who dealt in power, had strayed from the right revolutionary path.

I told Rodríguez I was sorry but I could not assume any responsibility in regard to his proposed plan. He was free to act as he pleased, of course, but I had to confine myself to the written instructions I had received from the Dirección Nacional, and those instructions pointed in a quite different direction. Rodríguez could hardly hide his displeasure, but he controlled himself and made no comment. In view of my attitude, Bisbé and Agramonte said that the Ortodoxos probably would not support the plan either. Rodríguez and Sotús said they had obviously wasted their time and left in disgust.

As the junta was in recess, I returned to New York to catch up on my public relations work. I was there less than four days, however, when I got word that the Civic Institutions had agreed to select a provisional president from a proposed list of five candidates and that the junta was ready to start discussing such a list. I returned at once to Miami.

The junta met promptly and I submitted the list of names that I had received from the Dirección Nacional: Urrutia, Pazos, Velasco, Carrillo, Miró Cardona. The Ortodoxos presented a somewhat different list of their own.

After a number of votes, name by name, there was general agreement on four: Pazos, Velasco, García Bárcena, and Miró Cardona. The inclusion of García Bárcena was little more than a sentimental gesture, as he had recently declared in an article in *Bohemia* that he favored an electoral rather than a revolutionary solution. When names were proposed for the fifth candidate, however, we reached an impasse. The only groups that supported Urrutia were the 26 of July and the Ortodoxo party.

I made it clear that the 26 of July's support of Urrutia was unchangeable. The Ortodoxos were equally firm. The Directorio Revolucionario seemed inclined to consider Urrutia if that would help to resolve the impasse soon, but none of the other delegations moved to join us.

I reported at length on the situation to the Dirección Nacional on December 21. Replies from Cuba to my reports and consultations, however, usually reached me with at least a week's delay, sometimes much more. It is this time element that caused the last meetings of the junta, as we shall see soon, to be a total waste of time and energy.

On Christmas Eve I wrote again to the DN to express my growing dissatisfaction with the amount of time I was required to spend with the junta. I asked to be relieved of the assignment as soon as possible. Yet I kept hammering on the Urrutia question: "My opinion is that under no circumstances must the 26 of July stop insisting on Urrutia. If the Dirección Nacional changes its mind in this respect, I beg that it be expressed through a delegate other than myself."

It was not only the junta that troubled me; as 1957 drew to a close I began to become aware of a feeling of discontent with the 26 of July Movement. Up to then I had unconsciously tended to dissociate Castro himself from the organization and its policies. I pictured him rifle in hand, fighting and risking his life for the new Cuba I had attempted to describe in *Nuestra Razón*, too importantly busy to be concerned with everyday decisions. This ennobled image was further enhanced by the apparent sincerity and selflessness of most of his utterances, whether appeals to the émigrés, statements for the press, or personal letters. I had not yet seen the other side of his moon. But I began to have an uncomfortable feeling that I was out of place in the organization. At first I thought this feeling originated in the coolness I sensed in some of my colleagues, including one or two whom I had considered my friends for many years. But this discomfort gradually revealed itself to be less personal than ideological.

In my Christmas Eve report I also discussed my difficulties with Léster Rodríguez. We had not seen eye to eye even before the formation of the junta, I informed the Dirección Nacional, and as a result of our differences the Committee in Exile was not functioning as a harmonious, coordinated whole. Rodríguez acted independently of the committee and failed to inform me about any of his activities. I did not expect to be informed about every military detail, I said, but the general direction of these activities ought to be known by the chairman of the Committee in Exile. My ignorance of a great deal of general information had frequently put me in an embarrassing position at the junta; other delegates often knew more about the 26 of July's activities than I did. Inasmuch as the Committee in Exile was serving no useful function, I proposed that it be dissolved and that the persons responsible for public relations organization, military affairs, and finances carry out their individual responsibilities independently, under the direct supervision of the Dirección Nacional.

That last week of December a number of communications arrived from Cuba, among them one that pointed to important developments to come. It was dated 9 December 1957 at Santiago de Cuba and signed by Armando Hart. Hart expressed satisfaction with the junta's decision to let the Civic Institutions designate the head of the provisional government, "exactly as the Sierra Manifesto says."

However, since the CI, after accepting in principle the designation of the Provisional Government, demands in turn that certain principles be agreed upon for the organization of such a government, we think it necessary that the position of the 26 of July be discussed again with Fidel Castro and the other members of the Dirección Nacional, because *our ideas on the matter might fundamentally alter some of the movement's plans. A new and different situation has been created contrary to what is declared in the Sierra Manifesto. . . .* This is the situation that needs to be discussed, so that we can instruct our delegates accordingly. [Italics mine.]

If a definitive statement on government organization should be required from the movement, Hart wrote, I was to ask for time until I received final instructions.

What were the "ideas" that "might fundamentally alter some of the movement's plans"? What "new and different situation" had "been created contrary to what is declared in the Sierra Manifesto"? Who or what had "created" it? Had Castro and the other 26 of July leaders changed their minds after the signing of that democratic proclamation five months earlier, or had they simply decided that now was the time to abrogate a declaration that had never expressed their true intentions? Hart's words are ambiguous, but there was no question that the "new situation" had occurred not in Miami but in the Sierra Maestra.

Hart's letter was really meant to warn me in advance of an impending decision, but it reached me too late. For more than two weeks I attended meetings of the junta and sent reports and made recommendations, completely unaware that the decision had already been made in the Sierra Maestra to give the death blow to the junta and all its works. That decision, in the form of a lengthy document in the handwriting of Fidel Castro (see Appendix A), had been formalized on December 14. I received the document in Miami on December 30. It was addressed to the leaders of the six other organizations that made up the junta, and in it Castro explained the 26 of July's reasons for withdrawing from the junta and proceeding independently on a revolutionary course. That was actually the turning point at which the anti-Batista process ceased to be political and became totally revolutionary.

Before coming to the details, let me just touch briefly on what had been going on meanwhile in Miami. My reports of those days had to do, as usual, with a variety of subjects. One was the question of Carlos Franqui, who was having difficulties in obtaining a visa to enter the United States. I wrote this comment:

Concerning the designation of a secretary of organization [for the Committee in Exile], I am well aware that Carlos Franqui has been named to that position. But Franqui is in Mexico, and apparently barred from entering this country for the time being. On top of that, there are those who fear that he may be subjected . . . to the suspicion of communism. Lately, however, I have heard from someone who ought to know that the Franqui case has been completely cleared of such a suspicion by the American embassy. . . .

Judge Urrutia and his family had arrived in Miami from Havana two days before Christmas, and on December 26 I wrote:

As I informed you earlier, we have welcomed Judge Urrutia. After looking around town for a place for him [and his family] to stay, we left him at a motel where he has to pay $50 a week. . . . Dr. Urrutia complains quite rightly that all these expenses are beyond his financial means. He is interested in finding a job. . . . Today we tried to get him in touch with one of the deans of the University [of Miami], hoping that something like a series of lectures could be offered him. Unfortunately, the acting dean was leaving today for California. Dr. Urrutia's situation in this regard is therefore serious.

On the other hand, nobody knows at the moment what is to come out of the Junta de Liberación. In my reports of 21 and 24 December I explained how the junta fell into an impasse as a result of the 26 of July's insistence on . . . [Urrutia's] designation. We here have felt hesitant about telling him the real cause of this impasse. Apparently Dr. Urrutia came with the idea that his designation was already in the bag. The truth, however, is quite different. So far there are three organizations that would not even let his name appear in the list of five eligible candidates. I am sorry to say that sending a man here under such circumstances, not knowing what the outcome of this situation is going to be, is acting with a little too much haste. . . .

I have transcribed these otherwise irrelevant passages only because they reflect my state of mind at that critical juncture. My very concern with minutiae and, above all, with the purity of a supposedly democratic endeavor shows that the official spokesman of the organization abroad was totally unaware that an entirely different reality was taking shape within the highest echelons of the movement. It would be naive to assume that their decision to break with the junta was made on the spur of the moment; it must have been long brewing in their minds, while they waited for the right moment to put it into effect.

Castro's sudden action not only caught me by surprise but made me a little apprehensive as well. Now there is a paradox here that demands clarification. Almost from the beginning of my involvement with the Castro group I had been very much concerned about the possibility that the movement might just drift away down the stream of conventional politics; this had been the usual trend of such undertakings in the past. No matter how unintentionally, I had found myself in the pedantic role of guardian of the revolutionary ideals. I had struggled against any involvement with the junta. Now the movement, through Castro's mouth, was making a 180-degree turn, apparently in the very direction I myself had been advocating all along. And instead of feeling happy about it, I became apprehensive. Why?

It is not easy to find a simple explanation. My concern grew gradually, under the cumulative effect of scattered incidents that individually might have had little significance: Faustino Pérez's remarks about fellows up in the mountains with Castro who would object to anticommunist pronouncements in the movement's manifesto; the lukewarm reception given the moderate *Nuestra Razón* and the reiterated announcements that a new manifesto was being prepared; Hart's enigmatic warning of "a new and different situa-

tion . . . contrary to what is declared in the Sierra Manifesto."
Here lay the basic cause of my apprehension. Much though I
disliked any entanglement with traditional politics, I dreaded a radical course far more. Add to all this the revelation that the movement's participation in the junta was only a pretense aimed at parting Prío from some of his millions and you have the seeds of my
discontent. There are two things that I did not fully grasp during
the sad junta episode: that I was being used, and that those who
were using me could not possibly have been doing so without Castro's personal advice and consent.

But let's turn back to the story as it developed. Castro's
handwritten message to the junta was brought to Miami by someone unknown to me, who delivered it to Luis Buch. Buch took it to
Chibás and then the two came to see me. When Rodríguez read
Castro's lengthy tirade, he termed it a "disaster" and bitterly criticized Castro and the Dirección Nacional. Rodríguez seemed to
have been completely won over by the politicians. He even muttered something about going over to Prío's side. In view of his
previous maneuvers, however, it was difficult to say whose side he
really was on. Felipe Pazos, too, was notified of the new developments, and, like Rodríguez, had sarcastic comments for Castro and
his blast against the junta.

The document itself was accompanied by a sort of introduction
in which the long-range intentions of the 26 of July leaders were
carefully couched in democratic rhetoric. If only for this reason, it
is worth transcribing in its entirety. It said:

The 26 of July Movement, by word of its leader, Fidel Castro, explains in
this document its thinking on certain political questions that lately have
caused great concern among the Cuban people and especially among the
gallant cadres of our organization. This declaration is a momentous decision in the history of the 26 of July Movement, which hereby presents itself as the only opposition group now capable of overthrowing the tyranny,
of establishing order afterward, and of offering the country a feasible program of historic realizations.

We shall discuss here only the following subjects: the keeping of peace
and order, the military question, foreign intervention, relations with other
opposition organizations, the independent position of the 26 of July, and
the only possible formula for a Provisional Government.

This exposition is only a first step. Soon other documents will be published which will deal with the following questions:

A. Program of political and institutional integrity.
B. Program of industrial and economic development.
C. Educational program.
D. Program of social reforms.
E. Foreign policy.

These questions will be followed by other pronouncements by the 26 of July on all matters of state.

We sincerely want to promote these programs within the democratic constitutional framework. That is why we now present our idea of the provisional state—one that will lead us to the full exercise of democracy and the rule of law, with a government free from political partisanship which will serve to guarantee and balance all legitimate interests.

The 26 of July has surpassed all others in heroism and sacrifice, and likewise in readiness to organize the masses, especially the younger generation. With all these definitive pronouncements it also demonstrates that it is more aware than any other [organization] of the necessity of a serious political articulation as a basis for the provisional stage. In addition, the 26 of July is the group that shows the greatest concern lest, in the struggle against the tyranny, the country fall prey to political anarchy and personal vengeance, in which lie the seeds of despotism as well as the germs that destroy democracy (as the very recent case of our sister republic of Haiti shows).

When the above-mentioned documents are published in the near future, it will also have been proved that, just as we have been the first and the most constant in action, we are likewise the first and the clearest in thinking.

In his tiresomely long exposition Castro lashed out at the other opposition groups for their failure, in his view, to provide adequate support for the guerrilla war in Cuba. He adopted the pose of the injured party. It was, of course, his way of covering up the fact that the 26 of July had hypocritically taken part in the negotiations for the sole purpose of getting Prío's financial aid but with no intention of living up to the agreements. Now that I had blocked that maneuver, Castro had no further use for the junta. From then on, Castro said, the 26 of July Movement would assume the sole direction of the fight against Batista as well as the responsibility for the future provisional government.

At this point, however, Castro engaged in flagrant contradictions. While proclaiming total power for his revolutionary forces, he declared that "the new [provisional] government will conform to the 1940 Constitution. It will guarantee all rights rec-

ognized by it and will be free from all political partisanship . . .
its main task will be to prepare the country for a general election
under the 1943 Electoral Code and the 1940 Constitution." It is
evident that at that time the 26 of July revolutionaries thought it
necessary to camouflage their intentions with democratic rhetoric.

Castro also took pains to explain in detail why the 26 of July
Movement had chosen Judge Urrutia as its designee for provisional president, and to state that that decision was firm and irrevocable.

It fell to me, as chairman of the Committee in Exile and official
delegate to the junta, to communicate Castro's message to the
leaders of the other opposition groups. Copies were hurriedly
typed. Chibás and I would make an appointment with each of the
junta delegations, formally read the document to them, and hand
them their copies.

Most of the leaders did not appear surprised, and they made few
comments. Our task proceeded uneventfully until we came to the
Ortodoxos, the last on our list. As a group the Ortodoxos had practically become a satellite of the 26 of July Movement, following its
directives almost to the letter. Most of them seemed convinced that
the 26 of July Movement was just a branch of their own party, and
some regarded Castro as an intrepid deliverer who was performing
a heroic act for which they themselves lacked the courage.

Agramonte, Salvador Massip,[2] Raúl Primelles,[3] and a few others
were waiting for us when Chibás and I arrived at Bisbé's rented
house in Coral Gables. I was about midway through my reading of
Castro's document when Bisbé suddenly rose from his seat, sob-
bing convulsively. Castro's harsh denunciation of the junta and of
politicians in general deeply shook him. He felt personally attacked
because he had taken upon himself the responsibility of selling to
his mostly reluctant colleagues—now with an obvious look of I-
told-you-so on their faces—the idea of cooperating with Prío's Auténticos, the political archenemies of the Ortodoxos. Bisbé had
been talked into taking this line by Léster Rodríguez, and he told
me he had assumed that Rodríguez was acting with the full
knowledge and support of Castro. Castro's letter was therefore a
real shock to him. He even blurted out that he was going to shoot
himself. Everyone in the room, of course, rushed to try to calm
him down. It was quite a scene. Bisbé was resilient, however, and
he soon adjusted to Castro's new position.[4]

Other reactions came later in the press. Varona and Cofiño were among many who made public declarations—some of them very angry—denouncing the 26 of July's abrupt turnabout, and particularly Castro's personal attitude. Faure Chomón issued a long fulmination against Castro and the 26 of July Movement on behalf of the Directorio Revolucionario. The FEU and the labor organizations also made public statements condemning Castro and his movement.

None of these people seemed to notice that by letting the junta disappear they were validating Castro's claim to the leadership of the revolution as well as proving their own inability to carry on without the 26 of July Movement. Only the Ortodoxos, as usual, took Castro's side. In a public statement signed by Bisbé as chairman they explained that although they had earlier favored the unity of the opposition, they had now decided to follow the 26 of July line. The time-worn metaphor of the tree and its branches was thus reversed: the Ortodoxos resigned themselves to the role of branch while the 26 of July became the tree. That was the end of the attempt at unity.

Because I had been the 26 of July's delegate to the junta, a considerable number of the protests against Castro's action which appeared in the Spanish-language press—in Miami, in New York, even in Havana—took the form of open letters addressed to me. People outside the movement seemed to have gotten the impression that the collapse of the junta had been to a large extent my own personal doing. At the same time, I also became the target of much criticism from members of the movement in exile: since I had been mingling with the politicians in Miami, they thought I had betrayed the movement and was to be included among those whom Castro had denounced. And while they were condemning me, the leaders in Cuba were expecting me to explain to the public the step just taken by Fidel Castro. In a letter accompanying the explosive message Hart wrote: "I am sending you herewith the original document signed by Fidel Castro on behalf of the Dirección Nacional of the 26 of July Movement in regard to the embarrassing questions that have occupied our attention for nearly two months of unending discussions. . . . Try . . . to give it as much publicity as possible. Take it especially to the *Diario Las Américas* [Miami] and the *New York Times*. We want you to explain the whole situation to Mr. Matthews on behalf of Fidel. Tell him that for us these are the only true bases for the integration of the opposition. Actually, the only existing opposition is in the 26 of July."

The Dirección Nacional evidently realized the extraordinary importance of its decision to abandon its cooperation with the other opposition groups and take an independent course. Hart said, "I believe this to be a most significant step for the 26 of July, because here the philosophy of the Revolution has been presented as never before."

There is indeed no question that that step marked a turning point of tremendous historical consequences in the ultimate development of the revolutionary process. At the same time, however, Castro and the other leaders in Cuba apparently still regarded the Ortodoxo party as a political factor to be reckoned with and considered Raúl Chibás to be still connected with that party (as indeed he was) even though he was an active member of the Committee in Exile. This dual membership seemed natural then to all concerned. Hart urged me, however, to win Chibás over fully to the 26 of July. Perhaps, Hart said, I should personally explain "our" attitude to the Ortodoxos; but he left the matter to my judgment.

On 1 January 1958 I addressed a formal note to Antonio de Varona, chairman of the junta, informing him of the official withdrawal of the 26 of July Movement from that body. That was the epitaph of the Junta de Liberación Cubana. Three or four days later I returned to New York.

# 8 The Making of an Image

There are two aspects to history: one from within the space-time capsule of actors and witnesses, the other from the distant perspective of future spectators. These last are in a much better position to assess the true dimension of events. As the saying goes, one may fail to see the forest because of the trees. Was I by now fully disenchanted with the Castro movement? Was I aware that the revolution was increasingly and consistently showing signs that it was turning to the extreme left? Of course not; my sense of smell was indeed telling me that something was rotten, but I could not pinpoint exactly where. I therefore kept on going, moved by the unconscious force of wishful thinking, listening to the echo of idealistic-sounding words and promises, and dismissing anything that looked suspicious as only human frailty. I was the typical middle-class reformer riding without realizing it on the crest of a full-fledged radical revolution.

Now that the episode of the Junta de Liberación was closed, I thought I would at last be free to devote my full time to the long-neglected task of public relations. It proved to be not at all difficult. With the heroic figures of Castro's bearded guerrillas already impressed on the public imagination, opportunities for publicity came my way without my having to seek them out. The American news media opened their doors to Castro's representative. Press releases personally drafted and typed by me were promptly accepted and disseminated by the Associated Press,

UPI, and other international agencies. When I thought there was reason to call a press conference, reporters from all major newspapers and TV networks would be there with their writing pads and their cameras. On 21 March 1958 commentator John Wingate interviewed me on his *Tonight* program on the old Dumont TV network. For half an hour I fielded his questions about the 26 of July Movement and its intentions for the future of Cuba. Was Castro a Communist? Certainly not! I defended Castro and the Cuban revolution as essentially democratic and emphatically denied that the movement was in any way influenced by communism. On the contrary, I assured Wingate, by its very new approach to old problems the Cuban revolution would act as a true antidote against the spread of communism. I took the same position before a Foreign Policy Association panel in Pittsburgh on April 20, aired on channel 11, and in a number of radio interviews.

I attended rallies of Castro supporters and was invited to address students at a number of colleges and high schools. At Columbia University, the Massachusetts Institute of Technology, and the University of Chicago, among others, my lectures were followed by question-and-answer periods. Almost invariably some student would write to me later to request further information on the Cuban revolution or to inquire how he or she could help.

I had never been so busy in my life. It would be presumptuous of me to suggest that my personal efforts helped in any large measure to make the Castro image palatable, even pleasant, to American public opinion. But I certainly tried hard.

I also wrote articles for the Spanish-language press of New York and Miami, and occasionally I had an opportunity to contribute to the English-language press as well. In a letter published by the *New York Times* on 8 November 1957 I protested the American government's shipments of arms to Batista. The letter ended with these two paragraphs:

It is a tremendous mistake. We all know that arming an unscrupulous dictator is against the principles and convictions of the American people; we all know that that is not the best way to unite us in the common cause of democracy and human dignity. But still it is done.

When are those who are responsible for this kind of unfortunate decisions going to realize that helping the Latin American dictators means preparing the ground for the bad seeds of communism? Let us hope that that realization will not come too late.

# No MAS ARMAS para

# el DICTADOR de Cuba

## TODOS AL PALM GARDEN

### 52 y 8th Avenida, N. Y. C.

## DOMINGO 10 - 2:00 DE LA TARDE

### H A B L A R A N :

DR. FELIPE PAZOS, Firmante del Manifiesto de la Sierra Maestra

DR. MARIO LLERENA, Secretario Relaciones Públicas Movimiento 26 de Julio.

DR. RAUL CHIBAS, Firmante del Manifiesto de la Sierra Maestra

Srta. JUANITA CASTRO, Hermana de nuestro Líder Fidél Castro

PADRE O'FARRILL, Sacerdote torturado por la Dictadura.

Y otras Destacadas Figuras Revolucionarias.

### I N V I T A :

## Movimiento Revolucionario 26 de Julio

Imprenta Defensores & Co., 234 Throop Ave., B'klyn 6, N. Y.

Handbill announcing an anti-Batista rally at the Palm Garden theater in New York, 1958.

How unexpected the turns of history can sometimes be! In the context of the late fifties I thought that helping *Batista* meant "preparing the ground for the bad seeds of communism"! The views expressed in that letter were shared by many others. Washington's complacency toward south-of-the-border dictators is an old, troublesome question. It has been raised with some bitterness by Latin American liberals ever since Bolívar's day. The pendulum, however, has swung to a point where Latin dictators no longer seek Washington's protective hand, but often find it safer—certainly more popular—to strike an anti-Yankee pose. To me the Castro movement was essentially a reinvigorated manifestation of the old longing for independence, democracy, and progress which somehow had time and again been frustrated. Such evils as Batista were the obstacles that stood in the way of that aspiration. The movement, therefore, became a living instrument of something that for years we had fondly referred to as "the revolution." I used to dwell on the idea that the antecedents of this movement could be traced back to similar ones in the recent past and even to the founders and heroes of the country from the early stages of its historical and political formation. Obviously, communism was totally alien and repugnant to this idea.

This was the picture I tried to project everywhere. The fact that in the American democracy it was possible for the representative of a foreign revolutionary organization to criticize the government freely and remain totally unmolested did not go unnoticed by me. I believed then that there existed a great affinity between this democracy and the Cuban revolution and that it was in the best interests of all of us to bring this community of interests into the open and make it the basis of a true relationship. In Washington Ernesto Betancourt made arrangements for me to meet a number of public figures, among them Congressman Charles O. Porter of Oregon. In the course of our first conversation I learned that Porter, a liberal Democrat, was interested in meeting Castro personally. He was willing to go to Cuba if it were at all feasible to do so. He also emphasized how important it was for the 26 of July Movement to have a public image entirely free from the suspicion of communism. I couldn't agree more.

I felt that the Dirección Nacional—and Castro in particular—should be informed of this conversation as soon as possible. In a report sent from New York on 7 November 1957 (this was before

Manuel Urrutia and the author at the Palm Garden rally. (World Wide photo.)

the junta commitments) I told of my meeting with Porter and added this:

At this very moment, as a result of influences set in motion by [Dominican dictator Rafael] Trujillo, an investigation is being planned in the Senate in regard to "subversive groups operating in the Caribbean." The real purpose is to have a pretext to accuse the revolutionaries of Communist infiltration. If the plan goes, we of the 26 may be touched by its effects, in spite of all clarifications.

For all these reasons—and some others—we ought to cultivate good relations with figures like Porter. I have learned too that he is much interested in seeing Alejandro [Castro]. But as this seems rather unfeasible now for obvious reasons, we could give him something else instead: a letter from Alejandro himself. May I suggest that this letter could be drafted as an acknowledgment of the democratic endeavors of Congressman Porter and of his interest in the liberty of the Latin American peoples as well as, above all, an opportunity to make the political goals of the movement known in such a way that the communist question will be completely dispelled. In short, it should be a letter likely to be published, intelligently written, not jeopardizing in the least our sovereignty and our revolutionary rights but at the same time erasing all pretexts our enemies could use to hang on us the communist stigma.

This letter should be sent to me so that I may deliver it to Congressman Porter personally as soon as possible. It could be handwritten, with a copy for me for the purpose of publicity, probably in the *New York Times*. . . .

The Dirección Nacional took notice of all aspects of the report except this particular suggestion. They ignored it completely—not a reference, not a word, nothing. Why? If the leaders of the movement, Castro above all, were so eager for favorable publicity, why did they not leap at the opportunity to welcome a sympathetic public figure from the United States, or at least to communicate with him? Press coverage would have been assured. Were they, perhaps, wary of any apparent association with American officialdom? But if so, why not simply tell me so? They may, of course, unintentionally have overlooked that part of the report. But one detail suggests in retrospect that their silence was in fact deliberate. I had emphasized the contact with Porter as an opportunity to dispel American fears that the revolution might be tainted with communism. As I came to realize much later, my comments and suggestions on the subject of communism were always ignored. Communism seemed to be a taboo subject in rebel territory. Only when specifically confronted by some correspondent (Andrew St. George of *Look*, for example) did Castro ever disavow communism, and

At the podium during a Castro rally in 1958 in New York. From left: the author, Felipe Pazos, Juanita Castro (a sister of Fidel).

then only in a mild, rather evasive way. And I was told later by eye-witnesses that the more I demonstrated my incompatibility with communism, the more alien and undesirable I became to the leadership of the 26 of July Movement.[1]

As the year 1958 progressed, it became increasingly apparent that the Castro forces were gaining strength and momentum and that the revolution was certain to triumph sooner or later. Popular support of the 26 of July mushroomed, while the elements around Batista, political as well as military, weakened and showed signs of demoralization. Outside of Cuba, too, things seemed to be going Castro's way. In the United States both the press and the government were becoming more and more favorably disposed toward the revolution. Thanks to the magic of the communications media, people all over the world were being conditioned to see the hirsute guerrillas of the Sierra Maestra as the legendary liberators of an oppressed and downtrodden people. Never had the techniques of image making worked more effectively. Even the unkempt beards and the long hair became—and still remain—the defiant symbols of nonconformity and rebellion.

Thus was the road to power being conveniently paved, red carpet and all, not only for Castro and his movement in Cuba but also for a revolution whose true ideological bases and political objectives had not yet been clearly defined or sufficiently exposed.

If I felt uncomfortable in my role, I attributed my discontent mainly to a loss of human values among some of the people in the organization with whom I had to deal. So, like a good moderate when the first gusts of the radical storm begin to blow, I buried my head in the sand of my original expectations and proceeded as best as I could with the job of building Castro's image as a patriot leading a democratic revolution.

My position as the official representative of the 26 of July Movement brought me in contact with a great variety of people, both inside and outside the organization. One of the most colorful was Manolo Couzeiro, an abstract painter who had been introduced to me in Havana in 1956 by Luis de la Cuesta of the FEU when I was secretary of the Cuban Committee for Cultural Freedom. At their request I had arranged to have the committee sponsor an exhibition of Cuban modern art which they were organizing. Carelessly and unconventionally dressed, a typical beatnik of the period, Couzeiro was a very friendly and affable fellow. He told me that he had been one of the people arrested with Franqui the time the police raided the clandestine paper *Revolución*. Couzeiro said that Franqui broke down under the threat of torture and gave the police the names of many persons involved in revolutionary activities, including my own, thus confirming the suspicions that prompted Franqui's wife to warn me that I might be in danger.

In New York Couzeiro was most eager to cooperate with me in the activities of the Committee in Exile, and I appointed him as a sort of coordinator among the 26 of July groups in the city. Instead of coordinating the groups, however, he was soon in deep conflict with most of them. I then reassigned Couzeiro to other jobs, particularly to gather material and make arrangements with the printers for the publication of *Sierra Maestra*, the official organ of the movement in exile and one of my pet projects. But allowing Couzeiro into this kind of responsibility was another of my mistakes. In an apparently innocent way, he managed to fan the flames of enmity within the Committee in Exile and to cast doubt on my personal motives. In the second number of *Sierra Maestra,* for instance, he rewrote the caption for a photograph in which Urrutia and I appeared together. When I read the copy after the issue was already being distributed, I was shocked and deeply embarrassed: the caption gave my name before Urrutia's, and referred to me in laudatory terms that contrasted conspicuously with those reserved for Urrutia. The wording could have been taken as a manifestation of a desire to curry favor on Couzeiro's part, but to a malicious interpreter it could have been clear evidence that I, as editor, was using the movement's organ for my own personal aggrandizement. I just hoped that the detail would somehow pass unnoticed. It did not. As I had feared, it was soon being cited as "proof" that I wanted to downgrade Urrutia and prepare the ground for replacing him as presidential candidate.

Finally I decided that Couzeiro had outlasted his questionable usefulness and was becoming a rather serious nuisance—and told him so. He laughed with mischievous glee about the photo incident and said I shouldn't take it so seriously—it wasn't really that important. But I stood firm, and finally he himself suggested that perhaps it would be better for him to leave the New York scene for a while. I agreed. He said he was thinking of going to Washington, where perhaps he could make some valuable contacts among American leabor leaders, and asked me for a letter stating that he belonged to the FON (Frente Obrero Nacional, the labor branch of the 26 of July Movement). I knew that he had been active in the FON in Cuba, so I gave him the letter and sighed with relief to see him go.

A few days later, however, Couzeiro was back in New York. He had something very interesting to report, he told me on the phone, but preferred to see me personally. His report turned out to be rather serious. Some "Communist elements" from within the American labor movement, he said, had approached him with an offer of aid for the Cuban revolution. According to Couzeiro, there were no strings attached. All the Communists wanted was to establish a relationship with responsible 26 of July leaders in exile as a means of channeling aid to the Cuban people. "After all," Couzeiro quoted the Communists as saying, "we are all fighting for the same goals."

In Couzeiro's view, this was a tremendous opportunity for the 26 of July Movement. He was sure, he said with a wink, that there was big money involved. The revolution was in desperate need of financial aid and we should take it anywhere we could get it. When I remained cold and unreceptive, he gave me a little lecture: revolutions did not necessarily have to submit to any old-fashioned code of ethics.

The possibility that Couzeiro might have come to the United States for the express purpose of soliciting aid from American Communists did not occur to me then. Considering him a fuzzy-minded Bohemian who thought he had found a gold mine, I lectured him in turn on the dangerous waters he might be getting into. Didn't he know about the typical trickery of the Communists? Above all, I warned him sternly against involving the Committee in Exile in any such dealings. Couzeiro did not mention the subject again.

Shortly after this, Couzeiro was instrumental in introducing me to a black man by the name of Arnold Johnson. The encounter took place in a 26 of July Club located on the second floor of a building near the corner of Amsterdam Avenue and Broadway. Johnson said that despite his name and his accented Spanish, he was Cuban. He was from Guantánamo, he explained, but had come to the United States very young. Johnson was very polite and well mannered and was always neatly dressed. As a veteran of World War II, he told me, he had taken advantage of the GI Bill of Rights to obtain an education. He had come now to meet the representatives of the 26 of July Movement, he said, moved by his patriotic interest in the Cuban crisis. He expressed concern for the lot of the poor people in Cuba, especially the blacks, and he wanted to help. As a first suggestion, Johnson offered to introduce me to a very influential member of Congress whom he knew to be sympathetic to the Cuban revolution: Adam Clayton Powell.

To the public relations director of the 26 of July, no offer could have been more welcome. That would be just fine, I said, and Johnson promised to make arrangements for an interview immediately. I suggested that Manuel Urrutia, our presidential candidate, should perhaps come along too. "Splendid," Johnson said, using a favorite word.

After I talked to Urrutia and the appointment was set, Johnson took us to the Baptist church in Harlem where Congressman Powell, who was also a minister, had his office. The meeting was a

A group welcomes Congressman Adam Clayton Powell at his arrival at the Havana airport in February 1959. Next to Powell are Arnold Johnson and the author (who had left the Castro movement the previous year but returned to Havana to engage in dissenting journalism). Those behind the militiaman at left are Protestant ministers. The man in the back row who seems to be touching ears with the militiaman is Raúl Fernández Ceballos, the Presbyterian pastor who embraced the Communist revolution.

fruitful one. Powell seemed indeed very much interested in the Cuban situation and willing to be of help in the anti-Batista cause. He was certainly a very practical man of action. He gave me several telephone numbers where I could reach him at any time and asked me to provide him with information that he could use in a speech in Congress. He mentioned specifically matter related to the "arms for Batista" issue, then receiving a great deal of public attention. Powell assured me he could make a good case against arming Batista. I promised him that I would soon be sending him some rather important material, and with that understanding the meeting ended.

I continued to see Arnold Johnson, who introduced me to a number of influential blacks with whom he was acquainted—

professionals, journalists, radio commentators, businessmen. Most of these people, like Johnson himself, lived in luxury apartments in affluent areas of Harlem. I realized that Johnson was well known and influential in the upper circles of the New York black community, although I never knew how he made his living. He also introduced me to a few of his white relations, among them some lawyers with an office in lower Manhattan and some staffers at CBS headquarters, then on Madison Avenue. Johnson arranged two interviews for me, one with a newspaper and one on a radio program. During my discussions with Johnson's acquaintances I noticed that all of them, black and white alike, exhibited a great deal of interest in current sociopolitical events around the world, with special attention now to the Cuban revolution. All of them fitted the mold of upper-middle-class American liberals. Johnson explained his interest in introducing me to these people on the incontestable grounds that they could give me valuable aid in furthering the public relations goals of the movement.

With Congressman Powell, Johnson seemed to maintain a close if somewhat curious relationship. On one occasion he confided to me that he was not exactly an admirer, much less a subordinate, of the colorful Harlem politician. He seemed to be trying to detach himself from any flaws I might have detected in Powell's personality. More than once I heard him make rather sarcastic remarks concerning Powell's sincerity and behavior—his womanizing, his junkets abroad, his flamboyant life-style. All the same, Johnson always concluded, "Adam" was a very shrewd politician and a most capable parliamentarian, and therefore we should not let all those other considerations prevent us from taking advantage of his present goodwill toward the Cuban cause—even if it might be motivated more by personal interests than by genuine concern for the Cubans.

For his own interest in the Cuban revolution Johnson invoked only patriotic and humanitarian motives. The closest he ever came to revealing any ideological leaning at all was once when he spoke admiringly of Eleanor Roosevelt, Adlai Stevenson, and other American liberals. He never commented on the strictly political or revolutionary aspects of the Cuban struggle; he spoke only—and constantly—of the sufferings of the poor, the black, and the destitute, those whom "the system" had deprived of the essential freedoms and necessities of life.

To all appearances, the contact between Congressman Adam

Clayton Powell and the 26 of July Movement's representative was exclusively Johnson's idea. He could have been acting on behalf of some group or party, though I have no knowledge that he belonged to any. It is possible that Powell himself, with an eye to an issue with a potential popularity dividend, asked him to introduce us. Whatever the case, my meeting with Powell turned out to be, in my judgment, the most significant development that took place while I was the 26 of July's delegate.

As the acknowledged spokesman for a foreign political organization, I was advised by Ernesto Betancourt to register at the Department of Justice. I did so promptly. Then, accompanied by Betancourt, I visited the Cuban Desk at the State Department on at least two occasions. There, in the form of a friendly conversation, I voiced the aspirations of the Cuban people (as I saw them at the time), and the State Department men in turn inquired about the political philosophy and intentions of the 26 of July Movement. They were always very courteous and appeared to be sympathetic. My position, as usual, was that the movement was genuinely democratic and not in the least influenced by communism. So, once again, this time before representatives of the government in Washington, I was presenting a golden image of a patriotic Castro and a popular movement whose primary aim was the establishment of true democracy and honest government in Cuba. Finally, of course, I took advantage of the opportunity to express to the State Department officials the concern of the Cuban people in regard to the provision of American arms and other military equipment to a corrupt and oppressive dictatorship.

While in Washington I also paid a visit to Congressman Porter at his office in the Capitol. Betancourt, our efficient local delegate, came along this time too. Congressman Porter promised to do everything he reasonably could to influence the Eisenhower administration to withhold military aid from Batista. I felt I owed Congressman Porter an explanation for the movement's failure to respond to his suggestion of a few weeks before, but he brushed aside my apologies. He said he understood very well how unpredictable the situation in the Sierra Maestra must be under the stress of guerrilla warfare.

The great impact in Congress, however, was caused by Adam Clayton Powell's speech on March 20 denouncing the American government's shipment of arms to Batistia. He backed his assertions primarily with the documentation I had provided him. As I had promised, I had sent him a memorandum containing, among other things, a piece of secret information that I had received in New York a few days earlier. This information came to me through the mail from a military attaché to the Cuban embassy in Washington by the name of Lieutenant Saavedra (I don't remember his first name). Saavedra had secretly visited me in New York some time before and had told me he believed he might be able to do something for the revolution. He had not specified what that might be, and naturally I had listened to his unexpected and unsolicited offer with the greatest circumspection. Evidently Saavedra either had access to classified matter at the Cuban embassy or had managed to sneak it out of the files. My memorandum to Congressman Powell included copies of the most important documents that Saavedra had sent me. There was, for instance, a copy of a document dated 19 September 1957, addressed to "Dir Log (G-4 EME) Hab. Cuba," signed "José D. Ferrer Guerra, MMP, Te Cor Agr. Mtar. y Aéreo, and headed "SUBJECT: Acquisition of 8 M4A3 tanks." The text made detailed reference to a series of contacts and petitions addressed to the U.S. Departments of State and Defense seeking approval for the sale of these tanks. The effort had apparently been unsuccessful for some time, as suggested by the last two paragraphs:

. . . Mr. Terrance Leonhardy, chief of the Cuban Desk at the State Department, . . . said by phone to Dr. Octavio Averhoff, counselor minister of our embassy here, that owing to recent developments in Cuba and because of the great number of telegrams protesting military aid to Cuba received at the State Department, the sale of said tanks to our government was being considered at higher echelons.

Today our ambassador, Dr. Miguel Angel Campa, was told during an interview at the State Department that the sale of the tanks could not be authorized and that the reason for this decision would be communicated by the American ambassador to Cuba to our minister of state.

Another letter among those sent to me, dated 18 December 1957, was addressed to the signer of the earlier document, Colonel José D. Ferrer Guerra, MMP, in Havana. It informed him that two contracts—one concerning "50 US Browning Machine Rifles M1918A2" and the other "10 Radio Receiving sets"—had been approved by the Departments of State and Defense and that the appropriate section of the army had been notified to comply. This communication was signed "Jorge Gutiérrez, Capt. Asst. Aux. Agr. Mtar. y Aéreo."

But the bulk of the material provided by Saavedra consisted of two series of copies of different classifications of arms and military equipment that had been shipped, or were being processed to be shipped, to Cuba. The first series was in English and was headed "Schedule of arms and other equipment sold by the United States to the Republic of Cuba during the last two years" (1956–1957). It comprised some twenty-odd items, of which the following are samples taken at random:

CONTRACT DA CUBA 553
  3,000 M-1 30 rifles and spare parts.
  1,500 75 mm. grenades.
  1,000 3.5 mm. rockets.
  1,000 60 mm. mortar grenades.
  5,000 81 mm. mortar grenades.
  1 complete battery of light mountain howitzer artillery.
  Shipment completed except for some accessories and spare parts.

    . . . . .

CONTRACT DA CUBA 559
  7 M4A3 tanks equipped with 76 mm. gun.

The series of copies in Spanish included a date for each item, presumably of approval of contract or perhaps intended date of shipment. Here are two samples:

CONTRATO OPC 64 (USAF)
SMG No. 115, 29 Feb 957
Arch. 7-C-1
  Bombas para la FAEC, por valor de $328,931.48.
  Todas las bombas fueron embarcadas excepto el renglón No.
  12 "100 Fuse Bomb Nose An-M103A1."
  El Departamento de la Fuerza Aérea Americana informó que próximamente pondrán a disposición de nuestros embarcadores el parque en cuestión.

    . . . . .

CONTRATO CUBA 64 (USN)
SMG No. 115, 29 Feb 957
Arch. 7-C-1 957
  300 rockets 5.1″
  Los cohetes fueron servidos con cabezas inertes, por lo que se está gestionando el cambio por cabezas explosivas.

My memorandum to Congressman Powell included copies of the documents I considered most important, a number of related press clippings, a translation of a letter from a prisoner in Cuba to his brother in New York describing atrocities committed by Batista military men in Oriente Province and witnessed by the prisoner, and, finally, my own personal assessment of the Cuban situation and recent political history. All these items were intended for Congressman Powell's personal information only. The prisoner's letter in particular—the original had been passed on to me by a close friend of the recipient—was not meant to be divulged but rather to give Powell himself a dramatic illustration of the Cuban plight. I furnished the name and address of the prisoner's brother in New York, even his telephone number, in case the congressman should care to verify the letter's authenticity or ask for further details. To my consternation, Powell had everything printed in the *Congressional Record*,[2] thus exposing the prisoner in Cuba, Antonio Santa Cruz, to the possibility of harsh reprisals. I believe no reprisals were actually taken, but the risk was enormous.

Powell's speech on the arms-for-Batista question appears to have caused no little commotion in Washington official circles. The congressman himself told me later that the exposure of the supposedly classified data raised a great deal of concern at the State Department as well as serious doubts about the reliability of Batista's diplomatic personnel in Washington.

A few days after the Powell speech, on March 26, Congressman Porter rose in the House to speak vigorously on the same theme. He began his speech this way:

Mr. Speaker, last week the gentleman from New York brought a grave matter to the attention of the House when he published on page 4407 of the *Record* a list of arms said to have been sent to the Cuban government from the United States in the last two years. The gentleman does not say if these armaments were purchased by the Cuban government or sent by the United States under our mutual security agreement with Cuba. In any case, he has done a service in opening up the question of United States policy at this critical juncture in Cuban affairs. . . .[3]

Porter dwelt at length on the subject of U.S. intervention in Cuba and also cited a number of articles and other sources that were put in the *Record*. The Cuban revolution was thus having resounding—and favorable—impact in Washington. In my most optimistic dreams I had never anticipated that I could generate so much favorable publicity in such high places. According to Powell and Porter, the revelation of the contracts for arms and military equipment played a significant part in bringing about a change of course in the Eisenhower administration's policy toward the Batista regime. Shortly thereafter, the shipments of arms to Cuba seem to have stopped completely.[4] The polished image of a patriotic Castro leading a democratic revolution against a bloody dictatorship was slowly but surely having its desired effect on American public opinion. And it was American withdrawal of support for Batista that determined his fall—and cleared the path to power for Castro.

# 9 The Ideological Enigma

**A**lmost a year had passed since I had had to leave Cuba and seek asylum in Mexico. During this time the original project that had led me to join the 26 of July Movement—the preparation of a political declaration of principles complemented by a program of revolutionary objectives—had been gradually forgotten, if not entirely abandoned.

As the Batista regime deteriorated, popular discontent grew toward open rebellion. The 26 of July was certainly not the only organized group engaged in revolutionary activities. One of the others, a branch of the Directorio Revolucionario, even opened a guerrilla "second front" in the mountains of the central province of Las Villas.[1] But it was the 26 of July Movement and its successful campaign in Oriente Province that unquestionably had captured the public imagination and thus earned the undisputed leadership of the revolution. By May 1958 it could safely be predicted that the Castro forces were bound to be in power in the not too distant future. All factors and circumstances were favorable.

The other side of this coin was the rise of a new myth. Despite the repeated frustrations of their recent past, Cubans were once again relapsing into the costly vice of hero-worshiping. Much faster than the most jaded cynic could have anticipated, the bearded Castro was becoming a figure of popular adoration surpassing the old appeal of Grau San Martín and Eduardo Chibás. The Cubans had found their "maximum leader."

The road to victory lay ahead, therefore, open and clear. At this stage, however, one question came often to my mind: Whatever became of that early preoccupation of the 26 of July revolutionaries with a written program that would serve to identify the movement ideologically and outline its plans for the building of a better Cuba? In the heat of the struggle and the anticipation of triumph, those concerns had apparently been abandoned. Or had they?

For those of us who had joined the revolution with utopian hopes of seeing a decent, progressive, truly democratic society firmly established in Cuba, the mere overthrow of the Batista dictatorship was no longer enough. In the anticipation of change, however, most people in and outside Cuba did not seem to care much about what kind of ideas or political philosophy might lie behind the Castro revolution, or if it had a program at all.

As I have already explained, my association with the 26 of July Movement had been the result of an explicit invitation to cooperate in the preparation of its revolutionary literature. One of the ideas then—I was specifically told so—was that such documents would act as a sort of binding contract that would subject the organization and especially its leader to a precise ideological and political course.

I found that argument convincing. In response to that commission I wrote *Nuestra Razón* and published it in July 1957 during my stay in Mexico. Although this document was supposed to incorporate ideas and suggestions given to me by Armando Hart, Carlos Franqui, and Enrique Oltusky, it actually reflected my own personal concept of the revolution: in each of its aspects the manifesto was essentially and formally democratic. Among other things, it took for granted the constitutional precept of government chosen by periodic popular election. It was based on the principle that the state exists for the benefit of the individual, not the individual for the benefit of the state. It stressed the importance of the rule of law.

But, as we have seen, the 26 of July hierarchy gave *Nuestra Razón* only limited—one might even say reluctant—approval. The only indication that Castro himself even knew of its existence came when he announced the use of its title for the official organ of the Committee in Exile. After circulating widely among the exile groups everywhere (but not in Cuba itself), the manifesto was soon forgotten, evidently for lack of endorsement by the leadership in Cuba.

The Sierra Manifesto, issued at approximately the same time, received wide publicity and had a corresponding impact. Among other things, it called for national unity and proposed ways for the return to constitutional, duly elected government; it was written in the Sierra Maestra itself, which had already become a symbol of heroic protest; and Castro chose to have it bear not only his own name but those of two public figures not then associated with the movement, Felipe Pazos and Raúl Chibás, who enjoyed great moral force and popular prestige.

In calling for the Civic Institutions to play a major role in returning Cuba to constitutional normality, the Sierra Manifesto gave the revolution a distinctly middle-class flavor. And in calling for general elections under the 1940 Constitution within a year of Batista's overthrow, it confirmed the general impression that the revolution to which Castro and his followers had committed themselves was essentially and unequivocally democratic. It appeared above all to be—in the best sense of the expression—a politically motivated revolution; that is, one whose primary objective was the establishment of a climate of political free play within the structural framework of the rule of law. In other words, the revolution had but one fundamental justification: to repair the damage done by the 1952 coup d'état and to reset in motion the constitutional wheels of democracy. Socioeconomic questions were only incidental and subordinate to this end. The truth is that they were confined almost exclusively to the slogans of hard-core militants and intellectual elites.

But as circumstances changed with the passing of the months, the original picture given out by the Sierra Maestra rapidly faded. The increasing momentum of Castro's guerrilla campaign upset the balance of anti-Batista forces in favor of the 26 of July Movement, which soon emerged as the undisputed determining factor in the Cuban conflict. From then until the movement reached power in January 1959 there was an almost total ideological and programmatic blackout. And very few people seemed to notice.

In a number of letters and documents Armando Hart, Marcelo Fernández, and other leaders referred to a committee (in which I was to be included) specially appointed to prepare the frequently announced definitive revolutionary literature of the movement. The "introduction" attached to the lengthy letter with which Castro broke with the Junta de Liberación Cubana at Miami in December 1957, it will be recalled, promised that the leadership would soon publish "other documents" that would deal with matters in five areas: political (which included what Hart called "institutional integrity"—a carry-over from the Chibasian lineage of Castroism), economic, educational, social, and foreign policy, in that order. These documents would be followed "by other pronouncements of the 26 of July on all matters of state."

They never materialized. No such "documents" or "pronouncements" ever came from the 26 of July Movement in Cuba after that date. To the best of my knowledge, they were not even started. For the general public, therefore, the Sierra Manifesto continued to provide what was presumed to be the true image of the movement. Any intimations such as the one contained in Hart's letter of 9 December 1957, that "a new and different situation has been created contrary to what is declared in the Sierra Manifesto," remained entirely confidential.

There were, to be sure, other documents, but they were neither ideological nor programmatic. I received, for example, a copy of a "Manifesto of the 26 of July Movement to the People," dated 12 March 1958 in the Sierra Maestra. It was signed by "Fidel Castro Ruz, Commander of the Rebel Forces," and "Dr. Faustino Pérez Hernández, Delegate of the Dirección Nacional." This manifesto was perhaps more significant for what it failed to say than for what it actually said. It began with a long tirade denouncing the Batista government for having denied permission to foreign and domestic correspondents to visit rebel-occupied territory. Castro and the others, evidently with a view to propaganda benefits, tried to make a big issue of a perfectly understandable situation. This blast was followed by a series of twenty-one brief statements, most of them advising the people of an upcoming general strike and instructing them what to do when it was announced. But nowhere in this manifesto—which the leaders referred to as "the Twenty-one Points Manifesto"—was there a single word concerning the ideological principles of the revolution or the movement's plans for the construction of the new Cuba.

Yet the 26 of July leaders seem to have attached great importance to this manifesto. An additional document that I received with it, Organization Circular CO-2, meant for leaders and active militants only, advised that the Twenty-one Points Manifesto was to be disseminated through all accessible media. The movement planned to print and distribute, "before March 31," more than half a million copies.

Organization Circular CO-2, by the way, turned out to be a far more interesting document than the Twenty-one Points Manifesto itself. It was dated 18 March 1958 at Santiago de Cuba and signed by "Zoilo [Marcelo Fernández], Coordinador Nacional." It consisted of two parts. The first told about the recent activities of the organization; the second was a detailed "Work Plan for the Month of March," in which the main topic was the planned general strike.[2]

It was the first part that contained the really significant material. It gives us a glimpse of what was going on at this stage inside the 26 of July leadership:

In the last days of February, as you all probably remember, there were insistent rumors that our comrade Fidel Castro was ready to negotiate with the [Batista] regime, offering a "peace formula" based on elections under the supervision of the OAS [Organization of American States] on condition that the government withdraw its military forces from Oriente Province. This obviously would have meant a fundamental change in the strategy of the movement.

For that reason, we decided to call a special meeting of the Dirección Nacional in the Sierra Maestra. The meeting took place during March 7, 8, 9, and 10. We discussed the strategy of the struggle in all its aspects, the tactics to be adopted at this time, and the political as well as the revolutionary circumstances in the country.

A fruit of this meeting was the enclosed document [the Twenty-one Points Manifesto], which possibly you have already seen by now. . . . This most important document must be reproduced in the largest possible numbers.

Comrade Fidel explained that at no time had the line of the movement been changed. He said that what he had proposed [the "rumors" mentioned earlier] to Nené León[3] [a politician supposedly acting as intermediary] and to correspondent [Homer] Bigart [of the *New York Times*] was in the nature of a tactical step, as it put the regime in the position of having to consider unacceptable conditions. The idea was to make the regime appear before public opinion to be rejecting the movement's peace proposals, thus causing it to be responsible for the continuation of the war. Fidel, however, admitted in the end that maybe he had chosen the wrong time to come up with his proposition, since the *radicalization* of the people made it unnecessary, even if it was only a tactical maneuver. The other members of the Dirección agreed that it had all been a mistake. [Italics mine.]

Both Castro and Che Guevara, the letter went on, reviewed in detail the current situation in the Sierra Maestra. The rebel forces were divided into four units under the command of Castro, Juan Almeida, Guevara, and Raúl Castro respectively. Interestingly, the units were numbered 1, 3, 4, and 6.

> In this meeting we are talking about, the revolutionary situation in the country was throughly analyzed, and so was the work accomplished by the movement. We looked back at the days when only twelve men were left, hungry and hunted, and the prospects of the revolution appeared gloomy. We were full of deep joy, however, at the realization of how the revolutionary process has kept on advancing, taking root in the hearts of the people until it has become the brightest hope of the Cuban republic.
>
> The strategy of the general strike and the insurrection was ratified, and a plan was laid out for *the progressive radicalization of the country* with a view toward a national revolutionary uprising. The main objectives of this plan are the following: to maintain sabotage and guerrilla warfare so as to weaken the regime militarily; to intensify the organization of the proletariat so as to weaken the regime in the labor unions; to expedite the resignation of members of the judiciary and of the executive branch so as to weaken the regime in its governmental structure; and to bring about such things as the paralysis of the means of transportation, refusal to pay taxes, a mass petition from the civic organizations for Batista to step down, etc., so as to weaken the regime psychologically and then give it the final blow. . . . [Italics mine.]

Organization Circular C-2 also gave valuable information on the way the guerrillas had organized life in the Sierra Maestra—their industries, schools, radio stations, and so on. But like the Twenty-one Points Manifesto, it almost completely ignored ideological and programmatic questions. Why? Was there any specific reason? Was it just an oversight, without any particular significance?

Let us pause here and consider the question for a moment. First, let us keep in mind that these two documents were the products of a meeting in the Sierra Maestra of the Dirección Nacional of the 26 of July Movement, called to discuss the scope of certain public political pronouncements made by Fidel Castro. All the big leaders of the movement must have been present on this occasion. We know that Castro and Che Guevara were there. We may safely assume that at least most of the others—Raúl Castro, Haydée Santamaría, Faustino Pérez, Celia Sánchez, Armando Hart—were there too; Marcelo Fernández obviously was there, since he signed the circular. We learn further that Che, who later turned out to be the main doctrinaire of the movement, participated actively in the discussions. The date itself is significant; the meeting took place in

March 1958, when the revolution had reached another checkpoint. Finally, for four days the 26 of July leaders "discussed the strategy of the struggle in all its aspects, the tactics to be adopted at this time, and the political as well as the revolutionary circumstances in the country."

The more one analyzes the various circumstances involved in this case, the more questions arise. It would seem only logical that a revolutionary movement, dedicated not only to the overthrow of a dictatorial regime but to the subsequent inauguration of a new constructive era for the country, would seize every opportunity to air its postulates and openly hammer home its slogans, if only out of the practical necessity of preparing the people for the revolutionary changes that were to be expected. Not so the 26 of July Movement. After the Sierra Manifesto of July 1957, it kept almost total silence on its intentions. Castro's occasional allusions to the matter served only to keep alive the original impression that the democratic principles implied in that declaration indeed represented the ideology and objectives of the movement. It thus becomes apparent that Castro and the organization were living under a double standard: one secret and confidential, the other for public consumption. One has only to compare Armando Hart's statement that "a new and different situation has been created contrary to what is declared in the Sierra Manifesto," written on December 9, with Castro's words in his letter to the junta, written on December 14, just five days later: "No matter how desperate our situation may be, or how many thousand soldiers are dispatched against us by the Dictatorship . . . we will never accept the sacrifice of certain principles that are cardinal to our understanding of the Cuban revolution. These principles are contained in the Sierra Manifesto." How are these two statements to be reconciled?

For the international press, Castro's voice maintained a loud and clear democratic tone. In his interview for *Look* (4 February 1958), cited earlier, he repeated the basic premises of the Sierra Manifesto. Asked to explain the rebels' plans once Batista was toppled, Castro answered: "Within a year . . . hold a truly honest election." And he added: "In a manifesto issued last July [the Sierra Manifesto] we called for the temporary government to free immediately all political prisoners, restore freedom of the press, reestablish constitutional rights." He emphatically disclaimed any radical intention on the part of the 26 of July Movement, particularly the nationalization of foreign investments. (Need anyone be reminded that

Castro was talking to the American press?) A similar interview was published in *Coronet* magazine.

To correspondent Homer Bigart of the *New York Times* (25 February 1958, exactly one year after Matthews's scoop) Castro disclosed a peace plan that stirred a great commotion among all revolutionary groups. "Upon withdrawal of the Government forces," wrote Bigart, "Señor Castro would agree to general elections under President Batista, provided the elections were supervised throughout the island by the Organization of American States." It was the repercussions of this particular statement that prompted the urban leaders of the 26 of July Movement to demand the special meeting of the Dirección Nacional reported in Organization Circular C-2. The Bigart interview contained many other interesting passages, some of which throw no little light on certain widespread misconceptions emanating from the early strategy of the Castro movement—this one, for instance: "Señor Castro showed some uneasiness when questioned about his economic and social platforms. The reason is obvious: he is a symbol of a middle-class reform movement rather than of economic and social revolution. His financial support has been derived mainly from wealthy and middle-income groups. . . ."

Bigart had put his finger on the sore spot. Castro's "uneasiness" shows simply that he had been caught playing his double-standard game. When questioned by his comrades, he explained his statements as only "a tactical step" aimed at "putting the regime in the position of having to consider unacceptable conditions." But Castro admitted error in timing. At that point the radical course of the revolution had been determined. Organization Circular C-2 leaves no doubt that every question concerning the nature and the true aims of the 26 of July Movement, whether political, social, or economic, was thoroughly examined and studied. "We discussed the strategy of the struggle in all its aspects," it says, "the tactics to be adopted at this time, and the revolutionary as well as the political circumstances in the country."

The movement thus assured its militants that its revolutionary identity remained intact. For the time being, however, the outside world would continue to see only its democratic mask. In Cuba the people outside the movement saw the revolution as simply the long-awaited opportunity of attaining honest constitutional government, while the growing number of middle-class liberals hoped for somewhat deeper reforms. None, however, not even the few who toyed with "socialistic" ideas, went beyond the democratic line. It was at this time that waves of professionals, teachers, businessmen, white-collar workers, and educated people in general rushed either to join or to support the 26 of July Movement. Many were, of course, from the intellectual elite. University professor Andrés Valdespino, who at first had refused to go along with Castro, now got on his bandwagon. So did economist Rufo López Fresquet, geographer Leví Marrero, and many others. Even Rafael García Bárcena, who personally detested Castro, became reconciled to the apparent trend of the revolution. It was at this time, too, that a curious clique of radical intellectuals, who so far had mimetically functioned in the Ortodoxo party, came out openly for Castro and the 26 of July Movement—Salvador Massip, Raimundo Lazo, Vicentina Antuña, Marta Frayde, and a few others. They were the exceptions that confirmed the rule. The highly influential middle class, tired of corrupt, mediocre politics and longing for a decent, progressive, yet free society, believed the Castro movement to be the honest instrument of such an ideal. They provided the moral and financial support without which it is extremely doubtful that the unsuspected Castro revolution could ever have reached power.

Despite Armando Hart's claims to the contrary in December, the question of an ideological manifesto was finally abandoned and even forgotten as the revolution gained momentum. In a communication addressed to the Dirección Nacional on 9 March 1958 I discussed at length the idea of a "revolutionary" government (as distinct from the nonpartisan one proposed in the Sierra Manifesto). Today I consider my proposal immature and extremely dangerous, but in the Cuban context of early 1958 it seemed to respond to a number of compelling circumstances, which I proceeded to explain in detail. One of the topics I mentioned was the role to be played by Judge Urrutia. He had originally, of course, been chosen as a nonpartisan figure (at least in theory) to preside over a provisional government in which all the anti-Batista groups would be equally represented. I suggested now that Urrutia be invited to accept openly the exclusive candidacy of the 26 of July as president of a "revolutionary government." I was not guided by any desire for a radical departure from my basic democratic philosophy but rather by what I then thought to be the immediate necessity of saving the revolution from extinguishing itself in a fruitless compromise with the past. That was, of course, the dividing line between expediency and the dangerous downhill area of revolutionary extremism. The ultimate outcome would depend on the prevailing ideological foundation of the leaders. I took it for granted that that foundation was solidly democratic.

The idea was remarkably well received in the Sierra Maestra. It seemed they were already thinking along those lines. In an unusually prompt reply, Marcelo Fernández wrote on March 30 that at the March 7–10 meeting "we considered precisely the ideas you now present about the possibility of creating a *revolutionary* government. That is what we have decided to do. The government will be headed by Urrutia, but the ministers and chief officials will have to be at least sympathizers of the 26 of July."

This decision was confirmed by a letter from Fidel Castro himself which I found on my return from a trip to Venezuela early in May. It was a long letter, handwritten on ten assorted sheets of stationary—some blue, some green, a few white—addressed to me and Raúl Chibás and dated April 26. Among other subjects, Castro discussed the formation of a "revolutionary" government that was a distinct departure from what he himself had proposed in the Sierra Manifesto and from the form of government that was generally assumed to be the goal of the movement.

Aside from its strategic import, the tacit significance of this letter is the importance that Castro and the other leaders around him attached to the organization abroad, especially to the Committee in Exile. This is made plain by the length and the timing as well as by the contents themselves (see Appendix B). Castro takes pains to paint for me and Chibás an optimistic picture of the progress of the war in Cuba and of the situation in "our territory" (most of Oriente Province). He wanted to reassure us, he said, because "I imagine you are worried about the adverse outcomes of these latest events." The general strike called by the 26 of July Movement in April had failed, and there had been other setbacks in the military field.

But no sooner had Castro finished telling us how well the revolution was progressing than he embarked on a long string of bitter complaints against the organization abroad, which "has failed completely in its duty to keep us supplied." Despite its general character, this charge carried an obvious reflection on the Committee in Exile, particularly on Chibás, who was head of finances. As I had never had anything to do, directly or indirectly, with the

First and last pages of letter of Castro to the author and Raúl Chibás telling of a new revolutionary approach to the question of a provisional government.

1º

sejo de Ministros y procede a designar representantes legales para el exterior. Con algunos magistrados de los
que renunciaron o están siendo expedien-
tados podrías organizarse el Tribunal
Supremo. Nosotros podemos garan-
tizar una sede fija y segura al Gobierno con facilidades, que tal vez no es-
peren para desempeñar su función. Este
planteamiento cuenta con el respaldo de
todos los compañeros de la Dirección y so-
lo del Dr. Urrutia depende el resto. Es
algo que él debe meditar y resolver, con
la absoluta seguridad de que su decisión,
si es contraria, no alterará en nada nuestra consideración y nuestro respaldo.
Es cuestión tan delicada que yo aconsejaría
tantear su criterio antes de hacerle el planteamiento y si no sustentara este punto de
vista dejar en suspenso la cuestión.
    Para no ser más extenso, solo quiero a-
ñadir que desde Costa Rica o Venezuela (visi-
tar Radio Continente de Caracas para mayor faci-
lidad de comunicación) es fácil hacer contacto
diario con nosotros a las 5 p.m. y a las 9 p.m.
por la banda de 20 metros. Los pilotos llevan
una clave. Sería para mí un placer extraor-
dinario saludarlo en cualquier ocasión. Estoy
instalado cerca de la planta. Tal vez desde Miami, tam-
bién podemos sintonizarnos.
    Reciban ustedes y Urrutia nuestro más
fraternal abrazo.  Fidel Castro

collecting, keeping, or use of money, or with the buying or shipment of arms or ammunition, these remarks did not seem to apply
to me personally.

Fund raising was an open activity—in fact, the paramount activity of all the Castro groups in exile. Collections of tens of thousands of dollars were constantly being taken up for the Cuban
guerrillas. And I knew of at least one man—my brother-in-law,
Fernando Hernández—who regularly sent small shipments of
arms and ammunition from Miami to 26 of July contacts in Cuba.
This isolated case alone contradicts the implications of Castro's
rhetorical question, "How is the expenditure of approximately
$200,000 going to be justified without our having received one
single weapon?"

As a result of that situation, Castro announced, he was taking
personal charge of all financial matters. "I have appointed comrade
Ricardo Lorié to take charge of this business under my personal
instructions." And he adds, "In addition to the funds we shall be
sending him from here, which we expect to reach over $100,000
in two months, it is necessary to put in his hands *absolutely all the
financial resources that can be obtained there.*"

That sounded as though the Committee in Exile was about to be
shaken to its very foundations, but as far as I could see, Castro's
directive brought no visible change in the activities of the committee or the groups at large. Lorié did come to see Chibás, but my
knowledge of the matter ends there. What one cannot fail to notice, however, is that Castro, in the same breath in which he com-
plains that the exile groups have not sent him enough money, tells
of placing $100,000 in the hands of his personal agent. Obviously
the guerilla group in the mountains was not exactly in a state of
indigence.

All this could be regarded as preliminary, however, to the central
point of Castro's communication. "There is yet another decision,"
he says toward the end, "that has been definitely made. We consider this to be an opportune moment for the establishment of the
Revolutionary Provisional Government. What would perhaps have
seemed inexpedient at some other time will now have a wonderful
psychological impact on both national and international public
opinion. . . ." Castro's wording makes it seem as though the importance of the decision lay not in its substance but in its *timing.*

This development should have pleased me greatly. As Marcelo
Fernández had pointed out, the idea was—or at least coincided

with—my own, although, as it turned out, it had been arrived at by a diametrically opposed line of thinking. But now the announcement left me indifferent. It was, of course, too late. My personal experience within the organization had considerably—and irreparably, it seemed—dampened my earlier enthusiasm.

Anyone familiar with the Cuban revolutionary process will agree that this letter from Castro amounts to an official confirmation of the momentous turn of direction—from moderate to radical—which had been taken by the Castro movement. The action had been signaled by the movement's dramatic break with the Miami junta the previous December. The guarded way in which Castro speaks of the leadership's decision to establish a "revolutionary government" shows that he is fully conscious of the significance of the change of course and concerned about its effect on world opinion when it becomes known.

His obvious uncertainty becomes even more manifest in a long passage in which he tries to anticipate Urrutia's reaction. There is one sentence that to this day is perplexing. Should Dr. Urrutia decline to go along with the idea of the revolutionary government, he says, "our consideration and our endorsement [*respaldo*] will in no way be changed." It is difficult to take the word *respaldo* in this context as strictly a personal compliment. Did Castro mean that in the event of Urrutia's refusal to preside over a revolutionary government the movement would continue to endorse him *as a nonpartisan candidate?* To do so would have required the immediate cancellation, or at least shelving, of the revolutionary plan. This seems extremely improbable. Yet that is what Castro said.

The repeated references to Urrutia in Castro's letter show a paradoxical aspect of his personality, probably hidden and unsuspected by most people. All those who witnessed the events at the time and were thus in a position to gauge the strength and popular impact already achieved by the movement will wonder. Castro goes beyond the elementary requirements of formality or courtesy and shows real concern. The possibility that Urrutia may refuse to go along with the revolutionary government causes him alarm. To be sure, Urrutia was a gentleman worthy of respect and courtesy. But Castro is writing not to Urrutia himself but to me and Chibás. After describing to us the idea of the revolutionary government, he says, "For all this we need the cooperation of Dr. Urrutia." In the next paragraph he is even more emphatic: "This proposition has the support of all the members of the Dirección

Nacional; the rest depends only on Dr. Urrutia." But did it really?

Only those who have known Castro personally may guess the explanation for his concern. Castro did not seem to be aware that the incredible progress of the revolutionary enterprise and his own unprecedented popularity would have made a refusal by Urrutia— or by anyone else, for that matter—appear insignificant. At that stage, Urrutia's withdrawal could not possibly have caused any major disruption in Castro's plans, and even less in the course of the revolution at large. But Castro was not so sure; the inner insecurity that he has always carried beneath his tough exterior overcame his judgment. And so he wanted to assure Urrutia of his *respaldo* in all events. He wanted to appear *nice* to Urrutia so as to neutralize him beforehand, if possible, in case of a refusal—lest, say, Urrutia denounce the maneuver and alert American public opinion to suspicious trends in the Castro revolution.

At the time he wrote, Castro assumed that the particular mission of briefing Urrutia about the new developments would be mine and Chibás's. There is every indication, however, that by the time the letter reached me, late in May, the judge had already been informed by Luis Buch, the ubiquitous courier for the Castro leaders in Santiago. It turned out that Castro's worries were unfounded. There is no known indication that Urrutia hesitated in the least to accept the plans for the revolutionary government.

Castro appeared to be unaware of any lack of harmony within the Committee in Exile. He mentioned in passing that Haydée Santamaría would be traveling abroad "to help the comrades there in the coordination of their work," but there seemed to be no connection with our internal conflicts (we shall see about this later).

This brings us to the one factor that gives the Cuban revolution its unique character: the Castro personality. Whatever way the political scientist or the historian may look at it, there is no escaping this fact. It is impossible here to separate the effect from its cause. It can safely be asserted, without fear of indulging in fanciful speculation, that if Castro had been cut to the usual pattern of young Cuban revolutionaries, or if he had not existed at all, there would have been no Cuban revolution—not of the kind it has turned out to be, at any rate. Castro's personality acted as the catalytic agent that transformed a popular protest of moderate democratic aspirations into a radical revolution in a country where originally there was no desire, no expectation, and no need for a radical revolution.

How did it happen? What answer can be offered to the riddle of the Cuban sphinx? Is he a patriot or a traitor, a revolutionary or a psychopath? No man, of course, can fully get into another man's mind. The psychoanalyst, we are told, can help bring out certain hidden areas of the subconscious—provided the subject cooperates. But it is not known that Castro has ever lain on the confessional couch. Yet when his background, his statements, his actions and reactions, and his ultimate orientation in life are carefully analyzed, a coherent picture emerges.

To the academic observer, everything that has happened in Cuba may appear to be the logical consequence of preexisting conditions. To the insufficiently informed, the final aspect of the revolutionary process, like a puzzle after the last piece has been put in place, may seem to present the complete design in all its details. As we have seen, however, Cuba's political and socioeconomic state at the outbreak of the revolution is not adequately described by the usual clichés of "underdeveloped country," "privileged wealthy elite ruling over miserable exploited masses," and the like. Should that have been the case, why did the radical revolution never materialize before? Certainly not for lack of able leadership. Starting at random with Julio Antonio Mella in the late 1920s, the extreme left in Cuba always had intelligent, dedicated leaders of fixed determination, many of them of high intellectual stature. To the name of Mella can be added such others as Rubén Martínez Villena, Juan Marinello, Gustavo Aldereguía, Salvador García Agüero, and Carlos Rafael Rodríguez; and at a more popular level but perhaps even more important were Blas Roca, Lázaro Peña, Aníbal Escalante, and others who figured prominently in Cuba's political life for decades.

Communists in Cuba, under the umbrella of democratic liberties, had every opportunity to organize and propagandize. They owned newspapers and radio stations. They held public rallies and openly tried to infiltrate all areas of society. During the first Batista era (1934–1944) they enjoyed unprecedented official favor. They were permitted to register as a legal political party (in fact, two parties)[4] and occupied positions in Congress and in the executive cabinet. Throughout this period, and with government acquiescence, the Communists held practically exclusive control of the labor movement (the secretariat of the powerful Cuban Confederation of Workers was in their hands). Yet the Communists always remained an isolated, incompatible, scarcely significant political factor within the mainstream of Cuban society. They were like a very active yeast that somehow could never succeed in permeating the dough around it and making it rise. They prospered only in the shade of someone else's power—as they did for a time when Batista welcomed them as his political allies. As soon as they were left without special government protection, they returned to their usual isolated state.

Neither the existing conditions, therefore, nor the considerable efforts of radical elements were ever sufficient to ignite the radical revolution in Cuba. Communism stirred to life again only when another propitious source of power arose on the political horizon. And this power arose not through the open expounding and gradual public acceptance of a radical ideology but rather through the mesmerizing talents of a unique leader: Fidel Castro.

So the question lingers on and becomes ever more intriguing: Who is this Castro, anyway? What is he *really*? To one who was in a position to judge the situation, the other members of the Dirección Nacional of the 26 of July Movement revealed themselves to be firmly set on a radical course early in 1958—the decisive year of the revolution. Castro's own position, however, remains shrouded in mystery. What were his real intentions then? Were his political overtures in February, which prompted the Sierra Maestra meeting in March, never seriously intended? Or was he yielding to group pressure in March when he claimed they had been nothing but tactical maneuvers?

Two hypotheses are possible. One is that Castro was always a convinced Marxist-Leninist, even before the start of the revolution. According to this view, all his democratic pronouncements were only tactical camouflage intended to protect himself and his movement as they advanced on the road to power. This hypothesis no doubt appears plausible. On 2 December 1961 Castro himself explained in a television speech that for many years, ever since his student days in the 1940s, he had been an apprentice Marxist-Leninist, but had had to hide his radical ideas in order not to jeopardize his chances of gaining power.

This statement, however, is probably only a half-truth, a convenient pronouncement for public consumption at a particular moment, rather than a complete historical fact. Many things cast shadows of skepticism on the supposition that Castro was a Communist throughout the revolution, among them the four-day discussion in the Sierra Maestra in March 1958. The other members of the Dirección Nacional—some of whom (Che Guevara, Raúl Castro, and Marcelo Fernández) were indeed Marxists—actually wanted to cross-examine Castro. Certain political statements that Castro had recently made filled them with anxiety, and they wanted to know what their leader really had in mind. It sounded like a plain case of deviationism, and they were calling him to account.

This crucial episode would make very little sense had Castro been at the time the Marxist-Leninist he said he was—as it turned out that most of his closest comrades were. The true Marxist-Leninist would have acted quite differently. Any public utterances made for tactical purposes would have been the result of group discussion and policy, not of the whims or the calculations of an undisciplined individual—not even if that individual were the leader of the group. If such moves as Castro had made were considered of value, they would have been made with the knowledge and the approbation of the group. There would have been no reason for alarm, no need to call the leader to account.

On the other hand, the incident does look like a classic example of typical Communist body pressure. Castro's comrades acted like experienced farmers trying to keep a spirited horse on his assigned furrow. The record shows that in this instance the horse (which, incidentally, happens to be Castro's nickname) submitted to the reins. From then on, while still maintaining a democratic face for the public and the great mass of his followers, Castro did behave like a willing and obedient Marxist-Leninist. The secret contacts that brother Raúl had been carrying on for some time with the high leadership—the "old guard"—of the Communist party culminated in the visit of the Communist intellectual Carlos Rafael Rodríguez to Castro in the Sierra Maestra in July.[5] It was presumably during this visit that definite plans for the communization of Cuba were made.

The other hypothesis is that at this time Castro's ideas were still fluid. He was engaged in a fight to the death against an illegitimate government and was justifying his action with the rhetoric most likely to win public favor (the Sierra Manifesto, for instance). But privately Castro was moved only by his lifelong ambition of building his own pedestal. Despite outward appearances, he had not yet committed himself fully to any specific political direction. By now he must have realized that the movement was unmistakably on the road to power. He was weighing the possibilities before committing himself to the one that would ultimately appear to make that power long-lasting and grandiose.

This view is consistent with Castro's background and record, and with some of his subsequent statements, in which fascist influences can be discerned.[6] For Castro an ideology is not an article of faith or a sincere political aspiration; it is only a means to his personal ends. Castro's protestations of Marxism-Leninism today cannot be taken more seriously than his vows of democratic devotion in the past. Who could assure us that his words and his poses are less tactical now than they were before? Castro is communism's Elmer Gantry. The colorful, fiery preacher of Sinclair Lewis's novel looked like a Christian and talked like a Christian. But though he was expert at feigning evangelistic zeal and held crowds spellbound, he was moved not by faith but by an unquenchable thirst for fame and power.

So with Castro. Whatever he appears to be politically or ideologically is simply the product of his ever expanding ego in relation to the prevailing circumstances. There is no question that Castro is a revolutionary, but he differs essentially from most great revolutionaries of history. For his primary concern is not the correction of what is wrong and the ushering in of what is right. He is not motivated by visions of a utopian society on earth, or by an altruistic desire for the well-being and happiness of people in Cuba and elsewhere. His actions are invariably geared to keeping him at the center of the world stage.

Many who have followed Castro's life trajectory since his early youth see in him a clear case of psychopathic behavior. The facts of his unhappy home life are well known. Fidel was one of several children of a somewhat irregular marriage. He had a number of stepbrothers. His father, a landowner in Oriente Province, was a bizarre, authoritarian Spaniard who could hardly communicate with or show affection for his family. He was not too scrupulous about the way he enlarged his property and increased the number of cattle in his herds. Fidel developed into a resentful, affectionless, independent youth. While a university student in the 1940s he showed more interest in the vendettas among pseudo-revolutionary gangs than in his books. He promptly joined one of those armed groups and soon distinguished himself in diverse acts of violence. A number of deaths are credited to him during this period. Indeed, all through his developing years Castro projects the image of a hyperactive individual with an uncontrollable urge toward the adventurous and the catastrophic. To the list of gangster activities of his student days a series of other notorious episodes can be added: an aborted expedition to "liberate" the Dominican Republic in 1947,[7] his participation in the famous *bogotazo* in Colombia in 1948, the assault on the Moncada barracks in 1953, and, of course, the *Granma* expedition from Mexico in 1956 and the subsequent guerrilla campaign in the Sierra Maestra.

Revolution, then, came to be Castro's supreme vocation. Castro sees revolution not as a last resort but as a channel for self-expression—an escape valve for his accumulated resentments and hates. He actually needs revolution as the addict needs his drug. In this sense, of course, the ends of revolution—be they good or bad, right or left—become accessory. What primarily attracts him is the iconoclastic, destructive turbulence that inevitably accompanies the revolutionary process. He positions himself on the wave of revolution and delights to ride on its crest, no matter which way the wind may blow. Once Batista has fallen, for instance, and the revolution is in power, the United States automatically becomes the new "enemy" that must be fought; once the island of Cuba is under total control, the revolution must be exported elsewhere—to Latin America, to the Middle East, to Africa . . . everywhere. For Castro there is no end, no rest. To paraphrase a theatrical saying, the revolution must go on.

But let us return to the critical juncture, the first half of 1958. If at that point in the Cuban drama Castro was still ideologically uncommitted, what influenced him to adopt the Communist line? The answer seems to be that in the circumstances in which he found himself, communism offered him the kind of stage and claque best suited to the cravings of his monumental ego. In the Sierra Maestra he had become used to being a legendary figure. He was very much aware of what the alternative would be. To him the prospects of donning a business suit and letting that image fade in the routine and the compromises of the democratic process must have appeared unbearably anticlimactic. To one used to the intoxication of revolution, the peaceful ways of constitutional democracy can seem dull and unrewarding. By adopting a totalitarian credo, on the other hand, he could expect to continue to be the "maximum leader" indefinitely—even if that meant having to turn to Moscow for the necessary financial support, and to accept the directives and the control that inevitably accompanied it. After all, he could always paraphrase the famous saying of France's Henri IV on becoming a Catholic: "Paris is worth a mass."

For all practical purposes, however, Castro became a Communist and has continued to act like a Communist. Has he, then, undergone a true conversion? Curiously enough, this remains highly questionable. Theodore Draper's keen observation that Castro has attached himself to different ideologies as each suits his purposes on the road to power is as valid today as ever.[8] Between Castro and communism there has been a marriage of convenience. Without Castro the Communists would never have attained power in Cuba; without the Communists Castro would never have gained the only kind of power that satisfies him. A turnabout at this point is extremely unlikely; time has passed and Castro has immersed himself too deeply in the red waters. Yet it will always remain a theoretical possibility. The Horse is still spirited and has to be kept under constant watch.

# 10 The Guevaras

**A** number of rather interesting questions concerning the ideological development of the 26 of July Movement in its early stages are indirectly raised by letters addressed to me from Lima, Peru, by Hilda Gadea de Guevara. Two things make these letters an element to be reckoned with in this connection: the simple fact that they were written by the wife of Ernesto (Che) Guevara,[1] at the time a major in the rebel forces in the Sierra Maestra, and Hilda Gadea's own political orientation and activities.

Some readers may wonder why so little is said in this book about such a colorful figure of the Cuban revolution as Che Guevara. The answer is that he did not emerge to public prominence before the last months of 1958, and then only as a guerrilla major. Whatever influence he may have exerted earlier on the character and course of the revolution remained unknown to all but Castro's inner circle. During the time of my involvement with the 26 of July Movement I met and corresponded with most of the leaders of the movement, but I never had any contact with Guevara. When I visited Castro in Mexico in September 1956 I met a number of his companions but heard nothing about Guevara, although I know now that he was already there. In the whole mass of papers and letters that I received from Castro and the others, Guevara's name is mentioned casually only once, in the circular describing the fateful Sierra Maestra meeting of 7–10 March 1958. He therefore plays no part in my story. In another sense, however,

Guevara is very much present in this narrative, for there seems to be general agreement that he played a large role in turning the revolution toward communism.

The first letter I received from Hilda Gadea de Guevara was dated 14 March 1958 (curiously, just a few days after the close of the policy-defining meetings in the Sierra Maestra). From then until the latter part of June I received at least ten letters from her (I believe some have been lost) and a few other documents. Hilda's communications deal mostly with the organization of a Peruvian committee to aid the 26 of July Movement in Cuba. But in the course of her remarks she touches upon a variety of other subjects—the Mexico period, the Apra movement, communism, her husband—in a manner that, in my judgment, cannot be overlooked in any serious study of the ideological trajectory of the Castro movement.

In her first letter she introduced heself ("I am the wife of Ernesto Guevara") and said she had been given my address by friends in Mexico. She was national secretary for statistics of the Aprista party, the non-Marxist reform movement founded by Víctor Raúl Haya de la Torre, and wrote a column on economic matters for *La Tribuna,* the party's daily. With her column in mind, she said, she had written to "General" Alberto Bayo, the Spanish exile who had trained Castro's men in guerrilla warfare in Mexico, asking for information about me.[2]

"If the situation in Cuba remains undecided," she wrote, "I would appreciate it very much if you would send me credentials stating that I am a member of the movement. As you surely know, I belong to it already in my heart. I was even in jail in Mexico when the federal police arrested Fidel, Ernesto, and the others.[3] I intend to organize a group of the movement's sympathizers here. I have already contacted a good many intellectuals and political and labor leaders. Some of them are even willing to go to Cuba and join the fight there."

She added some other details, including her telephone number in Lima and a telegraph address where I could reach her "in case of an emergency." She seemed to be quite worried about the presence in Peru of two Cuban exiles, Néstor Rodríguez Lamelas and Armando Cruz Cobos. Rodríguez, she said, claimed to be chief of the radio section of the movement, and Cruz Cobos had been "saying bad things about Fidel." She asked me to send her, if I could, information on the two of them. In most of her subsequent communications she reported in detail on their activities.

This brief letter is worthy of some consideration. To begin with, let us consider the fact that the wife of Che Guevara, who was soon to emerge as second only to Castro in the 26 of July Movement, should write to the chairman of the Committee in Exile requesting authorization to act as delegate for the organization in Peru. Evidently she had heard of the existence of the committee through my press releases to the international news agencies and had made inquiries about me to Bayo. When Hilda de Guevara left Mexico following the departure of the *Granma* for Cuba in November 1956, she presumably shared the general impression that the expedition was a quixotic venture with remote possibilities of success. To learn through the press of the Committee in Exile must have lifted her spirits and raised her hopes. It is obvious that at this time Che Guevara did not maintain, directly or indirectly, a line of communication with his wife in Peru, and that the importance of his role in the revolution had not yet fully developed, or at least had not surfaced. Otherwise, how to explain the fact that his wife sought credentials from such a marginal and distant agency as the Committee in Exile in New York? Her fear that other Cuban exiles—Rodríguez Lamelas and Cruz Cobos—might contest her right to represent the 26 of July Movement confirms that she was not yet aware of her husband's key position within the organization.

Let us now try to examine Hilda's own apparent political or revolutionary standing. A Peruvian of Indian heritage, she could be considered a woman of culture. She wrote informally in Spanish, yet with precision and even style. She wrote a column on economic matters for a daily newspaper. There can be little question that she was a woman of political discernment, not one who merely followed in her husband's steps. The Aprista party had named her national secretary for statistics. This picture brings one inevitable question: Why was the wife of a Marxist revolutionary an officer of a political party whose ideological foundations and tactics were bitterly at odds with those of Marxism?[4] By this time Hilda had already walked a long stretch with Che Guevara. She had been at his side during the 1954 events in Guatemala, where Che sought to organize resistance on behalf of the pro-Communist government of President Jacobo Arbenz when a U.S.-backed invasion of Guatemalan exiles, led by Colonel Carlos Castillo Armas, came across the Honduran border. After the Arbenz government fell, Hilda followed Che to Mexico, where they were married and where they later met Fidel Castro. That she did not confine herself to the role of devoted wife is further confirmed by her letters to me. Together with Guevara, Castro, and others, for instance, she was arrested by the federal police in Mexico City in 1956. Also significant is the fact that she corresponded with General Bayo.

All these details confuse rather than clarify Hilda de Guevara's true ideological stance at the time and, more important, that of the 26 of July Movement itself. Was she a Marxist whose connections with the Apra movement served to camouflage more radical activities? This possibility is remote, though it cannot be completely ruled out. She must have been familiar with her husband's ideas and pursuits. She participated in the meetings and discussions of the Mexico group. One could without difficulty conclude that not only Guevara but Castro and probably most of those around him in Mexico were already dedicated Marxists. And from here to an assumption that the Sierra Maestra venture was just the first act of a carefully conceived plot to communize Cuba is a short step.

Yet many arguments may be advanced against this assumption. The Sierra Maestra meeting of 7–10 March 1958 seems to indicate that the plot had not yet taken form. Further, such an assumption would presume in all those involved, including Hilda Gadea de Guevara, an extremely improbable degree of psychological sophistication and capacity for mimetic deceit. Although some of those in the Mexico group—Guevara, Raúl Castro, Bayo, and probably a few others—were later revealed to be dedicated Marxists, I am still inclined to believe that the idea of transforming the Cuban struggle into a full-fledged Communist revolution was still in embryo at this time. That the Communists were ready to manipulate events with a view toward taking control of the revolution is beyond question. That has always been their typical role. But the opportunity to do so was not yet in sight and there was no certainty that it would be in the foreseeable future. As for Castro himself, I believe that in Mexico he accommodated himself to the Marxist inclinations of his comrades but did not yet fully commit himself. For the time being, he would continue to proceed within the established concept of "revolution" as it was understood by most of the Cuban people—that is, just a middle-class reform movement.

I sent Hilda de Guevara the credentials she had requested, and she acknowledged them immediately, on March 28. Most of this second letter is dedicated to the activities of Rodríguez Lamelas and Cruz Cobos. We learn in passing that she was in contact with Haya de la Torre. She was very much concerned because the two Cubans had got in touch with him. "I'm going to alert Haya," Hilda wrote. She added a postscript that was longer than the letter itself, continuing vertically in the margins. She had discovered that the two Cubans were not, after all, the suspicious characters she had feared they were. She ended her P.S. with these words: "You don't have to thank me for my interest [in the Cuban cause]. I feel that I am one of you. This is so because I am an Indo-American, as we Apristas say. Even if my husband were not there fighting, I would feel the same. My moral support and my faith in the final triumph go all the way with you." There is feeling in Hilda's words but no hint that the cause she so warmly embraced was other than a movement that could be supported by any Aprista.

The next communication I received from Peru was an official document of the recently founded Peruvian Movement for the Liberation of Cuba. It was dated 22 April 1958 in Lima and bore a letterhead proclaiming that the group was recognized by the 26 of July Movement (apparently by virtue of the credentials I had sent Hilda). The document was addressed to me as chairman of the Committee in Exile, and its main purpose was to inform me of the founding of the organization. The members of its executive committee were named. The chairman was Carlos Enrique Ferreyros, a member of the Peruvian Congress. One of the secretaries was a well-known Aprista, Jorge Muñiz. The two Cubans, Cruz Cobos and Rodríguez Lamelas, had been included. Hilda was financial secretary.

The rest of the communication was concerned with details of a vast program of activities the committee was planning. One sentence stands out: "Our first concern has been to keep the press well informed about the development of the struggle of the Cuban people and to point out very clearly *the eminently antidictatorial and anticommunist position of the Cuban revolution* (our grounds for this are the pamphlet *Nuestra Razón* and the statements of Dr. Manuel Urrutia)." (Italics mine.)

The lengthy communication was signed by the chairman of the organization, Congressman Ferreyros. At the end Hilda added a somewhat obscure note in her own handwriting, saying that she had been given the post of financial secretary at her own request. She had also proposed Rodríguez Lamelas as delegate of the 26 of July Movement when it appeared that he was about to be left out of the committee. "At the opening of the meeting it was made clear that I was the one person authorized by the Committee in Exile in New York. I read the credentials you had sent me. This was necessary because of the confusion created by the formation of that Committee for Aid to the Cuban People, in which there was apparently Communist infiltration. I maintained then that only a committee of which I was a member could claim the authority to represent the 26 of July Movement."

What Committee for Aid to the Cuban People? Had Hilda mentioned it in some earlier communciation I never received? She seemed very much concerned that this group might be a Communist front and wanted to prevent any possible reflection on the 26 of July. In fact, it appears that the Peruvian Movement for the Liberation of Cuba had been formed as a countermeasure.

In a letter of May 7 she was more specific. I had acknowledged her letter and reminded her that she alone, not Rodríguez Lamelas, had been authorized to be the 26 of July Movement's delegate in Peru. Hilda replied that it had slipped her mind. "You can see how it is, however. . . . I mentioned that a Committee for Aid to the Cuban People had been founded . . . by people I didn't know. Having read in *La Tribuna* that I had received credentials from you, they called me. Naturally, I became distrustful. Immediately I contacted a number of friends sympathetic to the Cuban cause, and we had a meeting at the [Apra] party's office. At that meeting the Peruvian Movement was born, and it was made very clear that it had no connection whatsoever with any other committee. The other organization, which was suspected of Communist infiltration . . . , disappeared a few days later." The anticommunist stand of Che Guevara's wife in mid-1958 could not be plainer.

Practically all of the letters Hilda wrote to me then—I have ten in my possession, plus two from the Peruvian 26 of July Committee—are full of interesting details. I am citing here only a few passages with some bearing on the ideological issue. The second communication of the Peruvian committee, for instance, is a long document describing plans for a Latin American tour to be made by Rodríguez Lamelas and Cruz Cobos to promote the Cuban revolutionary cause. In the Latin American style, the document begins with rhetorical affirmations of democratic faith, independence, and the unity of the hemispheric peoples. In the section dealing with the specific details of the tour, we find the following under number 4: "Interviews with [leaders of] the political parties in each country, with the exception of the Communist or pro-Communist parties." In another section headed "Agenda," item *c* reads: "Creation of a continental organization, formed by the respective national organizations, for the struggle against the dictatorships and international communism." This document bears the signatures of all the members of the executive committee, including Hilda Gadea de Guevara.

In our quest for ideological clues in Hilda's correspondence, we naturally look for references to her husband. They are very few and inconsequential. In her first letter she mentions his name only to identify herself—"I am the wife of Ernesto Guevara." Then we find an indirect reference in the already cited postscript to her letter of 28 March—"Even if my husband were not there fighting, I would feel the same." There is a little family information in her letters of May 7 and 16: the illness of her father and her two-year-old daughter had forced her to postpone a visit to her husband's parents in Argentina which she had been planning. At the end of the May 16 letter she wrote: "If you have any news of my husband, I'd be most grateful if you'd let me know." The last reference to Che Guevara appears in one of the closing paragraphs of Hilda's letter of June 13: "I wonder if this would be asking too much, but would it be possible for you to send me the code to establish radio communication with the Sierra Maestra? I would be so grateful. I am very eager to talk with my husband. There is a radio amateur here who has agreed to try; all we need is the code. Rodríguez knows which band it is, but that's all."

Most of Hilda de Guevara's letters to me, incidentally, remained unanswered. "I have written you several letters lately," she complained on June 13, "and haven't got a reply." A crisis in the Committee in Exile was partially responsible for my neglect. The committee had been reorganized (as I shall explain in the next chapter), and by this time I felt totally out of place in the Castro organization. Using the new setup as a pretext, I reminded José Llanusa, the new delegate for organization, that correspondence with the various exile groups was his responsibility now. My disillusionment with the 26 of July Movement was reaching its climax and I was only marking time until I received a response from Cuba to my repeated letters of resignation. Nevertheless, on June 19 I wrote Hilda again, informing her of the changes in the Committee in Exile and explaining that I could not send her the radio code she had requested because I did not have it. Nor could I give her any news of her husband. I knew nothing about Che Guevara beyond what was public knowledge: that he was an adventurous Argentine doctor who had joined the Castro group in Mexico and had become a major of the rebel forces in the Sierra Maestra.

Hilda de Guevara's letters obviously owe their significance only to the role that her husband came to play in the Castro revolution. In view of their candor and the very special position of the person who wrote them, one may reasonably conclude that while communist influences certainly existed within the leadership of the 26 of July Movement at the time, the movement itself was not yet committed to communism. In other words, up to that point the Castro revolution still appeared to be guided by its original democratic concepts. This presumption, supported by the words of Che Guevara's wife, is unquestionably a most important consideration in the analysis of the Castro personality and the Cuban revolutionary process.

Much depends on the answers to a number of puzzling questions: Did Hilda not know that her husband was a militant Marxist? Was she sincerely committed to the anticommunist Apra movement in Peru? Why did she hasten to found the Peruvian Movement for the Liberation of Cuba upon learning that the Committee for Aid to the Cuban People was suspected of being a Communist front? Why did she approve of and sign all those statements containing anticommunist declarations?

One might speculate that perhaps Hilda de Guevara's anticommunist posture was only a masquerade intended to help neutralize the usual fears of radicalism encountered by all revolutionary endeavors. Yet the more one tries to conceive of this woman's attitude as a calculated pretense, the more difficult it becomes. But even if we admit the possibility, what need was there for her to try to hoodwink *me*? I was the movement's official representative abroad. She directed her request for credentials to me and assumed that I knew who her husband was and what he was doing. Had she been aware of any secret Communist conspiracy, or part of one, she would logically have presumed that I too was involved, so that all pretense before me would have been unnecessary and ridiculous.

On the other hand, the simple fact that Hilda was the wife of

Che Guevara and that with him she had shared in the Guatemalan experience and in the preparations of the Castro group in Mexico should be sufficient to suggest that she must have been familiar with her husband's Marxist commitment by this time. How are we to reconcile this presumption with the apparent sincerity of her own anticommunist stance? One plausible explanation has already been advanced: that communist leanings within the Castro circle at this stage, although obviously acceptable to the group, were still a matter of individual inclination and had not yet crystallized in a concerted plan. Husband and wife, therefore, while joining in the immediate struggle against a dictatorship in Cuba, could live with their ideological differences just as couples of different religions often do. (They did not, in any case, live with them long: Che divorced Hilda in Cuba to marry Aleida March, a Cuban he met later that year.) Such contradictions were not at all uncommon in the Latin American political scene. As I have already noted, a number of Ortodoxo leaders were Marxists, although the party was declared to be anticommunist. Hilda's participation in the Guatemalan episode cannot be taken as prima facie evidence that she supported communism. She had lived in Guatemala for a number of years, had even worked for the Guatemalan government in a minor capacity during the presidency of liberal Juan José Arévalo in the late 1940s. In the context of those years, support of the Arbenz government was not necessarily tantamount to being a Communist.

Hilda's last letter to me, replying to my suggestion that she address future communications to José Llanusa, the new secretary for organization, shows that she still considered me one of the main leaders of the movement—something I never pretended or expected to be: "I am very grateful for everything you have been willing to tell me. It has been very kind of you to answer my letters, when your time is occupied by so many things. Perhaps in the future, in order to avoid delays, it will be better for me to address myself to Mr. Llanusa, and only in extreme cases to you. I would like to be sure, however, that any person who communicates with me from the Committee in Exile has been duly authorized by you."

The personality that may be glimpsed in Hilda de Guevara's letters impressed me very favorably. Had my disillusionment not already reached a point of no return, they would have helped in no small measure to maintain my earlier hopes that, for all its ideological vagueness and the shabby intrigues of the exile groups, the 26 of July Movement still had its roots in Cuba's democratic tradition.

Che's wife was not the only member of the Guevara family to write to the Committee in Exile offering cooperation and asking for recognition. On 9 March 1958 Che's father, Ernesto Guevara Lynch, addressed a letter to Raúl Chibás, who passed it on to me. The senior Guevara wrote from Buenos Aires on the letterhead of Guevara Lynch and Company, a firm engaged in "construction, development, and real estate administration."

Señor Guevara sent his letter by hand to Miami with "a friend." He explained that a previous letter, sent in care of Jules Dubois,[5] had been returned because of an incorrect address. He had learned through the press that a young woman in Buenos Aires by the name of Disis Guira claimed to represent the 26 of July Movement in Argentina, and upon inquiry had discovered that she did indeed have credentials from the Committee in Exile bearing my signature. (She had written to me as chairman of the Committee in Exile, and, on the recommendation of people in Miami who knew her, I had sent her the requested credentials.) Señor Guevara seemed to be unhappy about this. He admitted knowing Disis Guira personally and having a good impression of her ("She is an admirable activist"), but her credentials seemed rather unconvincing to him (they were somewhat restricted). By reading between the lines one is led to suspect that Señor Guevara may have thought that by writing to Chibás, whose name was much more widely known than mine, he stood a good chance of obtaining for himself full authorization to represent the movement in Argentina—just as his daughter-in-law had done in Peru.

Guevara wrote that he had been working for a long time with a group of friends in support of the Cuban revolution. "Although we recognize the noble endeavors of other liberation movements in Cuba," he explained, "we consider the one headed by Fidel Castro the most effective and the one nearest to our thinking." However, he added, "without contact with my son Ernesto or with the leaders of the 26 of July, we have been a little disoriented in our activities."

In another paragraph Che's father came closer to his point:

Considering that we here . . . have started an organization for the purpose of collecting funds and obtaining arms (the funds collected so far are insignificant and the arms practically none), we think it indispensable that someone duly authorized by Fidel Castro or by any of his representatives there come to Buenos Aires to assess and direct what we have been doing. For my own part I can tell you that as a result of several radio broadcasts and articles in various newspapers in which the name of my son Ernesto was mentioned, popular sentiment has been aroused in favor of Fidel Castro's cause, and I have received offers of material aid for Castro from noted persons and institutions. So you will understand, Señor Chibás, how urgent it is to have a duly authorized person here to act in the name of the 26 of July Movement.

Then Señor Guevara provided us with his full curriculum vitae as a revolutionary and an impressive list of references. During the Spanish Civil War he had "collaborated with those opposing General Franco"; before the outbreak of World War II he had worked with President Roberto Ortiz "in a campaign to stop Nazi propaganda in America"; during the war he had "belonged to several committes to aid the Allies"; in 1940 he had been "secretary general for Acción Argentina in Alta Gracia"; during the Perón regime he had been a member of the Civil Revolutionary Commando Monteagùdo, had taken part "in all the plots to overthrow the Perón dictatorship," and "signed a great number of manifestos against dictatorships"; he had been a "leader of the P.P. in conjunction with Dr. Alberto González, who took part in the last revolution that toppled Perón"; lately he had been supporting the Paraguayan Revolutionary Commandos.

Among the people who could "confirm my words" were listed Alejandro Ceballos, minister of foreign affairs; Rodolfo Fitte, undersecretary of foreign affairs; Angel Cabral, minister of communications; Tristán Guevara, minister of labor; Rear Admiral E. Palma, undersecretary of the navy; and Rear Admiral Manrique, chief of staff. There can be little doubt that Che Guevara's father enjoyed important connections in Argentina's official circles. His list contains fourteen more names, most of them with no position specified, presumably also people of social or political prominence.

I do not remember acknowledging Señor Guevara's letter. I have found no copy of a reply among my papers. His letter had been delayed in reaching Chibás, and by the time Chibás finally handed it to me I was too preoccupied with my decision to leave the organization to carry on with my usual functions for the Committee in Exile.

The first thing that comes to one's attention in this correspondence is the striking parallel between Señor Guevara's letter and those of his daughter-in-law. The two initiated communication with the Committee in Exile at about the same time and their motives for writing were apparently the same: to obtain the committee's recognition of and authorization for their activities in support of the Cuban revolution. Both appeared most eager to campaign on behalf of the 26 of July Movement and both spoke of influential friends willing to help the cause. Finally, both referred matter-of-factly to their family relationship with Che, but neither of them seemed to imply that this circumstance called for any special consideration on the part of the Committee in Exile. In fact, both declared themselves to be completely out of touch with "Ernesto."

Could this string of coincidences (and there are more) have significance? It's hard to tell. I simply point them out as a curiosity. Someone looking for indications of a Communist conspiracy might suspect that Guevara's wife and father were acting in concert to lull the suspicions of the Committee in Exile, whose chairman had already indicated his disillusionment with Castro and was in a position to publicize his suspicions that the revolution was not the democratic affair it pretended to be. The problem with this interpretation is that Señor Guevara's letter was sent not to me but to Raúl Chibás, who was still several years away from his eventual disillusionment; and surely any conspirator would have been provided with the correct address.

One could more easily conclude that the Guevaras were what they said they were: liberal political activists sincerely dedicated to the overthrow of a corrupt dictatorship, eager to aid the reform movement in which their son and husband was engaged, and close associates of prominent liberals of impeccably anticommunist standing. If they in fact did not share Che's Marxist beliefs, there is no need to question their assertions that they had no contact with him at that time; when a man is secretly pursuing a course that members of his family would disapprove if they knew of it, he is seldom eager to keep in close touch with them. Hilda's wistful requests for news of her husband, coupled with his involvement a few months later with the Cuban woman he eventually divorced Hilda to marry, are facts that seem to speak for themselves. Yet there is a difficulty here, too. If Hilda and Señor Guevara knew that Che was a Marxist—and it is difficult to see how they could have failed to know—why would they unquestioningly assume that the organization with which he was fighting was free of communist aspirations? If Hilda did, as she claimed, move swiftly to dissociate the 26 of July in Peru from a group suspected of Communist infiltration, she was working at cross-purposes to her husband. Could she have been doing so knowingly?

I do not know the answers, and at the time I did not even ask the questions. In all but name I was through with the 26 of July Movement.

# 11 The Confrontation

**T**he Committee in Exile was created by Castro apparently for the purpose of providing a semblance of unity to the scattered groups of 26 of July exiles, émigrés, and sympathizers in all countries, but especially in the United States. It had two main functions: raising funds and channeling them to the Dirección Nacional in Cuba, and organizing the groups in such a way that they could influence American public opinion, especially the news media, in a way favorable to the Castro movement.

It would be difficult to assess in statistical terms what, if anything, the Committee in Exile actually accomplished. I personally believe that it contributed enormously to the favorable image the Castro movement enjoyed abroad. Ironically, the committee's public relations efforts were particularly instrumental in dispelling much of the suspicion that Castro and his movement were tinged with the red dye of communism. "Is Castro a Communist?" was an inevitable question in all press conferences, TV and radio interviews, public appearances, and conversations with government officials.

Yet the committee never met as such, not even once. Léster Rodríguez, who was responsible for military matters and had based himself in Miami, ignored it completely. Carlos Franqui was not in the United States at the time of its creation; when he finally arrived, months later, he, too, settled in Miami and soon began to act independently. Only Chibás and I, both living in New York, consulted each other occasionally on matters related to the organization, and then informally.

The big problem of the 26 of July Movement in exile was the direction and coordination of its members' activities. Organization was supposed to be Carlos Franqui's responsibility, but he did very little in this respect. A multiplicity of groups continued to flourish in every city with a substantial Cuban population in the United States and Latin America. They were forever quarreling, each claiming to be the only true representative of the movement—or rather of "Fidel."

The problem was due largely, I believe, to the political immaturity of the Cubans in general and not least of Fidel Castro. In the autumn of 1955 Castro had made a fund-raising tour of the United States, speaking at rallies in New York, Bridgeport, Tampa, Miami, and a number of other cities. Since he was still considered an Ortodoxo, the Ortodoxo committee in New York was chief sponsor of the tour. The personal contacts that Castro made during that trip became the foundations of the various 26 of July groups that sprouted throughout the following years.

In my communications to the leaders in Cuba I frequently described the bothersome situation and explained how it distorted and vitiated the true mission of the émigrés, not to speak of the Committee in Exile. Since the problem had existed long before the committee came into being, I was convinced that only stern directives from Castro could bring a solution. In a report in January 1958 I wrote: "The problem of organization . . . has been forgotten, or rather neglected. . . . The whole thing got off to a bad start with Fidel himself. . . . It now appears that Fidel tried to please everybody and so left a series of personal contacts and rudiments of organization. These in time became personalistic clans, jealous of each other and constantly fighting among themselves for the preference or the approbation of 'Fidel.' "

I suggested that the situation could be corrected only by an organizational structure clearly defined by the Dirección Nacional, from above, and I repeatedly called for action on the problem. My entreaties were given urgency by the fact that my position as chairman was taken too literally by most of the members of the various groups. They saw me as Castro's personal representative and, as such, the leader of the movement in exile. I tried in vain to dispel this idea. Acting as a "leader" in the popular sense was no part of my expectations and did not agree with my personal preferences. I had accepted an appointment to serve the movement in the broad area of public relations but never expected to find myself involved in the internecine quarrels of the Castro groups. Again and again I explained to them that my specific function in the committee was supposed to be primarily related to matters *outside* the organization and that internal questions belonged to another delegate specially designated for that purpose. But all my efforts in this regard proved to be only an exercise in frustration. They either disagreed or simply chose to ignore my arguments altogether.

At last a directive came from the Dirección Nacional in precisely the terms I had suggested, and I sighed with relief. Although this document, as usual handwritten and signed by Fidel Castro, has already been cited in another connection, I consider it worthwhile to reproduce it in full now. In answering my specific suggestions, Castro shows some characteristic aspects of his own way of thinking. The communication, dated 9 January 1958 in the Sierra Maestra, was addressed "to the Cuban exiles and émigrés" and said:

The 26 of July Movement has made its position clear in regard to certain gangs of politicians who have been maliciously pretending that they side with the Revolution while actually they have been deceiving the people ever since 10 March 1952.

This situation clearly indicates that our movement will go on bearing the entire weight of the struggle against the tyranny, unmasking once and for all the greedy and sneaky pseudorevolutionaries whose only aspiration is to profit from the blood of those who are dying in this heroic crusade.

The part of the Cuban exiles and émigrés in this struggle has also been defined: financial contribution, public denunciation of the atrocities suffered by the people, and a campaign in support of the Cuban cause directed at democratic public opinion in the Americas.

If the exiles and émigrés really want to help us, however, they must put an immediate end to all the rivalries and antagonisms that have been impeding the aid so much needed by our men, today more than ever, after our rejection [in breaking with the Miami opposition junta] of the onerous aid of embezzlers and corrupt politicians who, bearing great responsibility for the tragedy our country is suffering, beat their chests in the comfort of a foreign city and try to twist the course of the revolution.[1]

To make the aid of Cubans outside the country truly effective, some months ago the Dirección Nacional established the Committee in Exile in New York with full authorization to organize and direct all these pursuits as well as to designate its own delegates in every group or center of Cuban population abroad. Only through these delegates shall financial contribu-

Castro's handwritten letter "to the Cuban exiles and émigrés."

denuncia pública de los
crímenes que sufre el país
y la campaña a favor de
la causa de Cuba en la
opinión democrática de A-
mérica.

Pero es necesario, si lo oci-
tados y emigrados desean aun-
tar que cesen de una vez todas las rivalidades y reñta-
[...] que han estado pon-
gitando el auxilio que tanto
necesitan nuestros combatientes, hoy más que nunca des-
pues de haber rechazado

la ayuda previa de los
malvadores y políticos co-
rrompidos, que reponerse
[...] gran parte de la tra-
gedia que sufre la patria, hoy
se dan golpes de pecho desde
una cómoda ciudad estan-
do pretendiendo torcer el
rumbo de la revolución.

Para hacer verdaderamente
efectiva la ayuda de los au-
bonos que se encuentran fuera
del país, la Dirección precisa
que designe hace nuevo el
comité del Exilio que cada-

ca en New York y que tiene plenas facultades para organizar y dirigir todos estos trabajos, así como para designar delegados suyos en todos los grupos o centro de población cubana en el extranjero, o a los efectos de que estos a través de esos delegados se lleven a cabo las recomendaciones económicas y se orienten las actividades del movimiento fuera de Cuba.

A ese comité deben que-

dar subordinadas, abarcando totalmente, todas las actividades de los miembros de nuestra organización en el extranjero.

El Comité del Partido queda facultado para reestructurar todos los comités breves y se dará públicamente del movimiento a cualquier miembro que no cumpla sus instrucciones.

Para conocimiento de los aislados y emigrados cubanos comunicamos que el Comité del

**7**

Emilio tiene de Presidente al Dr. Mario Llerena y de Tesorero al Dr. Raúl Chibás.

Así mismo el Comité del Emilio tiene instrucciones de la Dirección del Movimiento. Publica un periódico que lleva el nombre de "Puerta Ra-..." que será nuestro órgano oficial en el extranjero.

Llamamos a todos los simpatizantes nuestros fuera de Cuba a cooperar con el Comité del Exilio y brindar apo-

**8**

nimadamente el gran empeño que los combatientes revolucionarios de Cuba reclaman de sus hermanos los exilados y emigrados cubanos.

Ratificamos una vez más nuestra decisión de proseguir esta lucha así terminará con la victoria o la muerte.

Por la Dirección Nacional del Movimiento 26 de Julio

Fidel Castro

Sierra Maestra, Enero 9 de 1958

tions be channeled and the activities of the movement outside Cuba be directed.

All activities of the members of our organization abroad must absolutely be subordinated to this committee.

The Committee in Exile is authorized to reorganize all the local committees and to separate publicly from the Movement any member who will not comply with its instructions.

Let it be known to all Cuban exiles and émigrés that the chairman of the Committee in Exile is Dr. Mario Llerena and its financial secretary is Dr. Raúl Chibás.

In addition, the Committee in Exile has been instructed by the Leadership of the Movement to publish a newspaper that, under the title *Nuestra Razón,* will be our official organ abroad.

We call on all our sympathizers outside Cuba to cooperate with the Committee in Exile and to work together to launch the great effort that our revolutionary soldiers expect from their brothers, the Cuban exiles and émigrés.

Once again we confirm our decision that this struggle shall end only with victory or death.

For the Dirección Nacional of the 26 of July Movement
FIDEL CASTRO R.

This document reflects almost literally the organizational approach I had been insistently recommending to the leaders in Cuba. I had it published and circulated among the 26 of July groups everywhere. And nothing changed. Neither Castro's exhortations to unity nor his threats of disciplinary action had the slightest effect. Complaints and grievances continued to pour in to me from Chicago, Los Angeles, Philadelphia, Bridgeport, Washington, Miami, Key West . . . and then Puerto Rico, Guatemala, Honduras, Panama, Buenos Aires, Lima . . . all telling essentially the same story of clashing personalities and disputed jurisdictions. Castro himself ignored his own instructions and continued to dispatch personal envoys and arrange contacts outside the regular channels of the organization. Reality thus canceled out theory.

And that was not all. The internal unity of the Committee in Exile itself was also irreparably broken. From January on, in most of my communications to Cuba I first suggested and then flatly stated my desire to resign. Only an idealistic sense of loyalty and an extreme concern for formalities held me. In a letter sent from Santiago de Cuba on March 30 Marcelo Fernández commented, "In a previous letter you mentioned the possibility of not continuing as chairman of the Committee in Exile. This is absurd, Mario.

At this meeting in the Sierra [March 7–10] the Committee in Exile was confirmed as it is presently organized. We have great faith in you four. You must resolve whatever misunderstanding may have arisen among you." But in spite of all the confirmations and conciliatory messages from Castro and the others, the moral gap that separated me from the rest of the Committee in Exile grew wider and deeper. In Miami, for instance, Franqui carried out activities as representative of the 26 of July Movement without informing me about them. I learned later that he had begun to send reports to the Sierra Maestra in which my character and activities were described in a rather bad light. It seems that Franqui had grown deeply resentful of the publicity surrounding my name. A similar attitude became noticeable in Luis Buch, who, although not a member of the committee, had little by little become a sort of ambassador at large for the Dirección Nacional. At first Buch displayed the marked humility of an Asian servant, but now suddenly he turned arrogant and unfriendly. Why, I had no idea. There seemed to be a vivid contrast between the attitudes of these people and those of the Dirección Nacional. As I had known some of the leaders in Cuba for many years, since long before Castro and the 26 of July Movement, I attributed the lack of cooperation and the animosity I was encountering to personal intrigues and jealousies.

The intrigues became serious, however, when some of my former friends suggested to Judge Urrutia that I was trying to undermine his position as presidential designate of the movement in order to obtain it for myself. The authors of the malicious fabrication resorted to such flimsy "proofs" as press clippings in which my name preceded his—as though the wording of press captions could have been under my control. This kind of thing was linked with some comments of mine on Urrutia's behavior in the United States in a letter to Marcelo Fernández in January 1958. My remarks, although critical, were in no way detrimental to Judge Urrutia, whom I considered a gentleman and a friend. But somehow they were leaked and intentionally distorted to indicate, as Marcelo himself wrote on March 30, that I had "certain reservations concerning Urrutia." I had no such reservations and had implied none. I had only become somewhat disappointed in the way Urrutia handled himself with the press as well as in his carelessness in letting himself get involved—against my advice—in the activities of the controversial *fidelistas* who did not recognize the Committee in Exile. I also made the mistake of sharing my concern with one other member of the committee; and the rumor started.

The ridiculous tale that I entertained hopes of taking Urrutia's place caught me totally by surprise. I learned about it accidentally from Urrutia himself. After Adam Clayton Powell's speech in the House denouncing the arms shipments to Batista in March, the congressman wanted Urrutia, Chibás, and me to join him in a press conference at Sardi's restaurant in Manhattan. The night before the conference I decided to give Judge Urrutia a ring to remind him of the appointment. Urrutia said somewhat evasively that he was not going. Surprised, I reminded him of the importance of the occasion, if only for its publicity value. But my insistence succeeded only in causing Urrutia to lose his calm. I was wasting my time, he said angrily. He clearly implied that he was not about to appear publicly with someone who was trying to replace him as the presidential designate. He not only was the confirmed candidate of the 26 of July Movement, he reminded me; he also had the support of most of the other opposition and revolutionary groups, which he proceeded to name one by one. (Evidently he was unaware that the groups he was naming, with the single exception of the Ortodoxos, had refused to endorse him.) Only then did I fully grasp what he was thinking. Suddenly a mixture of surprise and anger overcame me. Of all the 26 of July leaders in exile, I had given the strongest support to Judge Urrutia's candidacy. My immediate reaction was so vigorous that he could not disbelieve me. His suspicions appeared to fade and I believe he realized he had been the victim of mendacious gossip.

The incident was pushed to the back of my mind as we resumed our normal cordial relationship. Less than two weeks later we jointly expressed views that apparently had profound repercussions within the movement's leadership. Some members of the press in the United States frequently denounced Castro as a Communist or inclined toward communism, and it had become routine for me to deny such allegations. The critics suddenly found new fuel for their campaign in a manifesto of the Cuban Communists issued at the beginning of April in which, abandoning their tactical "nonviolent" line, they announced they were ready "to join all Cubans to end tyranny"—obviously an approach to the 26 of July Movement. There can be no question now that this step was taken as a result of previous secret negotiations and was aimed at conditioning the public mind for what would come later. But the news prompted Urrutia to suggest that we hold a joint press conference to counterattack all rumors of such a possibility. I agreed, and the conference was held at his apartment in the Hotel Walton in Manhattan on April 3. All major news agencies and TV networks as well as the New York dailies sent reporters and cameramen. Urrutia emphatically denied any kind of contact or understanding with the Communists and reaffirmed the democratic principles of the Cuban revolution. His statements appeared in practically all newspapers. The *New York Mirror* (4 April 1958) also quoted me as saying: "We flatly reject any cooperation whatsoever [with the Communists]. The Cuban Reds simply want to get on the bandwagon at this time. We would never have accepted this offer from the Reds at any time because our revolution is absolutely a democratic revolution."

The anticommunist views of the official presidential candidate of the Castro movement and its appointed representative outside of Cuba were, understandably, widely disseminated; so widely, in fact, that they caused quite a stir in the Sierra Maestra. It appears that there were indeed secret contacts taking place at the time between the 26 of July and the Communist party in Cuba. It is now known that the Communists had been in touch with the 26 of July Movement all along through Raúl Castro, although exactly when the actual negotiations started at committee level has not been established.[2] The pronouncements made by Urrutia and me no doubt sealed our fall from grace in the Sierra Maestra, although no immediate action was taken; we still had our uses. One of the delegates of the Civic Resistance Movement in New York, Víctor de Yurre, who in 1959 was appointed one of the three city commissioners of Havana, told me that he heard from a captain on Castro's staff that the guerrilla commanders in the Sierra, particularly Castro and Che Guevara, got "real mad" when they learned of our anticommunist declarations.

Later in April arrangements were made, at the request of the Venezuelan branch of the 26 of July Movement, for a visit to that country of the Committee in Exile and the presidential candidate. Luis Buch, the gray unofficial liaison man between the Santiago leaders (Hart and others who were not permanently in the mountains) and the Committee in Exile, came to New York to direct the preparations for the trip. By now Buch had practically become the center of gravity of the committee. Notwithstanding all the formalities and confirmations from Castro and the Dirección Nacional, my position as chairman became purely nominal. An irreparable communication gap had developed somewhere along the way. Buch ever more openly excluded me from private talks with Chibás and Urrutia. Was he acting under specific suggestions from above? Or had he simply learned in Santiago that I had fallen from grace and so felt free to ignore me? My guess is that he was merely reflecting the attitudes that he discerned among the other leaders in exile. I learned that my inclusion in the Venezuelan plans was due only to the express interest of the Venezuelan committee, which specifically asked for me by cable.

The main purpose of this visit to Venezuela was to initiate a campaign throughout Latin America in support of the 26 of July Movement. Venezuela had recently freed itself from the Pérez Jiménez dictatorship, and there seemed to be widespread public sentiment in favor of the Cuban revolution. The local 26 of July committee was looking forward to our presence there as an opportunity not only to arrange important contacts with sympathetic government and military figures but also to spur financial contributions. The committee was composed of some eight or ten Cuban residents of the country, most of them professionals, executives of large corporations, or independent businessmen.

One contact was indeed established whose importance surpassed all expectations. It was with Admiral Wolfgang Larrazábal, president of Venezuela at the time. The interview was obtained through the president's private secretary, who was a friend of Sergio Rojas Santamarina, secretary of the 26 of July committee in Caracas.[3] Urrutia, Chibás, and I were invited to lunch one day at the sumptuous military club on the outskirts of the city as the guests of three high-ranking officers of the armed forces who were sympathizers of the anti-Batista movement in Cuba. After lunch we were led to another room and there were introduced to the president. During the preliminary courtesies I was greatly surprised to learn that the president was familiar with my name and even with some of my statements in the press. I realized for the first time the incredible power and reach of the news media. Coming to the main subject of the occasion, we expressed our hopes for some kind of Venezuelan help to the Cuban revolution and diplomatically suggested that there were three main areas where help would be appreciated: some sort of international recognition of the rebel cause, permission for the Cubans to campaign and operate freely in Venezuela, and military equipment. President Larrazábal listened with a smile and then assured us of his personal goodwill. Although he made no specific commitment, we left with the impression that a positive response would be forthcoming, the details to be arranged at lower echelons.

By all criteria that meeting could be termed a great success. Its true significance lay primarily in the simple fact that it had taken place. No matter how secretly or unofficially, the president of Venezuela had consented to meet with the representatives of a revolutionary group ostensibly engaged in the overthrow of a recognized foreign government, and had expressed sympathy for the Cuban revolution.[4] The Cubans were practically given carte blanche to carry on in Venezuela their revolutionary activities against the Batista regime.

Something else happened in Caracas that added a great deal to my confusion regarding my personal relationship to the 26 of July Movement. Sergio Rojas was acquainted with a young Cuban radio amateur by the name of Tamayo who had a powerful short-wave radio in his high-rise apartment. Tamayo had succeeded in establishing two-way contact with the Sierra Maestra station on several occasions. At Rojas's suggestion, he tried again. Upon learning that we were in Caracas, the Sierra Maestra operators promised to arrange an opportunity for us to talk with Castro. A day or two later we were summoned to Tamayo's apartment and several of us, including Urrutia, Chibás, Rojas, and Justo Carrillo, were able to converse with Castro. When my turn came, Castro, to my amazement, was especially cordial, expressing support and encouragement that contrasted sharply with the cool reserve and even hostility of the other 26 of July figures in exile. He even reminisced about our meeting in Mexico two years before. This totally unexpected cordiality only mixed perplexity with my discontent. Was Castro being sincere? Was the souring of my relations with the others only the result of isolated personal jealousies and animosities? Or was Castro only trying to deter me from rushing into a premature resignation that, in his view, might have detrimental effects on the public relations of the movement? After all, it is axiomatic that revolutionary movements thrive on good publicity, for good publicity creates followers and admirers, and these in turn bring in the money without which the revolution cannot move. At the time I was unable to tell. Today, however, considering the known consternation in the Sierra Maestra at our anticommunist declarations of a few days earlier, the latter alternative seems likely.

Our stay in Venezuela was cut short by commitments in the United States. But it was agreed that we would return for a big tour through the country on the occasion of the Twentieth of May, the anniversary of Cuba's independence.

About a week after my return to New York I received a call from Luis Buch, giving me notice of an important meeting that I was expected to attend in Miami. Buch stressed that I should not fail to come. I promised that I would be there.

The reason for the meeting was the arrival of Haydée Santamaría, which had been heralded by Castro in his letter of April 26. Haydée was staying with some friends in a small house far from the downtown area. Among those present were Chibás, Buch, Franqui, Bebo Hidalgo, and José Llanusa.

The meeting itself, like most such Cuban affairs, was informal and disorganized. Dozens of people, many complete strangers to me, wandered in and out all day long, evidently to speak privately with Haydée Santamaría, the veteran guerrilla of the Sierra Maestra. I gathered that they were supposedly engaged in purchasing arms, transporting them to Cuba, and other clandestine activities. Throughout the day a persistent feeling of being out of place there overcame me. The old touch of comradeship, especially on the part of some with whom I thought I had enjoyed a long-time mutual esteem, was conspicuously absent.

In the afternoon the subject of the Committee in Exile was finally brought up. A plan for its reorganization had already been decided upon. The announced purpose was to make it "more effective," particularly in the collection of funds—Castro's perennial complaint. Franqui was to leave the committee and go to Cuba to assume certain bureaucratic duties in the Sierra Maestra. His place would be taken by José Llanusa, who appeared to be held in special regard by Haydée. *Sierra Maestra,* the organ of the movement in exile which I had founded and named, was henceforth to be the province of one Tony Buch, a distant relative of Luis Buch who came to the 26 of July from the Ortodoxo party via the Civic Resistance Movement.

All these changes were presented as accomplished facts. I was not consulted or asked for my opinion. Haydée, who obviously had brought the commandments down from the mountains and presented them to the others in a private caucus, chose not to be present at the time of the "discussion." This turned out to be almost a little kangaroo court, I being the accused. From their remarks it became immediately clear that I was being held responsible for the alleged failures of the Committee in Exile and that I was to be stripped of whatever hierarchical importance I might have enjoyed as its chairman and public relations director. I was responsible, it seemed, for the insufficient collection of funds. When I pointed out that Chibás was in charge of that department and they realized that I was totally invulnerable in this area, they turned to public relations, my assigned field of activity. Franqui insinuated that I had taken advantage of the position to advertise my own name. I was after publicity only for myself, he charged, instead of "sharing it with the others, too." It was almost laughable, and the tense situation took on a ridiculous air. I reminded Franqui—and the others—that if I was at all involved in activities related to publicity, it was simply because I had been requested and formally designated by Castro and the Dirección Nacional to carry out that specific work. Were they unaware of the various documents and confirmations that had been sent by the leaders in Cuba? It had been at Castro's request, not mine, that I became the official spokesman for the 26 of July Movement outside the island. My essential function was to establish contact with the news media, produce statements, give lectures, visit government officials, and gain favorable publicity for the movement in any other way I could. I could not help it if, as an inevitable by-product of such activities, my name became involved in the resulting publicity. The news agencies and the press in general paid little attention to anonymous releases, nor would they carry much weight with the public we hoped to influence. As for "sharing" the publicity with the other members of the group, they were free to issue statements of their own if they wanted to publicize their names.

Unable to back their charges with a single solid fact or valid argument, they unleashed a barrage of invective. I looked at Chibás, my friend since college days, who had been silent. He remained silent. Finally I said that they could do or think anything they pleased, and walked out of the room.

The concealed hostility had finally broken out into the open. Of course, the real problem was nothing I had done or failed to do.

Paradoxically, the success of my public relations campaign seemed to disturb them deeply, and bitter personal resentment was added to an ever more evident ideological incompatibility. It had become abundantly clear by now that the fact that I had joined the movement had never meant that I had abdicated my individual sovereignty, and that I was not one to accept directives unconditionally, whether from the "maximum leader" or anyone else, let alone submit to any kind of totalitarian uniformity. So, in typical totalitarian fashion, they staged their kangaroo court and tried to fabricate a case against me. Yet the movement was apparently not yet ready to make any charges against me publicly or to expel me.

As soon as I left the meeting I wrote a brief statement of resignation from my two positions on the Committee in Exile. When Haydée Santamaría returned late in the afternoon and inquired how the discussion had gone, I handed her the statement. Since she was a member of the Dirección Nacional, I thought it technically permissible for her to handle the matter. She was visibly taken aback by my decision. Evidently she had not anticipated it. Undoubtedly she realized that an announcement of my resignation could have adverse effects on the movement's publicity, especially at a time when plans were already under way for a propaganda and fund-raising campaign in Venezuela and perhaps in the rest of Latin America too. After my years of writing for the press and voicing opinions on Cuba's political life, my name was fairly well known and enjoyed general respect. Haydée reacted strongly against my taking that step. "True revolutionaries never quit," she admonished me with a touch of gentleness. In view of her attitude, I decided not to press the matter further at the moment.

By evening, however, I realized that I ought to talk further with her, after all, so as to have the question completely clarified. I had already sent another letter of resignation to the Dirección Nacional through a different channel. But on approaching her, I found her in a cold, unreceptive mood and changed my mind. I invented some excuse about having something to do downtown, bade her good night, and left. For the next two days I took part in some scheduled activities of local exile groups. Franqui remarked acidly on my total lack of enthusiasm. When the meetings were over, I took a plane back to New York.

In my letter to the leadership in Cuba, addressed to Faustino Pérez, I had written: "My resignation as chairman of the Committee in Exile is hereby submitted through you to the DN. I will not make it public until I have a reply from you." I never got the requested reply to this letter. In the days ahead I even considered again the possibility that the leaders in Cuba might be totally alien to the toxic atmosphere of the small circle in exile.

# 12 Not on That Bandwagon

**M**ost of us moderates, both in exile and in Cuba, did not realize that we had been left behind by the gradual radicalization of the revolution. When I say "we" I mean the great mass of middle-class, educated people who made the revolution possible, psychologically as well as actively and financially. I have been talking about my personal experience, but mine was not an isolated case. Thousands upon thousands like me throughout the island and abroad—professionals, teachers, students, white-collar workers, businessmen, industrialists—had been aroused to indignation by Batista's destruction of the country's constitutional system and then had been filled with hope by the prospect of a decent, constructive, democratic revolution such as the one in which Castro appeared to be engaged. These were the people who made Castro a national leader and gave their time, their efforts, their money, and frequently their lives for what they thought to be that kind of revolution.

As I have already pointed out, the seeds of radicalization were present in the Castro movement from the very beginning, but they did not start to sprout and take root until sometime during the first quarter of 1958. By all indications, the summit meeting of March 7–10 seems to be the most probable occasion when the revolution turned irrevocably to the extreme left. To be sure, there had been signs that something of the sort might happen or was happening, but anti-Batista sentiment and visions of a brighter future blinded most moderates to the red lights of danger. They kept marching along spellbound under the Castro banner, unaware of the Communist trap that awaited them at the end of the road.

I tried to go on with my usual activities while I waited for a response to my latest letter of resignation. At some moments I tried to convince myself with "revolutionary" logic that I should forget all about personal grievances and remain in my post like a good soldier. Perhaps the problem was only personal, after all. But then common sense told me again that the personal aspect was only an outer crust covering something far more serious underneath, and I felt that I no longer wanted to be a part of the Castro organization. Still, a foolish sense of propriety kept me from taking any public step until I heard from the leadership in Cuba.

So I became almost like an automaton. I went with Urrutia and Chibás on a second trip to Venezuela, as had been arranged. The local 26 of July committee had prepared a varied and extensive program. Urrutia and I were taken on a tour of the most important Venezuelan cities, from Maracaibo at the western tip of the country to Cerro Bolívar in the east. Emma Castro, who was in Venezuela at the time, joined us for part of the tour. There were receptions, banquets, rallies. The Venezuelan committee had had *Nuestra Razón* reprinted, and hundreds of copies autographed by Urrutia and me were distributed at the gatherings at which we appeared. When the tour was completed, Urrutia and I were invited to spend several days as guests of Sergio Rojas in Caracas. Luis Buch arrived later and also availed himself of Rojas's hospitality.

An important part of the Venezuelan program was a series of interviews with influential people—politicians, high-ranking military officers, journalists, businessmen, Catholic dignitaries, and so on. Representatives of other Cuban organizations also approached us to explore possible ways of cooperating with the 26 of July Movement. Delegates of the Directorio Revolucionario in particular were interested in discussing a formula for joint direction of the anti-Batista struggle (the old idea of the Miami junta, only without the politicians). To all these people I explained that such questions should be directed to the Dirección Nacional in the Sierra Maestra. This was technically true, but earlier I would at least have discussed their suggestions with them. Now I was only going through the motions. They could not hide their disappointment. Like many others, they were under the impression that my rank

The Venezuelan 26 of July committee and visitors in Caracas during the May 1958 Venezuelan campaign. From left: Francisco Villarreal, later ambassador to Chile; Carlos M. Piedra, later ambassador to Italy; Sergio Rojas, later ambassador to the United Kingdom; the author; Emma Castro, sister of Fidel; Manuel Urrutia, later provisional president; Gustavo Arcos, later ambassador to Belgium; Francisco Pi Vidal, later ambassador to Venezuela; and an unidentified member of the Venezuelan committee.

and position in the movement entitled me to handle that kind of negotiation.

In living contrast, however, Luis Buch on his own account started a series of meetings with some of the people I had brushed aside as well as with the local 26 of July leaders. The latter did not fail to notice the strange duality in the 26 of July representation in exile. Sergio Rojas in particular, a very intelligent and amiable gentleman, was quite surprised on learning about this situation. He told me that they had always assumed that I was one of the main figures of the 26 of July Movement and its only authorized representative outside of Cuba. That was why they had been so eager to have me take part in the Venezuelan campaign. Who was this fellow Buch, he asked, a political commissar? I explained to Rojas that I did not really belong to the high echelons of the movement but that this was not the core of the matter. Rather, a certain crisis had developed concerning my position because the movement seemed to be taking some unexpected and disturbing turns. I did not go into any more details with Rojas except to add that I had reached a personal decision and was only waiting for the right moment to make it known. Rojas was the first person to whom I confided my disenchantment with the Castro movement.

Then another opportunity of communicating directly with Castro by two-way radio presented itself. We were told of a small, independent exile group that owned the appropriate equipment and which had frequently established contact with the Sierra Maestra. The group broadcast news and anti-Batista material under the name of Los Indios Verdes (The Green Indians). Their leader, one Capó, was an engineer who had been a government official in Havana. He was willing to cooperate with the 26 of July.

One evening Luis Buch invited me to accompany him to the place where Capó and three other men operated the radio equipment. Buch wanted to let Castro know that an arms deal in which he was involved was making good progress. The communication was quickly established, and we heard Castro's voice. But then to my surprise, Buch appeared to have great difficulty in making Castro realize who he was. In trying to refresh Castro's memory, Buch referred again and again to *la prima* (the cousin), an improvised nom de guerre for Haydée Santamaría, his immediate contact. (Such radio exchanges were monitored by the Batista government, of course, so they had to be carried on in a carefully guarded fashion.) As Buch struggled to identify himself, it occurred to me that this was a splendid opportunity to tell Castro what was on my mind and of my decision to leave the committee. Why not? I said to myself. I had not intended to speak with him personally this time, but the opportunity seemed too good to miss.

As soon as Buch finished, I indicated that I wanted to talk to Castro too. One of the operators announced me, and I took the microphone. After the opening greetings, I told Castro in the somewhat indirect way that the circumstances required that I had decided to leave my position in the Committee in Exile, as he was doubtless already aware. This decision, I said, was the result of a growing discontent caused by a series of negative factors. I am sure he understood clearly what I meant. His reaction was immediate and struck me as even more remarkable than his cordiality of the previous occasion. Castro went into a long and emotional speech in which he praised my merits as a revolutionary and as one who "still has a lot to give to the revolution," and then benignly reproached me for even thinking of leaving the Committee in Exile. He spoke at length of the bravery and the sacrifices of those fighting in the mountains, of the ideals of a better Cuba that had brought us all together, of the special role of the exiles and émigrés, and of the need for all of us to forget discomforts and personal difficulties and join in a great push for victory. Quitting was not the mark of good revolutionaries, he said, echoing Haydée Santamaría. Finally, as if to dispel whatever doubts I might have had, he assured me of the total and sincerest support of every member of the Dirección Nacional, and especially of himself.

Castro must have talked to me for at least twenty minutes. The conversation—which practically became a monologue—was being recorded, but the tape came to an end and Castro was still talking. When at last he finished, I really didn't know what to think. The attitude of the leader of the revolution appeared to be the very opposite of that of the small circle of my associates in exile. To explain in detail my reasons for wishing to leave the movement was out of the question; that kind of discussion could not be carried on by monitored two-way radio. I wanted to believe him. Bewildered, I gave him the assurance he asked for and said I would try to weather my difficulties and stay on. The three Indios Verdes seemed awed by Castro's words. One of them breathed, "We should say a prayer." Buch said nothing.

It was extremely confusing. There had to be an explanation somewhere, but I could not find it. Yet, for all the strong tone of sincerity in Castro's praises and pleas, my urge to leave the movement remained unaltered. I no longer cared whether the situation changed or not. I only wanted to hear what Castro and the others might care to say about my decision, if anything. At least, I wanted my letters of resignation acknowledged. Then I would announce it publicly.

Difficult as it would have been for anyone listening to Castro on that particular occasion not to be moved by the tone of his words, the chronological facts witnessed strongly against his sincerity. The time was mid-May. Weeks before, at the very moment when the Communist party was making public approaches to the 26 of July Movement, after the leaders had secretly agreed to turn away from the democratic promises of the Sierra Manifesto, I had joined with Urrutia to denounce the Communists and publicly deny any Communist influence in the movement. Our statements had infuriated Castro. In addition, Franqui at least, with the tacit approval of other exile leaders, had been doing his best to undermine my reputation and status. It was therefore impossible to dispel my doubts that I still enjoyed the high esteem of which Castro had now so urgently assured me.

Why, then, did Castro beg me to reconsider? Why did he not simply let me go without further ado, or counter any move I might intend to make by announcing my replacement? I can only speculate. The answer, I believe, is sheer tactics. It wasn't yet my time (it wasn't Urrutia's, either). The movement's interests were better served by keeping me in place than by having me out. Although I personally believe my departure would have made little difference to the movement's fortunes, Castro may well have thought otherwise. He was always concerned about publicity and public opinion. The revolution was at a low ebb at the moment, having suffered some military setbacks. Castro must have felt that his enterprise could not spare the support of someone who had the ear of the news media. My departure at this time, especially in disgust, might trigger a chain reaction of negative consequences. He had invited me to join his organization because through the years I had built a solid reputation as an honest, insightful commentator on Cuban political affairs. I represented a decisively influential segment of Cuba's educated middle class, from which the movement derived most of its strength. As an individual I was of little importance, but my resignation might have an impact on a substantial number of others whose opinions mattered a great deal. Castro knew that many of my well-known former colleagues in the extinct MLR—Valdespino, Rumbaut, Marrero, others—were actively working for the 26 of July. So were many of my friends in religious, student, and journalistic circles. Castro may very well have feared that if I left the movement, or was dismissed without a convincing reason, at least some of these people might have started wondering why, and so might their friends and their friends' friends, and who knows how far this wondering might have gone?

Back in New York I pretended to go along, as much as I could, with the new setup in the Committee in Exile. I still expected to receive a concrete reply from Cuba at any moment. Under the supervision of Haydée Santamaría in Miami,[1] Llanusa, with the collaboration of Chibás, assumed the direction of committee activities other than public relations. They opened another 26 of July club farther north on Amsterdam Avenue and began issuing 26 of July ID cards to rank-and-file members. I signed the cards, thus apparently giving Llanusa the impression that I was going to accept my new role as decorative figurehead of the committee. He insistently urged me to talk things over with "Yeyé," even suggested that I make a special trip to Puerto Rico, where she had recently gone. I told him I felt there was no longer any need for me to talk with Haydée Santamaría. I had tried to do just that in Miami, without success. I also brushed him off when he attempted to give instructions concerning my own functions. He was much taken aback by my disregard for his newly acquired authority. I was told later by de Yurre, the Civic Resistance Movement leader in New York, that on one occasion he overheard Llanusa say, "I will destroy Llerena."

When days and weeks passed without any news from Cuba, I decided to write again, this time directly to Castro. I wrote under the lingering echo of his words through the radio in Caracas and with a last faint hope that there might truly be a difference between the Sierra Maestra and its emissaries among the exiles. On June 10 I prepared a six-page memorandum in which I summarized the circumstances in which I had joined the 26 of July Movement and enumerated the obstacles that I had encountered in the performance of my functions as chairman of the Committee in Exile. I gave my impressions of the meeting in Miami the previous month and referred to the Urrutia case. "I have learned of a certain rumor being circulated," I told Castro, "which depicts me as being opposed to Dr. Urrutia. I wonder in what wicked source that rumor originated." Then I expressed my own point of view on the matter. "I have a great respect for Dr. Urrutia," I said, "and consider him a citizen of exceptional virtues. But that doesn't mean that I will renounce my right to think for myself, especially when matters related to the interest and the future of our country are involved. Respect is in no conflict with truth. . . . I know how to administer my freedom of mind, and nobody excels me in discretion. But I would rather risk being misunderstood than submit myself to any kind of censorship."

The question of my resignation was advanced only as the inevitable alternative to the fulfillment of certain conditions. These

conditions amounted to a full vote of confidence for me to restruc-
ture and direct the activities of the Committee in Exile with no further interference. I viewed this memorandum as an ultimate test
of my relations with the movement. I thought I was giving Castro a
last chance to put things in their proper order. It is not easy to admit
that one has been wrong for years, to accept the fact that one has
expended his best efforts for a cause that has gotten irrevocably out of
hand, that all one's hopes must finally be abandoned. Hope dies hard.

After I wrote to Castro, I suspended all my activities for the committee. I even began to regret having written to Castro at all. I considered the rift beyond repair. About the only thing I did at that
time for the movement was acknowledge some of the last letters
from Hilda de Guevara.

Then on June 18 Betancourt called me from Washington to tell
me that he had received a phone call from Terrance Leonhardy,
chief of the Cuban desk at the State Department. The State Department was very much concerned about the tone with which the
rebel radio had been attacking the United States in its recent
broadcasts. Leonhardy had contended that the arms shipments to
Batista had ceased in March, and had said that the State Department would like to see a difference between the way the rebels
dealt with these matters earlier and the way they dealt with them
now. Leonhardy had complained also about the confiscation of
trucks and other materials belonging to the Nicaro Nickel Company in a recent rebel operation. He had warned that the State
Department might publicize the incident, which would raise
strong feelings against the rebel cause among the American public, or close the nickel plant, throwing many Cubans out of work.
Leonhardy had also complained that the rebel radio had been
using certain disturbing phrases—"capitalism that enslaves the
people" and the like. These were Communist slogans, Leonhardy
had pointed out.

Disturbed, I wrote once again to the Dirección Nacional, detailing the State Department's complaints. The Nicaro Nickel
Company was located in northern Oriente, an area that had come
under the control of Raúl Castro's forces. Confiscation of American
equipment was a very serious action. As for the "Communist
slogans," they might have reflected no more than the nationalistic
bravado that we all had become accustomed to during thirty years
of progressive demagoguery. Cubans had heard them so often

from people with no Communist connections that they would not automatically share the State Department's concern. Still, I wondered.

This communication was apparently ignored. By the end of June, however, from the headquarters of Raúl Castro in northern Oriente, I received three photographs intended as proof that the Batista government was still being supplied with arms by the American government. The photographs had been purportedly taken inside the U.S. naval base at Guantánamo. One showed a large American military truck backed up to the hatch of a Cuban Air Force plane; another Cuban plane was parked nearby. The insignia on the planes and the English words on the truck appeared to indicate that Batista was getting his aid through the U.S. naval base. The second photograph showed a requisition form that had apparently been removed from a record book at the Guantánamo base. It was dated 8 May 1958 and gave detailed instructions for the transfer of U.S. rocket heads and fuses to the Cuban navy. The third photograph showed another form, apparently from a U.S. Navy account book, related to the first.

I had had no previous communication with the Raúl group, which now appeared to have its own agents and lines of communication apart from those of the Fidel group. As I had practically withdrawn from all my usual activities, I did not take immediate action concerning this material. But it turned out that other copies had been sent directly to the news agencies at the same time. The State Department reacted in a statement released on July 3:

Press reports and other printed material purporting to show that arms from the United States are being supplied to the Cuban Government are erroneous. Since March 14, 1958, when a shipment of M-1 rifles was suspended, no arms deliveries to the Cuban Government have been made from the United States or by any agency of the United States Government outside of the United States save on one instance in May 1958. At that time, two unarmed Cuban transport planes landed at Guantánamo Naval Base in Cuba to exchange 300 small rocketheads for 300 of another type erroneously delivered by the United States Government in October 1957 in compliance with a Cuban Government purchase order of December 1956. One of these planes was furnished with sufficient fuel to return to its base.

Allegations that the Cuban Armed Forces are using the Base for their military operations or as a source of fuel and arms supplies are completely unfounded.[2]

Cuban Air Force planes at the Guantánamo airstrip early in 1958, allegedly loading arms and ammunition for the Batista government. Beneath the rear of the truck, unfortunately in shadow and therefore legible only in an enlargement of the photograph, hangs a sign bearing the words "Keep distance."

Page from requisition book of the Guantánamo naval station, dated 8 May 1958 and detailing war matériel "for pick-up by Cuban navy."

NSD, Guantanamo Bay, Cuba, Accountable activity for
CO, NS, Navy No. 11.., c/o F..., New York, N.Y.

R̶E̶Q̶N̶. NO. 325263-58

CASE NO. Cuba - 64

**Material to be issued on a reimbursable basis at a total cost of $6,450.00
as follows:**   Items:
        1. $5,190.00
        2.  1,260.00

Invoice in APA (52000) to NSD, Bayonne, N.J., and enter difference between
reimbursable price and book price as "Accounting Adjustment" under "Fiscal Gains"
or "Fiscal Losses," as appropriate.

Insert the following on transfer invoices: "For ultimate charge to Appropriation
17-11X8242.87, AMSAE     , Allotment    138/87005    , Expenditure Account 93048
and credit to Appropriation 17X1710.83·, POAN 1958 Program    Ammunition         .
Expenditure Account 98021.

Packing and handling costs are chargeable to the quarterly program 74 allotment
under Appropriation 17-118/91080.001, MAE. Request packing, crating and
handling allotment from BuSanda (Code F-6) in the event that a regular allotment
is not available.  Proper refund to MAP Appropriation 17-118/91080.001, MAE and
charge to Appropriation 17-11X8242.87, AMSAE     , will be effected by
NSD, Bayonne, N.J.  in accordance with separate instructions furnished that
activity.

~~Material may not be shipped to ultimate customer in commercial vehicle of trucks~~
Transportation is chargeable to Appropriation 17X4910.89, NMr 1958,
Allotment 58001, Expenditure Account (93511) 98003, for ultimate charge to MAP.

   NSD, Bayonne, N.J.

Take up the value of material in APA (52000) as a Transfer from Other Supply Officers.
Expend from APA (52000) on Invoice as a cost charge only to Appropriation 17X1710.83 ,
POAN 1958 Program   Ammunition    , Expenditure Account 98021.  Insert the following
on Expenditure Invoices: "For ultimate charge to Appropriation _____
17-11X8242.87, AMSAE    , Allotment  138/87005    , Expenditure Account 93048 ,
and credit to Appropriation 17X1710. 83 , POAN 1958 , Program   Ammunition    ,
Expenditure Account 98021.

Prepare Standard Form 98021 to reimburse Appropriation 17X1710.83     , POAN  1958
Program  Ammunition     , Expenditure Account 98021 and charge the MAP appropriation
cited on transfer and expenditure invoices.

Case No.  Cuba - 64    and Shipment Order No.    325263-58           should be
referenced on all correspondence and accounting documents pertaining to this
transactions.

Page from account book of the Guantánamo naval station giving instructions for invoices and
other details concerning war matériel for the Cuban government.

Not surprisingly, the State Department's denial did little but lend credibility to the rebels' allegations. The photos spurred Raúl Castro to undertake a mass kidnapping of American citizens in various parts of Oriente during the last days of June and the beginning of July. It is interesting to note that the State Department release of July 3 made no mention of the kidnappings, which were already in progress. As researcher Jay Mallin has pointed out, "Raúl Castro was able to indulge his delight in irritating the United States. He kidnapped Americans. He turned the water supply for the U.S. base at Guantánamo on and off. . . . He attacked the American owned Nicaro nickel works. . . . In effect, Raúl was leading the rebel movement into an increasingly anti-American position."[3] U.S. Consul Park Wollam traveled to rebel-held territory and entered into negotiations with Raúl Castro for the release of the kidnapped Americans, thus granting the Castro movement official recognition ordinarily reserved for duly constituted powers.[4]

The violent anti-Americanism suddenly exhibited by the Castro forces, expressed in words and even more eloquently in deeds, should have been a clear sign that the movement felt the time was ripe to demonstrate the radical turn it had taken. Yet the American government, most of the American news media, and the great mass of Cuban moderates who made the revolution run failed to grasp its ominous significance. Anti-Americanism was endemic in Latin America, and the original image of a democratic revolution and a democratic Castro had been so firmly engraved at the beginning that this evidence to the contrary was not sufficient to erase it.

By July it was almost a foregone conclusion that the revolutionary push was covering the last furlongs of the road to victory. The few who up to this point had remained cool or suspicious of Castro and his forces, among them politicians and leaders of other anti-Batista organizations, now were eager to get on the bandwagon. I was ready at last to get off it. On July 16, when five weeks had passed with no acknowledgment from Cuba, I addressed a letter to the Dirección Nacional which began: "I hereby advise you of my irrevocable decision to resign as chairman and as member of the Committee in Exile as of the above date." I briefly summarized the reasons I had given in detail to Castro in my memorandum of June 10. Somewhere in the text I suggested that I expected to continue as a rank-and-file member of the 26 of July Movement, but I was only indulging in polite rhetoric. The truth is that I did not. When the letter was finished I was filled with a wonderful sense of relief beyond anything I had anticipated. I realized that my separation from the Castro movement was total and absolute. I even began to wonder if I had ever truly been a part of it.

I sent signed copies of my resignation to Cuba through two different channels, one of them in care of Haydée Santamaría. As communications were subject to frequent delays, I allowed four weeks for it to reach its destination before making it public.[5] On August 13 I drafted my last press release as the authorized spokesman for the 26 of July Movement outside of Cuba and sent copies to the news agencies, networks, and newspapers with which I had maintained contact. The next day the *New York Times* printed it with comments. The *Diario Las Américas* of Miami made the news of my leaving the Castro organization the lead item on its front page. Thus ended my association with Castro and Castroism.

Through the years I have often reflected on the motives and expectations that led me into such incompatible company as Castro's. Those who came to solicit my cooperation told me that their intention was to try to prevent the development of anything that could be called, as it is now called, Castroism. In the abnormal situation created by Batista's coup in 1952, Castro's determination and audacity could be put to good use under the discipline of a written ideological and programmatic contract, so to speak. I provided the "contract," *Nuestra Razón,* but Castro never adjusted himself to its guidelines and it had no influence on the political philosophy or the final orientation of the movement.

Yet, did the theory itself actually fail? Not necessarily; the leader did accommodate himself to the requirements of a specific ideological program, and its advocates succeeded in using his unusual human potential and his tremendous capacity for persuasion and action. There was simply a shift in ideologies and allegiances. Somewhere along the way, the democratic charter of the presumably moderate revolution was quietly discarded, and the Marxist-Leninist plan that the leaders had kept hidden was brought out and put in operation instead. At the Sierra Maestra meeting in

NEW YORK TIMES, TH

# LLERENA LEAVES CASTRO UNIT HERE

---

Cuban Exile Resigns as Head
of Rebel Committee—
New Leaders Named

---

Dr. Mario Llerena, a Cuban exile, announced here yesterday his resignation as chairman and director of public relations of the Committee in Exile of the 26th of July Movement.

The committee is an organization of supporters outside Cuba of Fidel Castro, the Cuban rebel leader.

Dr. Llerena indicated that he had presented his resignation to the Cuban rebel leadership some months ago and that he had insisted July 16, after some discussion, that it be accepted.

He said he still held the ideals that led to his cooperation with the 26th of July Movement. But he added that he wished publicly to recover, in every way, his political independence.

First paragraphs of an item in the *New York Times* of 14 August 1958.

March 1958 a group of men with ideological commitments called to account an errant Castro who had shown disconcerting signs of political deviation, and the Horse obeyed the tug of the reins.

So there was a contract, after all. It was a marriage of convenience by which Castro declared himself a Communist and the Communists agreed to grant him endless power. Without Castro, the Communists could never have dreamed of a day when they would rule Cuba, let alone make the island a Soviet base; without the Communists, Castro would have become perhaps a revised version of Batista—for a time—but never the uncontested doctrinal dictator, with international influence besides, that he now is. The offspring of this union has been Castroism, a cross of personal, charismatic dictatorship and rigid, collective totalitarianism. One is tempted to call it Stalinism in Caribbean clothing. But the resemblance is only superficial. Stalin emerged from within the system, fully trained and indoctrinated, after having outdone others in the internecine power politics of the Kremlin; Castro came from outside the Red elite and had to start as a beginner.[6]

Castroism is in essence negative. It is based on a series of negative propositions: that freedom leads to decadence; that democracy is ineffective and ends in corruption; that the Cuban people are incapable of sound political judgment and therefore need a dictatorship; that the United States is an imperialistic monster and so must perpetually be regarded as an enemy. (These characteristics, especially the last one, fitted perfectly into the long-range world strategy of the Soviet Union, which soon became the protective stepmother of Castroism.)

This hybrid revolutionary creature was born out of deplorable Cuban circumstances and prospered in the resulting psychological climate. Its development and ultimate triumph resulted less from any intrinsic merits or particular message than from the moral deterioration of the existing political system. This condition had been worsened by the Batista coup of 10 March 1952, which killed the last chances of Cuban democracy to cure its own ills and thus invited revolutionary solutions. Attempts at overthrowing the illegitimate government were made, and insurgent movements and organizations sprouted profusely. Unfortunately, all proved to be too weak or too inconsistent to galvanize the people and deal effectively with the problem. They lacked, among other things, the magnetic force of capable leadership.

Then along came the strong-willed, charismatic caudillo. All he had to do was climb to the top of a mountain and manage to stay there long enough. After a while, he became the living symbol of national redemption. Once this image was worked out and sufficiently impressed on the people's minds—thanks to the combined action of public relations and the news media—the rest was only a matter of time. When victory finally came, it was not the result of any superiority of the rebel forces over the regular army. Rather, the psychological pressure generated by the image caused the official power to become demoralized and to disintegrate.

How did the Cuban people take to the whole Castroist phenomenon? The rich, who as a rule made a practice of getting along with the status quo, were traditionally made apprehensive by any revolutionary movement. Still, some, dazzled by the early promises of this revolution, became ardent Castro supporters. The poor too, for entirely different reasons, tried to get along with whoever was in power (once Batista was out, the poor came over en masse to Castro's side). It was the middle class that constituted the basic human reservoir of the revolution—the activists, the soldiers, the bomb-planters, the providers, the fund-raisers, the agents, the delegates, and the swelling ranks of the ecstatic Castro worshipers. The moderate middle class, in short, was the soul and muscle of the revolutionary effort. How did these people react to the conversion of their moderate revolution to a radical one? There was no special reaction. They simply failed to notice the ideological sleight of hand that had been performed before their eyes. Even if they had noticed it, their red-hot enthusiasm would probably have blinded most of them to ideological niceties, anyway. So, without realizing it, the middle class was actually used as the disposable booster of the camouflaged Communist rocket until it reached its planned orbit in power.[7] Then there was no longer need for a middle class.

What happened to the middle class as a segment of society took place also on an individual level. My own personal experience is a case in point. As a political commentator in the press (especially in *Bohemia*, the tremendously influential magazine of the 1940s and 1950s), I was often severely critical of the ills and inconsistencies, political and otherwise, of Cuban society. Later, as an active member of the 26 of July Movement, I once advocated a "revolutionary" provisional government in preference to a nonpartisan one. Could the Castro people have misread my true position all along and thought they saw in me a potential radical? I have frequently wondered about this. There were many intellectuals and influential citizens in general who, stirred by Castro's determination to overthrow Batista and seduced by the apparently moderate tone of the revolution, became active in the 26 of July Movement, and were thereupon used. Most of these people rendered the movement a double service: in addition to whatever they did, they brought with them the prestige attached to their names. This was in fact what the movement primarily sought and needed from them. It was extremely valuable—not to say indispensable—especially at the beginning, for it helped in great measure to neutralize and finally dispel the early image of the Castro group as a pistol-packing gang of hotheaded adventurers. Indeed, the involvement of that select minority opened for the movement—and for Castro in particular—the door of public acceptance. There can be no doubt about this.

After the revolution unveiled its Marxist-Leninist designs, a few moderates turned opportunist and jumped on the bandwagon; but most, when they finally realized what had taken place, began to cry foul, claiming that the revolution had been betrayed. So originated the concept of the "betrayed revolution," which became a bitter lament among disappointed Cubans. The expression might be, perhaps, semantically questionable. It all depends on what meaning one assigns to the term "revolution." From a moderate standpoint, the Cuban revolution amounted basically to the ethical reform of public life, complemented by a series of vaguely defined socioeconomic and educational reforms. The 1940 Constitution would need very little revision, if any; the popular clamor was for the restoration of the 1940 Constitution, not for its substitution. No major change was contemplated in the fundamental democratic structure of society, much less its transformation into a totalitarian order.

It is in this sense that the idea of a "betrayed revolution" acquires a ring of ethical legitimacy. For in taking advantage of massive popular support while conspiring to make Cuba a Communist satellite, Castro and his close associates did commit an act of treason—not only against the middle class that credulously carried them to power but against Cuba's historical legacy as well.

The radical nature of the revolution, therefore, passed unsuspected until it dropped its mask once it was in power. The mask was dropped only after an apparent majority of Cubans seemed ready to accept anything. Their euphoria at the fall of Batista, immensely increased by the legend of gallantry and pious zeal of the bearded liberator (his *barbudos* descended from the mountains with religious medals and rosaries around their necks), was incredible. When they began to awake from their trance, the totalitarian machinery was already assembled and everything was under control.

In the process, however, it became evident that Castroism, the Cuban variant of the radical revolution, is organically dependent on personality—the unique Castro personality. Whether Castroism could function without Castro remains to be seen. After nearly twenty years of unlimited power, the experiment seems to prove beyond the shadow of a doubt that Castroism is incapable of standing on its own feet—it must permanently depend on massive So- viet support—and that it has completely failed to realize the basic double commitment of the moderate revolution it betrayed and supplanted, namely, the spiritual and material welfare of the Cuban people. On the contrary, it has taken away their dignity and their freedom and it has lowered their standard of living.

# Epilogue

**A**fter my resignation I intended to remain in the United States indefinitely. I was convinced that Batista's fall was very close at hand, but I had no wish to be in Cuba to witness Castro's ascent to power.

Five months later Batista fled. Not long after Castro's triumphant arrival in Havana, I got an unexpected call from Raúl Fernández Ceballos, the restless Presbyterian pastor turned revolutionary. He inquired about my immediate plans, and I told him I expected to stay where I was. No, he said, I should come back to Cuba as soon as possible. My presence was necessary there, if only to contribute my views during the first stages of the new situation. He said he was in close contact with Marcelo Fernández, Faustino Pérez, Enrique Oltusky, and other old friends who now figured prominently in the new Urrutia government, and all agreed I should be there.

I was pleased, of course, but not persuaded. Then the Reverend tried a different approach. He said I should be in Cuba to face any misunderstanding that might arise concerning my unexpected resignation from the Committee in Exile; my absence would only serve to add credibility to the allegations of those who had already tried to discredit me.

That did the trick. I decided that I would go back to Cuba, after all. I knew I could go back to my old journalistic vocation. Through the printed word I would be doing the same thing I had done for years before the revolution. It was the beginning of 1959.

Urrutia was provisional president, pending elections. Miró Cardona was prime minister. Faustino, Hart, and other *fidelistas* occupied cabinet posts, but so did Agramonte and a number of other respected members of traditional parties. Bisbé was ambassador to the UN. This was no radical government. Perhaps my writings could help to keep it on a moderate course.

*Bohemia* welcomed me to its staff. So did *Diario Nacional,* one of Havana's newspapers, where I started a daily column. For a month or two all seemed to go well. As I had done in the past, I wrote mostly on political, cultural, and educational subjects. As the weeks passed I found much to criticize, but I avoided going into details regarding the recently established Castro regime. I meant to deal with principles and ideas in wide perspective and let readers draw their own conclusions. If the shoe happened to fit someone, so be it.

The first reader to react was Fidel Castro. On March 6, during an interview broadcast live at noon on CMQ-TV, he opened fire on me. He had begun to see enemies everywhere, and now he resurrected the old canard of my "presidential ambitions." It was a fiery, angry Castro, quite the opposite of the gentle, friendly fellow who had spoken with me by radio when I visited Caracas. He did not discuss anything I had said or even mention my name, but his detailed description left no doubt about the identity of the blackguard he was referring to. In case some dullard missed the point, however, my name was added in parentheses in the transcript published the next day in the official organ, *Revolución.*

That was the signal from the chief. Immediately Castro hatchet men—some I had never heard of—followed course from all sides. Columnists, radio and TV commentators, even cartoonists pictured me as one of the many "enemies of the revolution." For the first time in my life I found myself subjected to public slander and ridicule.

It was not a new method, of course. As I said in one of my articles, it had already been tried in Czechoslovakia when President Eduard Beneš was forced to resign. They would not respond to ideas with ideas, they would not refute, they would not argue: they would only try to defame and destroy the *person.* Castro personally attacked me in that manner at least once more. In one of his interminable monologues on television (he frequently spoke for five or six hours), he set aside half an hour or so to make me the target of his biting comments and diatribes. The catalyst was a lengthy article of mine which was to appear the following day in *Bohemia;* its title: "Democracy and Totalitarianism."

This kind of thing went on week after week. Mine was not, of course, the only case. All writers, teachers, and intellectuals in general who refused to renounce their freedom of thought suffered the same fate. Newspapers were taken over by the government one by one. So was *Bohemia.* When *Diario Nacional* was taken over, I shifted to *El Mundo,* then to *Prensa Libre. Prensa Libre* and *Diario de la Marina* were the last Cuban newspapers to stand up to Castro's power. After *Prensa Libre* (which literally means "free press") was occupied by the militia, there was nothing more I could do in Cuba.

During the year and a half that I managed to stay on the island, I witnessed firsthand the gradual, systematic communization of a traditionally freedom-loving country: the abolition of the political framework of democracy; the expropriation of businesses and enterprises; the occupation of all news media; the constant blare of propaganda and indoctrination; the kangaroo courts and the daily reports of executions; the organization of the citizens into militias and neighborhood vigilance committees. . . .

The most pitiable spectacle of all was the one offered by the deleterious effects of Castroism upon the minds of the people. This mixture of personal myth and Marxist theory succeeded in working the Cubans up to a delirium of revolutionary frenzy. It certainly was not a question of political or ideological discernment or of preferring one particular system to another, but rather of a human mass that suddenly became homogeneous and plastic in its wish to believe in the "maximum leader" and demonstrate its unconditional loyalty. All the frustrating experiences of the past with *caudillismo,* one-man rule, and police abuse were forgotten; so was the traditional concern for democratic procedures, constitutional government, and the rule of law. Instead, it was the old Cinderella story with an entirely new twist. Here Prince Charming promises to rescue the girl from all her miseries and give her a new, wonderful life. But once Cinderella falls in love with him, Prince Charming quickly restricts her freedom, orders her about, and subjects her to conditions a thousand times worse than any she has known before. And still Cinderella loves him.

This seemingly paradoxical aspect of the Cuban phenomenon is worthy of study and reflection. Perhaps if there had been less blind adulation and a little more political maturity among the Cuban people in the first critical months of Castro's regime, the hitherto hidden Communist conspiracy would not have dared to surface so openly and history would have taken quite a different course. As it was, the returns were far more abundant than the conspirators themselves had anticipated or were prepared to handle. There was only scanty, isolated resistance, and so they had precious time for mounting, oiling, and warming up the totalitarian machinery. The historical truth is that Castroism traveled to power not by way of a military victory or of a previously and sufficiently announced radical revolution but rather under the borrowed banner of a democratic, ethical reform movement, cheered on by a joyfully confused populace.

One must have lived through the phenomenon to grasp its full dimension and significance. Stickers saying "Thanks, Fidel" and "Fidel, this house is yours" were seen on most front doors. If you did not sing along with the general chorus, former acquaintances avoided you. When Fidel fulminated against someone from the television screen—as he came to do almost daily—crowds would take to the streets howling, "To the wall! To the wall!" President Urrutia, who had never belonged to the inner circle, made the mistake of complaining publicly of Communist infiltration in the bureaucracy, and Castro went on television to cover him with ignominious accusations, thus finishing his make-believe presidency. The same mob that the day before had been cheering Urrutia gathered now around the executive mansion to demand his head.

I, too, learned the taste of public vituperation. It was the price one had to pay for speaking one's own mind and not joining the screaming, frenzied parade of human lemmings marching on to their political suicide. I kept on writing my dissenting comments for as long as there was a newspaper that would publish them. By mid-1960, however, the last vestige of a free press had finally disappeared from the Cuban scene. It was replaced by a deafening crescendo of revolutionary propaganda. The atmosphere of incipient totalitarianism was thick and suffocating. I was never arrested or otherwise physically harassed, but friends in government positions confidentially advised me to leave the country while there was still time.

In June I returned once again to exile in the United States.

(Not long afterward, the spell beginning to fade, other Cubans would start to do the same by the hundreds of thousands.)

# Appendix A: Fidel Castro to the Junta de Liberación in Miami

To the Leaders of the Partido Revolucionario Cubano,
Partido del Pueblo Cubano,
Organización Auténtica,
Federación Estudiantil Universitaria,
Directorio Revolucionario,
Directorio Obrero Revolucionario:

A sense of moral and patriotic, even historic, obligation compels me to address this letter to you, motivated by facts and circumstances that have affected us deeply these past weeks, which in addition have been the most arduous and active since our landing in Cuba. For it was on Wednesday, November 20, a day when our forces were engaged in three actions within a period of just six hours (this gives an idea of the efforts and sacrifices that, without the slightest aid from other organizations, our men have to make here), that the surprising news and the document containing the principles, public and secret, of the Pact of Unity—which is said to have been signed in Miami by the 26 of July and the organizations to which I am addressing myself—were received here. As perhaps another irony of destiny, since what we need is arms, the arrival of these papers coincided with the strongest offensive so far launched against us by the tyranny.

The conditions in which we fight here make communications difficult. Nevertheless, the nature of this question—in which not only the prestige but also the historical raison d'être of the 26 of July have been put at stake—has made it necessary to gather the leaders of the organization together in the midst of the campaign to consider it.

We are fighting an enemy incomparably superior in numbers and in arms, and for a full year have been sustained only by that kind of dignity which comes from a cause one loves in all sincerity and is convinced is worth dying for. We have tasted the bitterness of being forgotten by those of our countrymen who, having all possible resources, have systematically (or should we say criminally?) refused to provide us with any help. Right in front of our eyes we have seen sacrifice in its purest and most selfless form, so many times experiencing the great sorrow of seeing our best comrades die, wondering which of those around us would be next to fall in new and inevitable holocausts without even getting to see the day of victory for which they fight so resolutely, with no aspiration or consolation but the hope that their sacrifice will not have been in vain.

Under these circumstances, you must agree that learning of a pact—so widely and deliberately publicized—that binds the future decisions of the Movement without their even having had the courtesy—not to speak of the moral obligation—of consulting its leaders and its soldiers has to be highly offensive and humiliating for all of us.

Acting in an incorrect manner always brings the worst consequences. This is something that should very carefully be kept in mind by those who consider themselves capable of such an arduous undertaking as overthrowing a tyranny and, even more difficult, succeeding in reorganizing the country after a revolutionary process.

The 26 of July Movement did not designate or authorize any delegation to discuss the above-mentioned agreements. It would not have refused to do so, however, had it been consulted on the matter. Our movement would have taken pains to send representatives with very definite instructions, realizing that it is something that bears so heavily on the activities, present and future, of our organization.

Instead, all we learned about contacts with some of those groups consisted of a report from Señor Léster Rodríguez, our delegate for military matters abroad, whose authorization is limited to this area exclusively. His report said: "In regard to Prío and the Directorio, I can tell you that I've had a number of meetings with them in order to coordinate plans of strictly military nature designed to arrive at the establishment of a Provisional Government respected and supported by the three groups. Logically, my proposition was for them to accept the Sierra Manifesto, which states that such government must be constituted in cooperation with the civic forces of the country. This brought on the first difficulty. When that commotion arose about the announced general strike (in Cuba), we called an emergency meeting. I proposed that we all act immediately with all resources at hand and try to decide the Cuban question once and for all. Prío said that he didn't have sufficient equipment to entertain any hope of victory, and that therefore it was crazy to accept my proposition. My answer was that he let me know as soon as he was ready to sail off, but meanwhile would he please let me carry on work within the 26 of July completely undisturbed. In consequence, there is absolutely no agreement with these gentlemen, and I don't think it advisable to have any in the future either. At a time when Cuba most needed their help, they refused to contribute the material they had—which has now been confiscated (by the authorities), and it is such a large amount that it moves one to indignation. . . ."

This report, which speaks for itself, confirmed our suspicion that we, the rebels, could not expect any kind of aid from those abroad.

If the organizations you represent had chosen to discuss articles of unity with some members of our Movement, such articles (which fundamentally affect the propositions subscribed to by us in the Sierra Maestra Manifesto) could by no means be given any publicity without previous consultation with and approval of the Dirección Nacional of our Movement. To act otherwise is to sign agreements just for publicity purposes, fraudulently invoking the name of our organization.

It so happened that when our Dirección Nacional, meeting secretly somewhere in Cuba, was preparing to reject the articles, both public and private, after having received them, it learned through clandestine publications and through the foreign press that they had already been made public as a mutual pact. The Dirección Nacional was thus confronted, before both national and international opinion, with an accomplished fact, finding itself in the position of having either to reject it, with all the ill and confusing consequences that would follow, or to accept it without even having expressed its own points of view on the matter. And, as anyone can logically guess, when those articles reached us here in the Sierra Maestra, the document had been known by the public for many days.

Faced with this dilemma, the Dirección Nacional—before proceeding to a public denial of those arguments—invited the Junta's consideration of a series of points taken from the Sierra Manifesto, and at the same time called a meeting in rebel territory in which the opinion of each member was weighed. There we arrived at the unanimous decision that has inspired this document.

Naturally, any accord for unity was inevitably to be welcomed by both national and international public opinion. Among other reasons, because abroad they do not know the real situation of the political and revolutionary forces opposing Batista, and in Cuba the word unity was enhanced with great prestige in days in which, mind you, the mutual relation of forces happened to be quite different from what it is today. And in any case because joining forces is always positive, whether enthusiastic or lukewarm.

For the revolution, however, what matters is not unity in itself but the principles on which it is founded, the way it is achieved, and the patriotic intentions that may inspire it.

To agree to such a pact of unity on the basis of principles we haven't even had a chance to discuss, to have it signed by persons who lacked the authorization to do so, and finally to give it publicity from the comfortable location of a foreign city, thus placing the Movement in the position of having to face people deceived by a fraudulent pact, is a dirty trick not deserved by a true revolutionary organization. That is deceiving the country and lying to the world.

And all that is possible only because of the simple fact that while the leaders of the other organizations signing that pact are abroad conducting an imaginary revolution, the leaders of the 26 of July Movement are in Cuba engaged in a revolution that is real.

These lines, however, could have been unnecessary; I would not have written them no matter how bitter and humiliating the procedure by which the Movement has been co-opted as a part of this pact. Discrepancies of form must never prevail over essentials. We would have accepted it anyway for the sake of all that is positive in unity, for what is worthwhile in certain plans conceived by the Junta, for all the help that has been offered us and which we so much need . . . were it not that we simply are in disagreement with some essential points of the articles.

No matter how desperate our situation may be, or how many thousand soldiers are sent against us by the Dictatorship in its present design to annihilate us (and even more earnestly since a condition becomes more onerous as circumstances become more demanding), we will never accept the sacrifice of certain principles that are cardinal to our understanding of the Cuban Revolution.

These principles are contained in the Sierra Maestra Manifesto.

To omit from the document of unity the express declaration that foreign intervention of any kind in the internal affairs of Cuba is rejected shows a very lukewarm kind of patriotism and unparalleled cowardice.

To say that we are opposed to intervention not only means to demand that it not be carried out in support of the revolution, as that would be a violation of our sovereignty and furthermore a diminution of a principle that affects all the peoples of the Hemisphere, but it means also to demand that there will be no intervention in support of the Dictatorship, as there has been by sending it planes, bombs, tanks, and modern equipment with which it keeps itself in power. This we and above all the peasant population of the Sierra Maestra know very well, as we have suffered the consequences in our own flesh. In short, if we succeed in barring intervention, the tyranny will be automatically defeated. Or are we such cowards that we won't even dare demand that there be no intervention on the side of Batista? Or so insincere as to solicit it ourselves underhandedly, to have others do what is our own and exclusive duty to do? Or so mediocre that we do not know how to say a word on the matter? How, then, can we call ourselves revolutionaries and, with claims of engaging in a historical act, sign such a document of unity?

The express declaration rejecting any type of Military Junta to take charge of the Provisional Government has been omitted from the document of unity.

Since it would come with the false illusion that Cuba's problem can be solved simply by the Dictator's absence, nothing could happen to the country at this moment so terrible as the replacement of Batista by a Military Junta. Such a solution, agreeable only to the country's enemies, is being considered by certain civilians of the most despicable kind, formerly associated with the 10 of March [Batista's regime] and separated from it today perhaps because they went even further in ambition and despotism.

If experience has proved that all military juntas in [Latin] America drift again in the direction of autocracy; if of all evils that have afflicted this Hemisphere the worst is the establishment of military castes in countries with fewer wars than Switzerland and more generals than Prussia; if one of the most legitimate aspirations of our people in this crucial hour—in which its democratic and republican destiny will be either saved or lost for many years— is to keep, as the most precious legacy from our founders, the civilian tradition that began with the Independence Revolution itself and will be broken the very day in which a junta of men in uniform take over the government of the republic (something that was never intended, either in war or in peace, by the most glorious generals of our independence); will we sink so low that, for fear of hurting someone's feelings (which is rather imaginary as far as those honest military men who might decide to support us is concerned), we would be ready to suppress such an important declaration of principles? Is it so difficult to understand that an opportune declaration could check in time the danger of a Military Junta, which could serve for nothing but to prolong the civil war? Let me tell you then that we are making it perfectly clear that, should a Military Junta take Batista's place, the 26 of July Movement will resolutely continue fighting its war of liberation. Better to have to fight longer today than to fall tomorrow into a new, unfathomable abyss. We will accept neither a Military Junta nor a puppet government in the hands of the military! The civilians are to govern with decency and honesty; the soldiers are to go to their barracks; and everybody is to do his duty!

Or are we perhaps waiting for the 10 of March generals, to whom Batista would gladly turn over the government (when he feels it can no longer be defended) as the most convenient way of assuring that change will do the least possible damage to his interests and those of his associates? How blinded can the Cuban politicians be by ignorance, absence of noble ideals, or just lack of a will to fight?

If you do not trust the people, if you do not have faith in their great reservoirs of strength and fighting spirit, you have no right to lay hands on their destiny just to twist it and turn it at precisely the most heroic and promising times of our history as a republic. Let not the ways of base politics, or the low ambitions of certain politicians, or their thirst for personal advancement, or their premature division of spoils meddle with the revolutionary process. It is for something better than that that men are dying in Cuba. Let the politicians become revolutionaries if they wish; but let them not turn the revolution into bastardly politics, for too much blood has been shed and too many sacrifices are being made by our people at this hour for them to be rewarded with such bitter frustrations in the days ahead!

In addition to these two fundamental principles that have been omitted from the document of unity, we are in total disagreement with still others of its aspects.

Even accepting clause B of secret article no. 2, referring to the powers of the Junta de Liberación, which says, "To name the President of the Republic who shall assume the office in the Provisional Government," we cannot accept clause C of the same article, which includes in those powers: "To approve or disapprove, in toto, the Cabinet designated by the President of the Republic and whatever changes may be made in it as a result of a total or partial crisis."

How can anyone conceive that the powers of the President to name and substitute his secretaries should be subject to the approval or disapproval of a body alien to the sphere of the State? Is it not clear that, as the Junta is composed of representatives of different parties and organizations, and therefore of different interests, the designation of the members of the Cabinet would be turned into a distribution of positions as the only means of reaching agreement in every case? Can an article be accepted which implies the establishment of two executives within the State? The only guarantee that all segments of the country must demand from the Provisional Government is the limitation of its mission to a definite basic program; also that it will act as a moderating power during the period of transition toward complete constitutional normality.

An attempt to intervene in the designation of ministers implies intention of controlling the administration for the benefit of political interests. This is something that can be understood only in the case of parties or organizations lacking in popular support, which can survive only in the traditional atmosphere of petty politics. But such a situation is in contradiction to the political and revolutionary aspirations of the 26 of July Movement.

The mere existence of secret articles that refer not to aspects of the organization of the [military] campaign or plans of action, but rather to questions of such national concern as the structure of the future government—and which therefore should be openly proclaimed—is in itself unacceptable. Martí said that in revolution the methods are supposed to be secret, but the ends must always be public.[1]

Another point that is just as unacceptable to the 26 of July is secret article no. 8, which says: "The revolutionary forces, with their arms, shall be incorporated into the regular armed forces of the Republic."

In the first place, what is meant by "revolutionary forces"? Is an

ID card [identifying the bearer] as policeman, soldier, or marine to be given to anyone who comes out at the last hour with a gun in his hands? Will they be given uniforms and invested as representatives of authority who today have their arms stored away only to take them out on the day of victory, while doing nothing when a handful of their countrymen carry on against all the forces of the Dictatorship? Are we to include in a revolutionary document the very germ of gangsterism and anarchy that were a disgrace to the Republic in a not too distant past?[2]

In the territory under our control experience has taught us that keeping law and order is a matter of primary importance for the country. It has been demonstrated that as soon as the enforcement of order is relaxed, a number of problems appear, and crime, unless checked on the spot, springs up everywhere. The opportune application of severe measures, to the enthusiastic approval of the people, put an end to the upsurge of delinquency. It used to be that the neighbors, accustomed to seeing an enemy of the people in every officer of the law, offered protection and hospitality to those running away from justice. Today they see in our soldiers the defenders of their interests, and order prevails. The citizens themselves are the best law enforcers.

Anarchy is the worst enemy of a revolutionary process. It is absolutely necessary to start fighting it now. Anyone who refuses to see it this way does not care about the outcome of the revolution. Of course, those who have made no sacrifices do not care. The country must understand that there will be justice, but within the strictest order, and that crime will be punished, wherever it may be found.

The 26 of July Movement demands for itself the function of maintaining law and order and of reorganizing the armed forces of the Republic.

First, because it is the only organization having organized and disciplined militias throughout the country, as well as an army in the field with twenty victories over the enemy;

second, because our soldiers have shown a spirit of fairness free from any hatred of the military, respecting the lives of their prisoners, taking care of those wounded in action, never torturing an enemy, not even when they have learned that he is in possession of important information, and throughout the war have maintained this attitude with an equanimity that is without precedent;

third, because the Armed Forces must be permeated by that

spirit of justice and nobility which the 26 of July has cultivated in its own soldiers;

fourth, because the restraint with which we have acted throughout this campaign is the best guarantee that honest military men have nothing to fear from the Revolution, nor will they have to pay for the crimes of those who have dishonored their uniforms.

There still remain some other aspects of this document of unity which are difficult to understand. How can an accord be reached without a definite strategy of action? Are the Auténticos still considering the putsch in the Capital?[3] Will they continue to store away arms and more arms that sooner or later fall into the hands of the police, instead of passing them on to those who are doing the fighting? Has the position maintained by the 26 of July concerning the general strike finally been accepted?

As we see it, there has also been a deplorable underestimation of the importance, from a military point of view, of the campaign in Oriente Province. What is being fought now in the Sierra Maestra is not a guerrilla war but a war of battalions. Being inferior in numbers and equipment, our forces try to take maximum advantage of the terrain, keep a constant watch over the enemy, and achieve greater speed of movement. No need to say that the question of morale has tremendous importance in this kind of war. The results have been astonishing—and will someday be known in their every detail.

The entire population is in revolt. If there were arms, our men would not have to worry about patrolling any district. The peasants would not let one single enemy soldier pass. The Dictatorship, which is obsessed with dispatching heavy forces, might suffer disastrous defeats. Nothing that I could tell you about the bravery that has been awakened in our people would be enough. The Dictatorship takes barbarous reprisals. The mass murder of peasants compares easily with those the Nazis perpetrated in any European country. The war bulletins from the general staff announcing rebel casualties are invariably preceded by a massacre. For each defeat they take revenge on the defenseless population. This has put the people in a state of absolute rebellion. What has hurt, what has made our soul bleed many a time is the realization that nobody has sent these people one single gun, that while the peasants here, begging desperately for arms, see their houses burned down and their families murdered, there are caches of arms in Cuba which are not used to kill even one miserable cop, and time is permitted to pass until the police capture them, or the Dictatorship is overthrown, or the rebels are exterminated.

There are some among our countrymen whose attitude could not be meaner. But they still have time to make amends and try to help those who are fighting. As for us personally, the question is unimportant; let no one worry that we may be moved by interest or pride. Our destiny has been decided already and no uncertainty can trouble us: either we die here to the last man while in the cities a whole young generation perishes, or we overcome even the most incredible difficulties. For us there is no longer any possibility of defeat. Nothing can take away the year of heroism and sacrifice that our men have gone through. Our victories are there, and nothing can cause them to be forgotten. Our men, firmer than ever, are prepared to fight till the last drop of blood. Defeat is for those who have denied us all assistance; for those who, having given us their word at the beginning, then left us alone; for those who, without regard for dignity or ideals, spent their time and their prestige in shameless dealings with Trujillo; for those who, having the arms, hid them away like cowards at the hour of action. They are the ones who are wrong—not we.

One thing we can assert with all certainty: had we seen other Cubans fighting for freedom, persecuted and about to be exterminated; had we seen them resist day after day without giving up or weakening in their attempt, we would not have hesitated one minute in going to their help and dying with them if necessary. For we are Cubans, and Cubans do not remain impassive when others are fighting for liberty—even if it is in a different American country. Do the Dominicans gather on some islet with the intent of liberating their country? For each Dominican, ten Cubans assemble. Do Somoza's henchmen invade Costa Rica? There go the Cubans to fight. How can it be, then, that now that a most arduous struggle for liberty is taking place in our own country there are Cubans in exile, driven from their native land by tyranny, who deny help to their fellow Cubans who are fighting?

Or is it that their help is subject to onerous conditions? Is it that in order to count on their help we have to offer them the entire Republic as a prize? Is it that in order for them to help us we have to give up our ideals and turn this war into just a new art of killing our neighbor, a useless bloodshed that may not bring the motherland the reward she expects from so much sacrifice?

The leadership of the struggle against the tyranny is and will continue to be in Cuba—in the hands of the revolutionary fighters. Those who, now and in the future, may wish to be regarded as leaders of the Revolution should be in the country, directly facing the responsibilities, risks, and sacrifices that the present situation demands.

The exiles must cooperate in this struggle. But it is rather absurd that we should be told from abroad which hill we must take, what sabotage we are to carry out, or the time, circumstances, and manner in which we can unleash the general strike. It is not only absurd but ridiculous. Help can be provided from there—raising funds among the Cuban exiles and émigrés, campaigning for the Cuban cause in the press and before public opinion, etc.; the crimes of which we are victims here can also be denounced from there. But let nobody try to conduct from Miami a revolution that is being carried out in every town and hamlet throughout the island, with fighting, agitation, sabotage, strikes, and the thousand other ways of revolutionary action that are included in the strategy of the 26 of July Movement.

The Dirección Nacional is ready, as it has repeatedly stated, to confer in Cuba with the leaders of any opposition group in order to coordinate specific plans and produce concrete forms of action that may contribute to the overthrow of the tyranny. The general strike will be carried out through the effective coordination of the Civic Resistance Movement, the National Labor Front, and any other group free from political partisanship,[4] all in close contact with the 26 of July Movement, which so far is the only opposition group in a combatant position throughout the country.

The labor section of the 26 of July is active in the organization of strike committees in every labor and industrial center. These committees are to be integrated with opposition elements of all shades as long as they support the strike and are disposed to cooperate. The aggregation of these committees will result in the National Labor Front, which will be the only representation of the workers recognized as legitimate by the 26 of July.

The overthrow of the dictator will mean the disbanding of the present spurious Congress, the executive committee of the CTC [Confederación de Trabajadores de Cuba], and all mayors, governors, and other officials who directly or indirectly owe their positions to the false elections of 1 November 1954 or to the military coup of 10 March 1952. It will also mean the immediate release of all political prisoners, both civilian and military, and the prosecu-

tion of individuals responsible for crimes or any kind of wrongdoing in complicity with the tyranny.

The new government will conform to the 1940 Constitution. It
will guarantee all rights recognized by it and will be free from all
political partisanship.

The executive branch will assume the legislative functions assigned to Congress by the Constitution, and its main task will be to
prepare the country for a general election under the 1943 Electoral
Code and the 1940 Constitution. It will also develop the basic ten-
point program put forth in the Sierra Manifesto.

The Supreme Court shall be dissolved: it was incapable of facing
the antijuridical situation created by the coup d'état. Some of its
present judges may be reinstated later, provided they have defended the constitutional principles or maintained a firm attitude
against crime, wrongdoing, and abuse of power during these years
of tyranny.

The President of the Republic will decide how the new Supreme
Court shall be constituted. The Court will then proceed to reorganize all the courts and autonomous bodies, dismissing from their
positions all those who are found to have been in manifest complicity with the Dictatorship, at the same time starting prosecution
in all cases that so require. The new officials will be designated according to what the law prescribes in each case.

During the provisional period, political parties will have but one
right: freedom to expound their programs and to campaign and organize within the ample scope of our Constitution, as well as to
participate in the general elections that will be called.

The need to designate a person to occupy the office of President
of the Republic was already expressed by us in the Sierra Maestra
Manifesto. It was the opinion of our movement then that this person ought to be chosen by the Civic Institutions. As five months
have passed without that step having been taken, and it has become more and more urgent that the country know who is going to
succeed the Dictator—and this question cannot remain unanswered any longer—the 26 of July Movement issues its own answer and presents it to the people as the only formula capable of
guaranteeing legality and the fulfillment of the preceding articles
of unity and of the Provisional Government itself. That person
must be Judge Manuel Urrutia Lleó, of the Provincial Court of
Oriente.

The reasons for this decision are the following:

1. He is the member of the judiciary who has rendered the highest honor to the Constitution. Sitting on the bench during the case against the Granma invaders, he declared that it was not unlawful to organize armed rebellion against the regime, but rather perfectly legal according to the spirit and the letter of the Constitution and the Law. This attitude on the part of a judge has no precedent in the history of our struggles for liberty.

2. His lifelong dedication to the honest administration of justice gives assurance that he has sufficient experience and character to serve as a harmonizing factor among all legitimate interests when the tyranny is overthrown by the action of the people.

3. None is so free from political partisanship as Dr. Manuel Urrutia. His position as member of the judiciary bars him from belonging to any political organization, and there is no other citizen with his prestige who, without partisanship, has sympathized so much with the revolutionary cause.

In addition, the fact that Dr. Urrutia is a judge makes this formula the nearest to the constitutional procedure.[5]

If our conditions—the disinterested conditions of an organization that has gone further than any other in sacrifices and which was not even consulted when its name was used to sign a unity manifesto that it had not approved—are rejected, we will keep on fighting as we have done so far, with no other help than that of the suffering people and no other support than that of our own ideals.

In the last analysis, after all, the truth is that the one organization that has maintained the whole country in a state of war is no other than the 26 of July Movement. The members of the 26 of July alone have taken the rebellion from the wild mountains of Oriente to the western provinces; only members of the 26 of July Movement are carrying out sabotage, implementing executions of policemen, putting the torch to the cane fields, and carrying out many other revolutionary actions; it was also the 26 of July Movement that was able to organize the workers for revolution throughout the country;[6] the 26 of July is also the only organization capable of carrying out the strategy of the general strike; the 26 of July was the only organization to contribute to the formation of the Civic Resistance Movement, in which the civic groups of almost all communities in Cuba are joined.

There may be those who think it arrogant to say all this. But it happens that the 26 of July Movement has also been the one organization that has declared it does not wish to participate in the

Provisional Government and that it is ready to give all its moral and material support to the qualified citizen who will take charge [of the executive office] during the necessary provisional period.

Be it clearly understood that we decline to accept bureaucratic positions or participation in the Government. But let it also be known, once and for all, that the members of the 26 of July Movement do not renounce and will never renounce—from the Sierra Maestra down to the underground and to the graves where our dead are in command—the right to provide leadership and guidance for the people. And renounce we do not because it is not we but a whole generation that with the Cuban people has the moral debt of finding substantial solutions to their great problems.

We are prepared to win or die all by ourselves. The struggle will never be so arduous as when we were just twelve men, when we did not yet have the support of the brave and organized people who are now behind us here in the Sierra, when we did not have, as we do today, a powerful and disciplined organization in every part of the country, when we did not have such massive support as became evident at the death of our unforgettable Frank País.

To fall with dignity no company is necessary.

For the Dirección Nacional of the 26 of July Movement

FIDEL CASTRO R.

Sierra Maestra, 14 December 1957

# Appendix B: Fidel Castro to
## Mario Llerena and Raúl Chibás

Sierra Maestra, 26 April 1958

Dear Friends:

I had already thought of writing you this letter when I heard on the radio that you had left for Venezuela with Dr. Urrutia. Anyhow, the bearer has been instructed to find you wherever you may be.

I imagine you are worried about the adverse outcomes of these latest events.[1] I hope getting news from us will bring you some reassurance. Even though the strike failed, we have made numerous gains in the military field and our position is now stronger. But the Dictatorship has recovered some of its morale and is getting ready to come after us with all its might. All indications are that the attack will be directed against the area of this unit. There is no doubt that our situation is far better today than in the days when you, Raúl, were here with us.[2] You'd be amazed if you could see how we have progressed in all respects. The bearer could tell you a lot about it. I have only one bitter complaint—not about anything that concerns me personally but because of the consequences of the matter. It is that the Movement has failed completely in its duty to keep us supplied. To the selfishness and at times even trickery of other organizations[3] we have to add the incapability, the negligence, even the disloyalty of some of our own comrades.[4] Our organization abroad has not been able to send us one single rifle, one single cartridge.[5] The only thing that's been received here, a few weeks ago, was something that we ourselves arranged and paid for. From Cape Cruz to Santiago de Cuba, from Mayarí to Baracoa, from Cauto to Victoria de las Tunas, the territory [Oriente Province] is totally under the control of our units. Nevertheless, there is still a lot of fighting to go through. Many brave fellow soldiers have died and are dying every day. The last one was Ciro Frías, a gallant captain of our forces, victorious in several encounters, a peasant boy of exceptional character. He was one of the first to join us; was killed in action in Imías, in Baracoa territory. Sometimes I get the feeling that we are going to lose our best soldiers one by one. I carry these things deep inside me, and the realization that very few share this sorrow fills me with distress. It wouldn't be this way if all the rivalries, jealousies, and differences among our comrades which have impeded the arms supply had disappeared. How is the expenditure of approximately $200,000 going to be justified without our having received one single weapon?

Moral considerations aside, however, the fact remains that once again it falls to us to save the revolution in one of its gravest crises. The threat of a military coup looms again after the failure of the strike. It is a recurrence of the idea that only the military can overthrow dictatorships—in the same way that they also set them up and subject the people to the fate of military dependence. The rejection of this notion must be made a permanent objective in a policy for Latin America to be adopted by the Cuban Revolution as a reaffirmation of the rights and sovereignty of the peoples. The strike turned out badly not only because of lack of organization but also because armed action is not yet strong enough. The explanation is that we have to fight only with the weapons we can seize from a well-equipped enemy at a painful cost in lives. If there were rebel units operating all over the island, as there are in Oriente, no measure would be drastic enough to repress the action of the people, and the strike itself would become the inevitable consequence of the paralysis of the country by the action of the war. No government will ever be able to withstand the total and indefinite disruption of its communications system, just as no living organism can survive the cutting off of its arteries. This objective could have been accomplished if only a few hundred guns had been sent to us. This, by the way, would be a task incomparably easier than introducing them clandestinely, since we have under our control large areas totally occupied where planes can land and take off, or drop the weapons by parachute, without a single one being lost. How then to explain the fact that our organization [abroad] has not been able to send us that kind of help?

Now the [Batista] regime, with a proper strategy, will surely try to crush us. Only they don't seem too sure they can do it, as is shown by certain peace feelers than I have rejected and will continue to reject, not only emphatically but even proudly—a thousand times more so after the fiasco [of the strike]. I am one of those men who feel far more spirited in the difficult times than when victory seems to be around the corner.

It is imperative to strengthen the revolution in its military aspect. For the time being, let's not even talk about a general strike. The strike, or rather the paralysis of the country, will be a natural consequence of the revolutionary military campaign—and they won't be able to hinder it by printing the newspapers elsewhere, or with mobile radio units, etc. The Dictatorship, which has powerful forces at its disposal to counteract the strike, has none against the military forces of the revolution.

This view has already been accepted by the majority of the comrades in the Dirección Nacional, and no doubt it will also be the opinion of those whom I haven't yet consulted.

As a first step, we have decided to assume ourselves the task of arms supply. To that end I have appointed comrade Ricardo Lorié[6] to take charge of this business under my personal instructions. Through this same channel I am advising him to get in touch with you immediately. Haydée Santamaría, too, will go abroad to help the comrades there in the coordination of their work. Our delegate has been briefed about all means and facilities for the fulfillment of his mission. In addition to the funds we shall be sending him from here, which we expect to reach over $100,000 in two months, it is necessary to put in his hands *absolutely all the financial resources that can be obtained there*. That money should not come solely from private sources. You must try to get aid from [the governments of] some of the Latin American countries. The Committee in Exile must devote itself to this task with the assurance that here lies victory.

Bebo H.[7] will continue his mission of supplying the militias in the way he has arranged and with the funds that will be assigned to him as the opportunity arises.

There is yet another decision that has been definitely made. We consider this to be an opportune moment for the establishment of the Revolutionary Provisional Government. What would perhaps have seemed inexpedient at some other time will now have a wonderful psychological impact on both national and international public opinion, precisely because it is a reaffirmation of faith in the midst of reverses which will also raise the fighting spirit. When the Dictatorship claims that we are defeated, we respond by announcing to the world the establishment of the Revolutionary Provisional

Government in the free territory of Cuba. Such a government will have a great task to perform now. There is today enough territory under our control to require administrative organization and important legal measures. We have a radio station with an extraordinary rating outside Cuba. There is a possibility of obtaining the recognition of some countries. For all this we need the cooperation of Dr. Urrutia.

Once the government has been established, we shall take gradual steps to win the support of other [opposition] groups. Then we shall have unity in its ideal and active form—through the Revolutionary Provisional Government of the Republic of Cuba.[8] But this cannot be announced prematurely, for it would throw us back in the middle of the same old perennial disputes. It's got to be accomplished as we move along.

Dr. Urrutia could arrive directly in our territory, be proclaimed President, set up a Council of Ministers, and proceed to name diplomatic representatives abroad. With some of the judges who resigned[9] or are being subjected to proceedings, he could organize the Supreme Court. We can guarantee the Government a permanent and safe territory, with facilities you probably wouldn't expect in these mountains for the performance of its functions. This proposition has the support of all the members of the Dirección Nacional; the rest depends only on Dr. Urrutia. It is something that he must consider and decide, with the absolute assurance that, should his decision be negative, our consideration [for him] and our endorsement will in no way be changed. This is a question so delicate that I would advise exploring his feelings before presenting the proposal to him, and if he doesn't go along with this point of view, just leave it there.

I must close. Let me add only that from Costa Rica or Venezuela (for better communication you can visit Radio Continente in Caracas) it is easy to make daily contact with us at 5 P.M. and 9 P.M. on the 20-meter band. The pilots have a code.[10] It would give me extraordinary pleasure to exchange a word with you sometime. I am quartered near our [radio] plant. Maybe we could get in touch through Miami too.

Our most fraternal *abrazo* for you and Dr. Urrutia.

FIDEL CASTRO R.

# Appendix C: *Nuestra Razón*

## Manifesto-Program of the 26 of July Movement

This document is published in the midst of the battle's roar. As the vanguard of the Revolution, the 26 of July Movement fights on all fronts against the mercenary forces of the Dictatorship.

High on the unconquered peaks of the Sierra Maestra, Fidel Castro, with an outpost of Cuban youth, is writing a real epic of patriotism and glory.

There appears to be an inversion of terms at this stage of the Cuban revolution: action has come before the exposition and development of ideas.

But it is not really so. The ideas on which this struggle is based have existed in the conscience of the Cuban people ever since the beginning of a national sentiment. They are the same ideas that inspired our wars of independence and later achieved pure and complete expression in the political thinking of José Martí.

The ideological source of the 26 of July Movement is Martí.

Yet it has become necessary now to gather into some kind of programmatic manifesto those old ideas of Martí's and raise them as living thought against the dramatic present of Cuba.

Such is the purpose of this document.

It does not presume to be definitive, nor, of course, does it hope to exhaust all aspects and details of a future government platform. But it does present the general guidelines of our struggle as well as the basic objectives of the Revolution.

As shall be seen, it is a manifesto that indicates causes and directions. The 26 of July Movement has in preparation other documents that deal in full with economic, educational, and agrarian questions, and with such other questions as must inevitably be included in any serious and complete program of national policy. These documents will soon be presented to the Cuban people and the judgment of the whole hemisphere.

Meanwhile, here is our card of introduction—our sincere and professed vow before the altar of the Motherland.

## 1. The Present
A Solemn Promise

The fundamental objective of the 26 of July Movement is the realization of the unfulfilled ideals of the Cuban nation. In that task it relies on the contribution and participation of the younger generation of Cubans, who are eager for new horizons in the chronic frustration of the Republic. Such is its credential and its distinctive mark.

In declaring itself torchbearer of the revolutionary generations of the past, the 26 of July Movement explains the reasons for its present struggle and the direction it is following on its way toward the future. That direction is one of national affirmation, human dignity and democratic order. We who belong to this movement are bound only by a solemn vow of our consciences as free men. We are moved neither by folly nor by inflexibility: only by a deep and reasoned conviction of the justice and necessity of the Revolution and by a blood-tested faith in the higher destiny of Cuba.

The Four Riders

That destiny has been broken today by an anti-Cuban and immoral power in which are concentrated all the vices and negative elements that have always worked against this nation's hope of being a land of freedom and dignity. The colonial mentality, foreign economic domination, political corruption, and military intemperance have come together, like the riders of the Apocalypse, to subject the country to a power machine of control and exploitation grotesquely disguised as a republican system.

The Defenseless Republic

But in fact the republic does not exist. These calamities, brought together as a by-product of a most ordinary form of one-man rule, prevent the functioning of the democratic system while subjecting the people to a deliberate and effective process of degradation. The failure of the most important means of public expression is quite evident. The political parties and the press in particular, with rare exceptions, have notoriously succumbed to the pressures or the subornation of power. Consumed by mediocrity, resignation, or cowardice, they have proved completely useless to the country in its difficult hour. Cuba has thus fallen into the condition of a defenseless private concession, entirely at the mercy of an armed band that grows fabulously rich while trading with the national patrimony as if it were a private commodity.

The March 10 coup has totally eradicated the rule of law. Sheer physical power (which could not even invent an ideological pretext) prevails over any law, judge, or court. Civil liberties are nothing but words, and the most fundamental rights of any civilized society—home, property, the physical and moral integrity of the individual, life itself—perish under the brutal foot of the "restrictive" corps. The abuses and tortures of the SIM, the Buró, any of the countless official agencies of hired thugs, the barracks, and the police stations throughout the island have no need to envy the torture chambers of the totalitarian regimes.

But to those crimes against civilization, against legal order, and against human dignity (with the consent and complicity of submissive courts) one must add those committed against the economic resources of the country. Those in power not only carry the plundering of the public treasury and the organized exploitation of vice and contraband to incredible extremes but also extend their claws to such vital centers as the National Bank, the pension funds, and the gold reserves of the country. The mountain of appropriations earmarked "for the armed forces," the tremendous increase in the public debt, the nickel concessions, the telephone monopoly, the secret oil concessions, the Isle of Pines concession and others, and the fantastic so-called Canal Vía-Cuba, all typify the irresponsibility of the band of brigands that, headed by Batista, seized power on 10 March 1952, and illustrate the irreparable damage they have already done to the present and future of the national economy.

The Youth Reserves

Only the younger generation of Cubans has stood without bending before that gale of horror and shame. This is highly significant. It confirms the imperative necessity of reform that this country is experiencing. Because of the failure of its civic defenses—the political parties with their leaders, the news media, and the courts—the younger generation has had to come forward and literally assume a combat position. With this authority, sealed with blood and with the lives of those comrades who have fallen in the struggle or have been executed by the henchmen of the dictatorship, we declare that nothing and nobody will make us shun the responsibility that has been passed to us, and that we shall be faithful to the ethics and program of the Revolution.

A True Revolution

Let it also be understood that what we have in mind is a true Revolution. We are not engaged in this struggle simply to expel from power those who illegally hold it or to acquiesce in a mere substitution of rulers. Nor will we facilitate a return to the corrupt situation that led to the tenth of March. We will not accept a protectorate in place of a sovereign country, no matter how it may be disguised, or a band of exploiters in place of a democracy. We aspire to something more than that: we want a true and deserving nation in the hemispheric community; we want honest and functional democracy; we want an independent productive economy.

We therefore cannot content ourselves with the childish consolation of words. We are working on a program of serious political, economic, agrarian, and educational reforms. We resolutely go to the roots of Cuba's problems: to the effective reorganization of its democratic system; to the application of technology as well as honesty to public administration; to a search for more appropriate ways of making use of our natural resources; to a just and scientific system of land distribution; to an efficient nationalization of public utilities; to an intensive plan of agricultural and industrial development; to a new foreign trade policy; to a structural reform of the educational system.

The "Necessary War"

That is, in essence, the nature of our struggle. Right now we are occupied in the preliminary task of removing the stone from the road. The illegitimate power that today obstructs and frustrates Cuba's destiny exhibits the same features as the colonial power of the past, or worse. Rebellion, therefore, is as justified today as it was in 1868 and 1895, perhaps more so.

Actually we are resuming the unfinished Revolution of Martí. That is why we extol today his "necessary war," for the same reasons he proclaimed it: against backward colonialism, against the protective arms of tyranny, against grasping and corrupt politics, against those who barter away the national economy . . . against all the evils that derive from this dismal amalgam.

Positive and Negative Forces

We are aware that we are engaged in an unequal contest. With a free hand in the public treasury, the enemy has acquired an impressive amount of military equipment. The dictatorship tries also to gain strength in two other respects: under the pretexts of "order" and "anticommunism" (the old worn-out clichés of the Latin American dictatorships), it seeks to obtain U.S. support; and by encouraging a ready-made political opposition, it expects to present the necessary legal and electoral facade.

It is interesting to note that while in the United States, public opinion and the government itself seem to be awakening to the "strong man" fraud, in Cuba the false opposition, incompetent and shortsighted, is ready to play along with a Batista whose days in power are inevitably numbered.

Everything indicates, therefore, that we stand alone before the illegitimate power. The line has been clearly drawn: on one side, the negative forces of colonialist regression; on the other, the positive forces of the Revolution.

This distinction will no doubt have a historically healthy effect. It will enable the people to know, beyond any possibility of confusion, who truly serves them and who betrays them. The government usurpers have at their disposal all the resources of power and the support of their natural allies among the discredited professional politicians; we rely on our dignity as free men and on the justice of the revolutionary movement.

That is our cause.

## 2. The Cuban Nation

The right of Cuba to constitute itself a sovereign and independent nation is fully justified on all geographical, historical, political, economic, and sociological grounds. This is the first as well as the basic affirmation of our struggle. Without it, the historical progress of the Cuban people in the last hundred years would be totally devoid of sense.

The fact that the struggle has not yet reached its end means simply that the conditions of *territorial sovereignty, political organization, domestic economy,* and *distinctive culture* which are the basis of the national concept have not yet been fulfilled. These conditions exist only imperfectly and incompletely, hindered by the negative realities that have always stood in the way of Cuba's national destiny.

The Three Forces

To understand Cuba's historical progress one must take into account the three great political forces that move it. These forces are the *Spanish,* the *Cuban,* and the *North American,* which are manifested respectively in the colony, the republic, and the intervention. Their reciprocal action made itself felt from the beginnings of a national conscience early in the nineteenth century; it is still felt at the present time.

In the Colony

Félix Varela, "the one who first showed us how to think," was also the first to voice the message of an independent Cuba. His thinking thus represents in his times the third concurrent force in the political development of the island. By then, the beginning of the nineteenth century, Jefferson had already said, in a noted letter to President Monroe (1823): "I confess that I have always looked upon Cuba as the most important acquisition we could make." Varela, however, in one of his articles in *El Habanero* (1825), flatly rejected Jefferson's idea: "I am against the annexation of the Island to any government; I would like to see it as much an island in the political sense as it is in nature."

That is the relationship in which the three political forces of the Cuban process first appear under Spanish rule. In the colonial context, the words of Jefferson and Varela raised a most important alternative, one that would be present throughout the later course of Cuban history. All the logic of geography and the clear will of the Cuban people, however, prove that independence is the one proper position and the only one fully suitable to this country.

In the Revolution

In 1898 we witness another historic occurrence of extraordinary significance. The three forces come together again in time and space. After more than thirty years of struggle (fifty if one begins with Narciso López), Spain is forced to haul down the flag over the last of its possessions in the New World. During that period, Cuba, in its pursuit of liberty, had paid a high price in martyrs and heroism, in ideals and programs. Yet, at the symbolic moment of the end of the war, Cuba was excluded from the conference in which its political status was determined.

That decision set an unfortunate precedent. The final outcome appeared to be determined more by the intervention of the United States than by the bloody sacrifices of the Cubans. The island was thus liberated from Spain's political yoke thanks only to the aid of "the mighty neighbor." The antecedents and consequences of that episode could perhaps be explained by the logical relation of the facts; but the result was that from then on the former colony was burdened by a status very much resembling that of a protectorate, and by an ironic and costly "debt of gratitude" that would in time serve to cloak countless wrongs and injustices.

In the Republic

The history of Cuba as a republic continues to be determined in large measure by the uneven interaction of the three forces. It is true that Spain was no longer in the picture as a political entity; but it remained as an active presence in the colonial mentality of the most powerful and influential social groups, which were driven by colonial nostalgia toward the new magnetic pole of metropolitan influence: the United States.

Then, under the pretext of the Platt Amendment, came the interventions. When Washington was not actually intervening, the real power still lay in the hands of the American ambassadors. González, Crowder, Guggenheim, Welles, Caffery exercised more authority than the presidents, with the consent—even the approval!—of the latter. Washington became the new power seat to which Cuban rulers, caudillos, and politicians servilely turned their eyes.

We therefore have no moral right to complain. While the politico-economic expansion of the great American nation can be considered a natural phenomenon of the period, it must be admitted that on the Cuban side (save for a few voices as gallant as they were isolated) it met with no resistance at all. On the contrary, it was invited and welcomed.

If the Republic thus came to be a pitiful caricature, only the Cubans are to blame. The political parties are mere personal alliances, lacking in ideology and even in a national doctrine. Politics is conceived as an exhibitionistic contest of ambitions, or as an exercise in tropical Machiavellianism. Meanwhile, the national wealth falls without difficulty into foreign hands. The land, the mines, the sugar industry, the public utilities go to owners for whom the country is nothing but a promising reservoir of riches waiting to be exploited. Cubans are pariahs in their own land. Independence constantly dwindles, crushed under a mountain of betrayals and apostasies.

## The 1930 Generation

Then came another flare-up of the original unfinished Revolution. During the 1930s the younger reserves of the Motherland come forward once again to strain against the unbroken chains of the past. This time students and workers form the vanguard of the movement, thus showing the discontent of the second republican generation, breaking violently with the sad colonial realities then incarnated in the regime of Gerardo Machado.

With the so-called 1930 Generation, notwithstanding its romantic immaturity, we must acknowledge a favorable advance in the republican enterprise. More was done for the national and public interest during the "hundred days" of [Grau's] revolutionary government than by all the other governments of the past thirty years. Not only was the Platt Amendment abolished, but many measures were adopted which, although commonplace in most civilized countries, represented extraordinary progress in Cuba. The eight-hour workday, ·the right to strike, minimum employment of nationals, university autonomy, the reduction in the cost of electricity . . . these things gave the Cuban people for the first time the feeling of being masters of their own destiny. In addition, it was demonstrated that Cuba could exercise full sovereignty without causing the sky to fall.

The end came soon, however, when the colonial elements, prevailing in the armed forces and in the cliques of political parasites, recaptured power and strangled the newborn assertion of nationhood. With neither experience nor organization, the standard-bearers of the 1930 Generation drowned in their own credulity. Their leaders did not know how to defend the Revolution against its traditional enemies—the armed forces and political corruption—and saw power snatched from their hands by, of all people, the Batistas, the Mendietas, the Menocals, and all the rest of the reactionary parade.

## Constitutional Interregnum

The revolutionary movement of the 1930s, although lacking in organization and rather vague in its objectives, managed to leave its mark on the constitutional document that brought it to a close.

The new sentiment of sovereignty it had awakened in the people caused the situation to develop into a legal order that included many social advances while at the same time establishing an adequate democratic mechanism. For the first time in the Republic the will of the people really counted, and a system functioned which was based on popular suffrage and open competition among political parties.

These circumstances permitted the coming to power of the group that seemed most closely identified with the movement: the Partido Revolucionario Cubano (PRC), "Auténtico." Soon, however, what has always been the weakest spot in the Cuban struggle made itself felt once again: lack of organization, of discipline, of a true revolutionary mentality. The two consecutive Auténtico administrations, those of Grau San Martín and Prío Socarrás, were two great disappointments, two incredibly wasted opportunities. They not only left unsolved the basic problems of the country—economic, industrial, agrarian, educational, military, etc.—but ushered in an unprecedented era of scandal and corruption which again opened the door of power to the counterrevolutionary forces, again significantly under the leadership of Fulgencio Batista.

Back to Point Zero

If any spark remained of the revolutionary fire of the 1930s, the reactionary coup of the tenth of March extinguished it altogether. Just one blow was sufficient to bring down the weakened democratic structure of Cuba. The republic lay defenseless for lack of efficient instruments of civic resistance—political parties, courts of law, the press—and the counterrevolutionary elements joined together in a sinister league of military ambitions, political trash, and unscrupulous financial interests. These conspirators encountered no slightest difficulty in winning to their side the costly and corrupt military machine, which happily cooperated in this new act of treason.

Events took their logical course. Hordes of decadent politicians, some hurriedly recruited, some brought back from obscurity and oblivion, rushed joyfully to make up the civil facade of the military dictatorship. In an instant, Cuba was back to point zero of its historical trajectory. The country became in fact (though not in theory, since the new power was completely devoid of political philosophy) a Caribbean version of the police state. The armed forces played their true role of mercenary army of occupation. And democracy ceased to exist.

## The Failure of the Political Parties

The case of the political parties deserves special attention. One of Cuba's great weaknesses is that it has never had a true political party. The Partido Revolucionario Cubano founded by Martí was created exclusively for the immediate requirements of the revolution, and it did not go beyond that. It therefore could not assist the Republic at its inauspicious birth, much less guide it during its difficult early years.

It is painfully ironic that the closest thing to a party Cuba ever had, on the very eve of the Republic, was the Autonomist party, an organization that disdained independence, founded by arrogant intellectuals without faith in their country.

For the first thirty years of the Republic, Cuba's parties were simply masses of ignorant or credulous people clustered around some caudillo or charismatic figure. These aggregates, whatever name they took, were manipulated by cliques of unprincipled, profit-seeking politicians who squabbled over the crumb of power tossed to them by Washington.

Something that looked a little more like a true party appeared after 1930: the PRC, "Auténtico." Very soon, however, the revolutionary image of the Auténticos blew up like a soap bubble during its first experience in power. The facts are too recent and too well known to warrant a detailed description.

The discrediting of the Auténtico party moved Eduardo Chibás, one of its most popular and prestigious leaders, to found the Partido del Pueblo Cubano, "Ortodoxo." As the name suggests, the main purpose of the party was to fill the niche that the Auténticos had so lamentably abandoned. In reality, however, the Ortodoxo movement was never more than a curious phenomenon of political psychology, lacking in ideological content and in program. Only the strong personality of Chibás, with his honest and defiant image and his clean record in the struggle against the Machado dictatorship, could succeed in holding together what was in fact a heterogeneous conglomeration of incompatible elements.

Chibás's tenacious insistence on high ethical standards in Cuba's public life attracted to the Ortodoxo ranks a formidable and unprecedented abundance of popular support. After the Auténticos' lavish misuse of public funds, Chibás wielded his symbolic broom with a will. But the unexpected death of the popular leader, followed by the military coup of March 10, brought the great inner weakness of the Ortodoxo movement into the open. Not only did the party prove to be incapable of standing up to the crisis provoked by Batista and the military, but it could not even preserve its own organization or take advantage of its enormous mass support.

Organized Labor

As a result of the ineptitude of the political parties, the abdication of the judiciary, and the submissiveness of the press in the face of Batista's coup, the country found itself without civic defenses. To this list one must add the subservience of organized labor, a consequence of the philosophy of class struggle (i.e., putting the group interest over the national interest) which has prevailed in the Cuban labor movement. Although individual workers, as human beings and as citizens, are capable of feeling and understanding their country's problems, collectively they cease to function, turned off by sophistic arguments and by leaders who willingly collaborate with the illegitimate power.

Hypocritically claiming that they are guided only by "class interests," the false labor leaders—of whom Eusebio Mujal is typical—actually keep the workers under a reign of terror. They control them with the help of the repressive police apparatus of the regime, take charge of the unions or federations that do not submit to the official "discipline," and obtain from the Ministry of Labor the coercive legal regulations that enable them to wield dictatorial control over the unions.

Union elections are either indefinitely postponed or conveniently rigged. So too workers' "congresses" and all other labor activities: they are held with puppet delegates under police protection, in the style of the prearranged assemblies of the totalitarian regimes. Since 1952 the Cuban workers have been unable to hold their traditional annual parade, not simply because the government prohibits it by force, but because the collaborationist leadership of the CTC [the official labor organization] agrees that it should not be held.

Despite the government's iron grip, surprisingly, the civic and patriotic unrest has found a response in many Cuban workers. Strikes protesting the excesses of the dictatorship (with the complicity of organized labor) have been staged by sugar workers and bank employees, despite fierce government repression. There has been open rebellion among rank-and-file workers of the telephone and electric power companies.

These positive showings encourage the hope that the Cuban worker will soon abandon the class isolation and negative indifference to which he has been led by unscrupulous, profiteering leaders, and will join fully in the national whole, whose stability and well-being are so closely tied to his own.

## The Commercial Settlement

The league of antinational elements which came to power with the March 10 coup cancels *ipso facto* all of Cuba's chances for economic independence. The colonialist interests impose upon the country a type of subservient economy whose main features are the following: (*a*) a system of concessions and great monopolies in the area of public utilities; (*b*) enormous new concessions, such as the Canal Vía-Cuba; (*c*) unconditional grants of the country's most important mineral deposits (nickel, manganese, iron, oil) to foreign companies; (*d*) a policy of privileges and laissez faire for big foreign investors; and (*e*) a plan to abrogate and annul laws that benefit the worker.

This reactionary plot obviously shifts the center of gravity of the national economy out of the country, establishes a system of unrestrained exploitation, and nullifies the rights of labor and the social security of the people. Independence, with all its political, cultural, and spiritual involvements, is traded for the condition of the commercial settlement.

The reasoning on which this position is based exhibits an astonishingly gross and brutal materialism. It consists of the proposition that the opportunities for employment and the circulation of money that would result from those policies, notwithstanding the inevitable emigration of profits—the mortgaging, in short, of the future for the sake of the present—would amply compensate for the loss of those subjective values of national integrity which would have to be sacrificed.

The fallacy of this proposition is equaled only by the cynicism of those who favor it. For it cannot be asserted that all the values of national integrity (the supreme reason for the struggle) are exclusively *subjective*, nor is submission to foreign economic power the only or the best means of distributing jobs and material welfare to the people. In the last analysis, the question is not one of conflicting economic theories. The real issue is the fact that the gang in power, eager for foreign support at any price, does not hesitate to pay for it by irresponsibly and criminally handing over the country's natural resources and economic sovereignty.

### Sierra Maestra

Only one thing can save the country from all these dangers and evils: the determined and active upsurge of the younger generations, under the banner of a national doctrine and a firm patriotic conviction. On them rests the arduous task of completing the unfinished Revolution and of repairing the damage inflicted on the country by the March 10 catastrophe, as well as by the apathy, cowardice, and submissiveness displayed by those whose inescapable duty was to reject it.

With the avenues of democracy closed, there is no worthy course left open but insurrection, which is as justified today as it was during the struggles for independence in the past, and for the same reasons.

The action in the Sierra Maestra, with its epic realism, is therefore highly symbolic. It represents the action of the fresh, uncontaminated blood of the nation against the toxic humors that sap and destroy it. Whatever the outcome of the present armed confrontation, it has already been demonstrated that insurrection is more than a dream and that the highest mountains of Oriente are now witnessing one more episode of the "necessary war."

It must be emphasized that the Revolution is not a simple reform or punitive movement, dedicated only to the overthrow of the brigands who usurped power. Its aspirations reach far beyond that. As necessary as it is today to use the knife to cut out the cancer that has caused so much suffering, it will be equally or more necessary tomorrow to apply the appropriate remedies for the reconstruction.

The Sierra Maestra is the indispensable first step toward a brighter and better tomorrow—the logical antecedent of the revolutionary program.

The struggle, then, has two complementary phases: the destructive and the constructive. In one the accursed apparatus of tyranny must be reduced to ashes; in the other we must raise over its ruins the free-standing structure of the true Republic. We are still in the first of these stages. For how long we do not know, but we must be prepared for a long and painful struggle. The one thing we are sure of is that we shall achieve victory, and that then the constructive work of the Revolution will begin, in deep devotion to the great Motherland yet to come.

## 3. *Thesis of the Revolution*

The Revolution is the struggle of the Cuban nation to reach its historical goals and to achieve complete fulfillment. This "fulfillment," as we have seen, lies in the harmonious blending of three elements: *political sovereignty, economic independence,* and *cultural differentiation.* The first defines the condition of the state; the second affirms the need for self-sufficiency; and the third has to do with the special characteristics and appropriate mental attitudes of the people.

### The Insurrection

The Revolution is not exactly a war or an isolated episode, but rather a continuous historical process that presents distinct moments or stages. The landings of Narciso López in the mid-nineteenth century, the wars of 1868 and 1895, the revolutionary movement of the 1930s, and now the struggle against the Batista dictatorship—all are part of one and the same national Revolution.

Armed struggle is not necessarily an inherent element of the Revolution. In theory, and even in situations of constitutional normality, the revolutionary objectives can be realized through the democratic mechanism. But since this has been totally vitiated and rendered ineffective as a result of the seizure of power by the negative, antinational elements incarnated in the military dictatorship and its political accomplices, the revolutionary aspirations can find no way but that of insurrection.

### Essential Goals

What the Revolution seeks is simply *the establishment of a social order that will be just, decent, good, and pleasant for human beings in every lawful and necessary aspect of life.* In this case, of course, it is proposed that this ideal be realized on the island of Cuba and for the Cuban people.

The revolutionary concept has political, economic, social, and cultural aspects. It includes nearly all areas of human interest and activity. Human beings have as much right to a free soil as they have to their bread; as much right to live in a society governed by the rule of law as to enjoy cultural opportunities suited to their personal inclinations.

With these considerations in mind, we believe the essential goals of the Cuban Revolution to be the following:

(a) A free and sovereign country
(b) A democratic republic
(c) An independent economy
(d) A distinct national culture

None of these goals can be achieved apart from the others. There can be no country without a national economy, no republic without a culture of its own—and vice versa. Each one is a part of the whole, and all are necessary if the national concept is to become a tangible reality.

## Ideology

*A constitution is a living, practical law that cannot be constructed of ideological elements.* —Martí.

Where ideological definitions are concerned, the 26 of July Movement prefers to avoid abstract formulas and worn-out clichés. The ideology of the Cuban Revolution must arise from the very roots and circumstances of the people and the country. It should therefore be neither the imported thought of other climes nor the refined product of the mind conceived apart from existing reality. On the contrary, its ideas must spring from the land and the human flesh of Cuba.

In the spirit of this same principle and taking into consideration the essential goals stated earlier, we can nevertheless declare that the 26 of July Movement is guided by political thinking that is characterized by *democracy, nationalism,* and *social justice.*

These concepts, however, must be carefully defined, for political categories are often misused and their true sense distorted, and in recent decades many crimes have been committed in their names.

As for *democracy,* the 26 of July Movement considers the Jeffersonian philosophy still valid and subscribes fully to Lincoln's formula of "government of the people, by the people, and for the people." Democracy thus cannot be the government of a race or a class or a religion, but of *all* the people. In addition, the Cuban Revolution inherits a democratic tradition from the Founders of the country. "All men are equal," reads the Proclamation of 10 October [1868]. And the same idea can be found later in the Monte-

cristi Manifesto and in all the documents and constitutions of the
Republic.

As for *nationalism,* it is a natural outgrowth of the special geographical and historical circumstances surrounding Cuba's acces-
sion to independence. It is the "willing to be a nation" of a people
that has been strong enough to win its liberty. Cuba, which obtained nominal independence in 1902, has not yet obtained economic independence. The lands, the mineral resources, the public
utilities, the credit and loan institutions, the transportation ser-
vices—in short, the most important national assets—today turn the
greater precentage of their profits over to foreign interests. The na-
tionalist position here consists of rectifying this unfair situation,
seeing to it that the country receives a fair share of its own national product. As an appropriate complement of this pledge, nationalism will also be manifested in the areas of culture and education.

By *social justice* the 26 of July Movement means the establishment of a social order in which all the inalienable rights of the
*human being*—political, social, economic, and cultural—will be
fully satisfied and guaranteed.

To this general concept, however, certain further considerations
should be added concerning the material conditions that are the
*sine qua non* of every human right. The history of the economic
development of the nations during the nineteenth and twentieth
centuries shows that the capitalist system of free enterprise tends
inevitably toward the accumulation of wealth in a few hands, with
the consequent exploitation of the rest. It is this experience that
has caused the most developed nations—including the country
most representative of capitalism, the United States—to resort to
techniques of economic planning to ensure the production and
consumption of goods in accordance with the needs of the entire
society.

The 26 of July Movement favors the adoption of a system of economic planning that will free the country from the evils of a one-
crop economy, foreign concessions, privileged monopolies, latifun-
dia, and other manifestations of the commercial-establishment
economy; in other words, a system that will offer the Cuban people
the same opportunities for progress and material well-being that
are enjoyed by the citizens of the great civilized countries.

As a summary of these general considerations, the 26 of July

Movement declares that these concepts spring from what is doubt-less the essence of the political thought of José Martí: the principle of the *full dignity of the human being.* Everything in the area of human activities and interests—country, politics, economy, educa-tion—comes together at this point. It is in this conviction, in this devotion to Martí, that the philosophical foundations of our strug-gle are to be found.

This ideological position breaks down into the following guide-lines:

### 1. National sovereignty

*If the family of American republics has any role at all, it is not to follow one of them like a flock of sheep.* —Martí.

Sovereignty is the right of a nation to choose its own direction and control its own destiny. Without this basic condition, every-thing else—state, government, culture—lacks national sense; it is folly. The paramount objective of the Revolution, therefore, is to affirm the full sovereignty of Cuba.

In an international political sense, of course, this condition has been officially recognized, particularly since the abrogation of the Platt Amendment in 1934. But Cuba is still forced to endure actual situations that, without reaching the point of direct intervention, constitute essential violations of its sovereignty. The existence of foreign bases and military missions on national soil, economic pressures, and the lack of restraint on the part of diplomatic envoys who take the liberty of publicly taking sides and passing judgment on domestic political matters are obvious and eloquent examples. These things weaken and demoralize the national spirit and interfere with the true understanding that ought to exist be-tween neighboring countries.

A country must enjoy full sovereignty over its own territory, its form of government, its political decisions, whether national or in-ternational, its economic policies, its education, its culture, and every kind of human activity that has to do with its historical pro-cess.

There can be perfect harmony between sovereignty and the ideal of hemispheric and universal brotherhood. In truth, national sovereignty is both an indispensable condition and a guarantee of cordial and peaceful relations among nations and their govern-ments.

### 2. *Economic independence*

*The only wealth and liberty that last and bring good are those that are created and won with one's own hands.* —Martí.

Economic independence means a country's ability to be self-sufficient within the established system of international relations. Economic independence is the indispensable foundation of political sovereignty. Cuba has enough natural resources to aspire to economic independence, the same as the other sovereign nations of the world. This aspiration in no way hinders but rather opens the door to a rich international trade, profitable and satisfying for everyone.

The principle of economic independence requires that *the greatest possible percentage of the profits of national production remain within the country.* When for whatever reason the bulk of these profits flows abroad, the balance of payments is disturbed and the country consequently becomes increasingly subservient and impoverished; the means of production are developed not in the interests of the country but for the benefit of the private interests that control them. Once that pattern is established, the country loses its economic sovereignty and becomes for all practical purposes a commercial colony.

In order to avoid the disastrous consequences of such a situation and ensure a steady level of prosperity, not subject to abrupt shifts or unpredictable events abroad, the state will exercise a policy of control over natural resources, public utilities, banks, insurance, foreign investments, and all forms of production and credit. The state will also reserve the right to choose, within the established international framework, the conditions of its foreign trade.

### 3. *Labor*

*The general happiness of a nation is based on the individual independence of its people.* —Martí.

Although the 26 of July Movement does not defend the doctrines of economic determinism, it nevertheless proclaims that there can be no democracy or social justice if the individual lacks the means to satisfy his material needs comfortably. It is the movement's belief, therefore, that the state is morally bound to provide those means, primarily in the form of a high level of production and opportunities for well-paid employment.

In this sense, work is considered both as a right in itself and as a means of individual progress. Rather than a pretext for fragmenting society into mutually distinct groups, work will be a factor of national unity, inasmuch as it is an indispensable element in national production. The right to work shall always be accompanied by adequate, just, and increasing economic compensation, and by a body of legal regulations based on the principle of the full dignity of the human being.

The right to organize and to strike shall also, of course, be guaranteed by law. But when labor is recognized as an integral part of the production process, its class opposition to capital will be abolished or drastically reduced. In other words, when the role of labor is upgraded and the privileges of capital are limited, there will develop between them a state of harmony and solidarity which will considerably increase the index of productivity and provide benefits for all.

### 4. Social order

*We must prevent the sympathies of the Cuban people from being twisted and enslaved by any class interest, or by the unbridled authority of any military or civil group, or of any particular section of the country, or of one race over another.* —Martí.

The 26 of July Movement takes its position on social questions from Martí. Its ideal in this regard is the *organic unity of the nation.* According to this concept, no group, no class, no race, no religion can place its own interest over the public good, or consider itself unconcerned with or apart from anything that may affect the social whole or any of its parts. The ancient Romans recognized this principle in the expression *salus populi suprema lex,* which amounted to saying that the general welfare of the people was to be the model that guided the letter and the spirit of the law.

The concept of society as an organic whole means that everyone, without privileges or exceptions, shares in the advantages and responsibilities of progress. This participation in benefits and responsibilities will be brought about through a more just, more dynamic concept of property (especially land), capital, and production, together with the elevation of labor to the rank of participating agent in both the management and the profits of industry. Thus the things that cause class antagonism will disappear, or at least diminish appreciably, and all people will unite on the basis of common interest.

Social unity, on the other hand, is based on what may be considered the highest aim of the Revolution: *the spiritual and material welfare of man.* All the rights of the individual, including, of course, the right to a decent standard of living, are implicit in the ideal of the Revolution. In the furtherance of the happiness of the individual and his harmonious relations with the community, the conditions necessary for the integration of the nation are established and the subjective values of the Motherland are secured.

### 5. Education

*The measure of responsibility is found in the extent of education.* —Martí.

Education is the long-range strategy of the Revolution (insurrection or political action is the immediate or short-range tactic). Since there can be no Motherland without a national conscience or democracy without responsible citizens, we must have a patient and systematic educational program dedicated to providing these indispensable conditions.

The state must therefore take an active interest in education. The 26 of July Movement sees education as *the deliberate, organized process of instructional and environmental factors which, in addition to providing general knowledge and vocational guidance, will seek to awaken in the individual the fundamental qualities of citizenship and patriotism.*

This definition embraces the four aspects that Cuban education must include: the cultural, the vocational, the civic, and the national.

It is easy to see that education cannot be reduced simply to pedagogical technique. In a country such as Cuba, still striving for national fulfillment, education must also be directed toward other important goals, some *subjective,* some *objective.* Outstanding among the former are the values of Liberty and Motherland, both complementary to the basic principle of *human dignity;* among the latter, first place is of course taken by the cultural, vocational, and technical training that will enable the citizen to face and deal effectively with the country's social and economic problems.

Herein lies the explanation for the great revolutionary importance of the educational process, and for the special care and interest that the state must take in the philosophy or thought that guides it. While education, if it is to be an instrument for reaching national and civic goals, cannot be limited to its technical function but must have some moral or philosophical content, this content must be kept free from church or sectarian influences, which would seriously endanger democratic liberties. The moral content of education will be the kind that is universal in character, common to all men regardless of belief, and the natural ally of the principle of Liberty. The implicit impartiality of the democratic state, moreover, requires that public education be absolutely free of religious control or content, so that there can be no occasion, for reasons of conscience, for undesirable discriminations or divisions among the future citizens.

In setting forth these concepts, the 26 of July Movement underlines the exceptional importance it assigns to public education, and indicates its intention of devoting its most careful attention to educational curricula and programs.

### 6. Political activity

*Government is only the organization of national resources in such a way that the human being can attain his goals with dignity and employ to maximum advantage the elements of public prosperity.* —Martí.

The 26 of July Movement holds resolutely to the ideal of the democratic republic, inspired by the credo of Liberty and sustained by the character and ability of its citizens. The movement seeks the establishment in Cuba of a form of government and a regime of individual rights and public liberties that will exist not only as words written in the Constitution and the laws but in full and impartial operation in the practical realities of life.

In order to arrive at this ideal state, however, it is first imperative conscientiously to eradicate the evils and injustices that now debase Cuban politics. The principal causes of this peculiar situation are *parties that lack ideological content, corrupt politicians, personal rule, low civic involvement of the masses,* and *political apathy;* their fruits are *vote fraud, the mockery of suffrage, police excesses, military control, messianism,* and *dictatorship.*

The eradication of these evils involves a double task: on the one hand, revolutionary action in the form of legal sanctions that will severely punish all crimes against public liberties and individual rights; and on the other, a systematic campaign of civic education aimed at raising the political culture of the masses at least to the minimum level required by the democratic system.

The next step will be the adoption of a political-electoral structure (electoral code) that will contain the measures necessary for the adequate functioning of the system within the rule of law. To this end the 26 of July will draft an electoral code designed to guarantee the vote as a fundamental right of citizenship, at the same time providing for the educational measures that will enable this vote to be at all times the free expression of a sound and informed opinion.

This position of the 26 of July Movement responds to its ideological determination to inaugurate in Cuba an era of truly democratic political activity: competition of ideas among political parties and representative government founded on the free and legitimate expression of the people's will.

### 7. Civil authority

*Power in a democratic republic must be exclusively in the hands of civilians. . . . A country cannot be founded the way a military camp is run.* —Martí

All the guarantees of the democratic system—present in essence in all the great historic documents of the West, from the Declaration of Independence (1776) and the Déclaration des Droits de l'Homme et du Citoyen (1789) to the Charter of Human Rights of the United Nations—presume the establishment of a firm civil authority that will ensure their fulfillment.

With the increase in military and police power as the decisive factor in public life (the primary cause and effect of the March 10 coup), Cuba has sunk to the lowest depths of political primitivism. Except for its absolute ideological void, the government headed by Fulgencio Batista reproduces point for point the horrors of the totalitarian regimes.

This state of affairs, moreover, clashes openly with Cuba's best historical tradition. The founders of this country always, by conviction and by temperament, believed deeply in civil authority. Céspedes, Aguilera, Agramonte, Gómez, Maceo, García, Sanguily, Varona, Martí . . . even those among them who, like the Bayardo [Agramonte] and the Titán [Maceo], won unfading laurels on the fields of battle, were men who set aside their rank and bowed respectfully before the civil majesty of the Republic. But that is not all. The Cuban civilian position does not confine itself to the personal area of biography; it is also part of the political philosophy of all the constitutions and other political documents of the Revolution. The October 10 Proclamation, the Montecristi Manifesto, the Articles of the Cuban Revolutionary Party, and the constitutions of

Guáimaro, Jimaguayú, and La Yaya adopt and reflect the civilian spirit that prevailed throughout the formative stages of Cuban history.

### 8. Freedom of conscience

*Liberty is the right every man has to be honest, and to think and speak without hypocrisy.* —Martí.

The Revolution embraces, as one of the essential components of democracy, the principle of freedom of conscience. Every citizen shall be free to hold the belief of his choice, to have a religion or to have none, as long as his conduct does not debase human dignity or jeopardize the rights and liberty of others.

When the state recognizes any religion as official, grants it special privileges, or permits it to intervene in public affairs, the principle of freedom of conscience disappears and democracy loses its stability.

This position has its roots in the political thought on which the Western democracies are founded. It is a vital part of the French Revolution and appears in the national formation of the United States, where its most distinguished defender is Thomas Jefferson, the author of the Declaration of Independence. In the history of Cuba it goes hand in hand with the affirmation of civil authority and is clearly discernible in the thinking and conduct of the Founders as well as in the juridical literature of the Revolution. Here the names of all the great patriots of the past could again be cited; but it is sufficient to remember Martí's numerous references to the subject, particularly the one that summarizes them all: "No nation can be happy without the separation of Church and State."

Nevertheless, and despite the fact that the separation of church and state is a principle officially recognized by the Republic, this principle is constantly violated in Cuba, especially in the form of privileges, many of them financial in nature, granted to church interests. Under the guise of piety, something that is consubstantial to the democratic system is thus weakened and undermined: the unequivocal separation of the state from all religious creeds.

On this question, the 26 of July Movement adopts and proclaims the thought of Martí. It will spare no effort to bring about the conditions that will put into effect the principle of freedom of conscience, and its expression in political terms: separation of church and state.

## 9. Public morality

*Honesty is the only useful policy, and the only one that endures.
. . . Public affairs must be taken out of the hands of those who
traffic with them.* —Martí.

The Republic was born with the colonial inheritance of political
corruption. Since it also lacked the moral or philosophical influences to counteract that handicap, time has only aggravated the
evil. It is not at all surprising, therefore, that public affairs in Cuba,
as Martí observed, frequently fall into the hands of traffickers and
thieves, for whom democracy is only a market for contemptible
and shameless profiteering.

The Cuban Revolution must therefore complement its ideological stand with a serious ethical concern. Corruption in the public
sphere might not be an essential evil in itself, since it can be easily
eradicated (in theory, at least) by legal and educational means; but
it does constitute a danger in that it frustrates constructive policy
and opens the door to other, much worse evils. Crimes against
public morals, if allowed to go unpunished, destroy the people's
faith and undermine the foundations of democratic institutions.

The 26 of July Movement believes this problem requires a double programmatic approach: a full investigation into misuse of
public office, with sanctions of confiscation, among others, for
those found guilty of enriching themselves illegally; and a combined plan of political, electoral, and administrative techniques to
eliminate or minimize the possibilities of crime. The procedural details will be duly fixed by law; the important thing now is to bear in
mind that the revolutionary effort cannot achieve its objectives
unless it is accompanied by a firm and systematic ethical course of
action.

## 10. International policy

*Sound inter-American understanding demands that each nation
develop with the freedom and autonomy necessary to a healthy
state, even if on crossing the river they get their clothes wet and
on emerging they stumble, without jeopardizing the liberty of any
other people—which is the door through which others will enter to
jeopardize their own. Nor must they permit any rapacious and ir-
reverent nation, under the cover of business or any other pretext,
to annul and dominate them.* —Martí.

The Cuban Revolution is historically within the purest American
tradition. It is a fortunate fact that the republics of the Western

Hemisphere, north and south, are united by the same ideals and the same destiny. To preserve and develop this community of interests, the whole hemispheric family must work together.

The independence of Cuba, therefore, like that of all the other peoples of the Americas, cannot be seen as an isolated fact. It is part of a larger process whose paramount goal must logically be the integration of all in a higher unity of liberty and mutual understanding.

Such, in a few words, is the international position of the 26 of July Movement, in particular its inter-American position. Accordingly, Cuba, in its relations with other American republics, including of course the United States, will assume an attitude of rapprochement rather than distance, of friendship rather than enmity. This position, moreover, whenever the common historical ideals so require, will have priority over any other kind of nonhemispheric international relations.

Having set down these basic points, we must turn to certain explanations. While independence could be taken ideally as a stage in a process leading to plural integration (not yet realized), that does not mean that it can or should at any time be abolished or curtailed. On the contrary, that desirable state of harmonious unity of the whole can never be reached without the complete maturity of its parts—a maturity that in this case means *national fulfillment*. In other words, independence is not an obstacle: it is the way. A fraternity of equally free republics can be thought of as good, beautiful, and possible; an association of colonies or satellite states can be none of these.

The 26 of July Movement believes with Martí that "sound inter-American understanding demands that each nation develop with the freedom and autonomy necessary to a healthy state, even if on crossing the river they get their clothes wet and on emerging they stumble . . ." It also believes that this "freedom" in no way hinders a satisfactory understanding among neighboring countries, but rather encourages it. If in the process of managing their own destinies the nations, in Martí's metaphor, "get their clothes wet" or "stumble," that is simply part of the process of learning to use and perfect their liberty, and is always preferable to the hypothetical advantages of leading strings.

In regard to the specific question of the relations between Cuba and the United States, the 26 of July Movement proposes its own doctrine of *constructive friendship*. This is to be understood as an ethical standard to be employed in our dealings with each other, especially in the economic and cultural areas, which will be beneficial to both countries while leaving intact the national values of each.

Strictly speaking, the term "imperialism" is no longer appropriate to American realities; but there remain some forms of economic penetration, usually accompanied by political influence, which closely resemble it, and which cause irreparable harm to the moral and material welfare of the affected countries.

Fortunately, such a situation can be overcome without damage to any legitimate interest. The new concept of *constructive friendship* will permit Cuba to be—as so many geographical, economic, and even political factors urge it to be—a faithful ally of the great nation to the north, and at the same time to preserve its right to control its own destiny. Through new and fair agreements we can, without unnecessary sacrifice or humiliating submission, multiply the advantages that derive from proximity.

*Constructive friendship,* finally, can be expressed in a simple formula: it is a combination of the process of national fulfillment with an increment of Cuban–U.S. relations guided by a pattern of equity and justice. This is what is really meant by "sound inter-Americanism"; it clears the way for the aspirations of the National Revolution, and it opens the door to a reasonable, fruitful, and lasting understanding.

## 4. The Future

Today, five years after the 10 March 1952 coup, Cuba is going through the most critical phase of its history. Either the Revolution succeeds—thanks to the almost exclusive effort of the younger reserves—and ushers in a new order of dignity, liberty, and national reconstruction, or Batista's band of usurpers prevails (although they disguise themselves with a false show of propriety, with the complicity of the pseudo-opposition), thus adding a new frustration to the destiny of the Motherland by compelling the struggle to go on indefinitely.

As a revolutionary force, born and baptized with blood in the midst of tragedy, the 26 of July Movement aspires not only to overthrow the illegitimate power and cleanse the corrupt political environment that nurtures and sustains it, but to achieve power itself in order to launch the program of indispensable changes that constitute the positive side of the Revolution.

The history of republican Cuba shows a most unfavorable balance in the accounts of the parties and political organizations. The slogans and promises were never anything but demagoguery and electoral lures; the "programs" were never anything but lifeless words on the printed page.

One of the factors to which the 26 of July Movement owes its existence is the imperative necessity of overcoming this situation. The Cuban people will not find their true direction as long as they lack a political instrument that represents the national will in the deepest ideological and programmatic sense. Disdaining the theatrical rhetoric of the hawkers of cheap politics, the 26 of July Movement resolves to get to the root of every problem in order to find the appropriate solution, in accordance with its position and its doctrine.

This position and this national doctrine, as well as the basic tenets of our ideology, have been outlined in the preceding chapters. All that remains now is to present, though necessarily very briefly, the principal measures that will be included in our program:

Political Measures

- *Government policy based on sacred respect for the Constitution and the law.*
- A system based on the independence of the three branches of government.
- Legislation geared to avoid the calamity of one-man government.
- Reforms intended to ensure true popular representation in the Legislative Branch.
- A system of civil liberties and full recognition of human rights.
- Democratic organization of political parties.
- Legal measures that will guarantee the exercise and validity of suffrage.
- A new electoral code.
- A system of disqualification and other legal sanctions against those guilty of crimes against democratic order.

Economic Measures

- *Government policy aimed at ensuring the economic independence of Cuba.*
- Development of new sources of production and employment.

- Agrarian reform that proscribes the latifundium system and encourages the formation of a middle class of rural landowners.
- Creation annually of centers of production (factories, small industries, centers of mineral exploitation, farms) capable of giving productive employment to young people reaching working age and to the unemployed. The goal: 100,000 new jobs every year.
- Diversification of agricultural production and measures to assure a market to farm products.
- Study and promotion of the cooperative system.
- Recovery of subsoil resources.
- Nationalization of public utilities.
- Encouragement of investment of domestic capital.
- Progressive increase of mean productivity per worker and mean per capita income.
- Effective development of the national merchant marine.
- Expansion of foreign trade.

Social Measures

- *Government policy inspired by the principle that society is an organic whole.*
- The upgrading of labor to the category of associate agent in the production process.
- A system of progressive, systematic increases in wages and salaries.
- Unification of the social security system and extension of its benefits to all citizens.
- Guarantee of the right to strike.
- Measures to establish democratic unions and prevent the control of workers by unpopular elements.
- Study of a system of public health, public hospitals, and socialized medicine.
- Changes in the penal system to transform the penitentiaries into rehabilitation centers.
- Total eradication of organized gambling, including the national lottery.
- An educational plan of racial understanding and integration.
- A social assistance program of an educational character, based not on charity but on the recognition of human dignity.
- State financing of home acquisition.

Educational Measures

- *Educational policy inspired by the concepts of human dignity, liberty, and motherland.*
- Structural and functional organization of the entire educational process.
- Compulsory education from age 5 to 15.
- Compulsory basic secondary education following the primary stage.
- Multiplication and academic unification of professional and technical schools.
- Licensing of some of these schools as the only means of access to the corresponding branches of university studies.
- Lowering of the high school diploma to its proper function: an entrance requirement for certain branches of higher education.
- Functional readaptation of university careers.
- Multiplication of schools and educational centers in accordance with demographic requirements.
- A special study of school architecture, to find the style best suited to the climate of Cuba and the character of the Cuban people.
- A plan for the selection and upgrading of teachers.
- Adequate salaries for teachers, with progressive increases.
- Professionalization of the Ministry of Education.
- Elimination of excess bureaucracy in administrative as well as teaching personnel.
- A scientific study of the education budget.
- Revision and improvement of school texts.
- An intensive plan for the elimination of illiteracy.
- Special attention to rural education.
- Creation of "school cities" with an urban-rural character.
- Enactment of a National Education Law.

Judicial Measures

- *Government policy directed toward the formation and establishment of a judicial system capable of guaranteeing the rule of law and strict compliance with its statutes.*
- Investigation of all present members of the judiciary on the basis of a rigid code of ethics.
- Study of the present system of judicial process with a view toward simplifying and speeding the administration of justice.

- Revision of codes and statutes in order to make them responsive to modern social needs.
- Study of a penitentiary system that will contemplate the moral, intellectual, and vocational rehabilitation of the prisoner.

International Measures

- *Government policy based always on full affirmation of national sovereignty.*
- A foreign policy directed at achieving and maintaining an international order of justice and peace, with special emphasis on the improvement of inter-American relations.
- Revision of those treaties and agreements that may be detrimental to the sovereignty or independence of the American nations.
- Proposal of measures that will favor trade and economic relations among the American states.
- Study of a plan for the educational unification of the Latin American countries.
- Study of an inter-American monetary unit.
- A program for inter-American cultural exchange.
- Proposal of measures against totalitarianism and dictatorships in the Americas.
- Proposals of measures and international agreements directed toward the promotion and protection of the democratic system.
- A foreign policy dedicated to the defense and application of the Charter of Human Rights of the United Nations.
- Affirmation of the right to political asylum.

*Havana, Cuba*
*November 1956*

# Notes

## Introduction

1. In August 1931 various opposition groups and individuals, mainly old-time politicians but also students, newspapermen, and intellectuals, attempted to overthrow General Gerardo Machado. Former President Mario G. Menocal and Colonel Carlos Mendieta were the main national figures. Other well-known participants were Sergio Carbó, Emilio Laurent, Aurelio Hevia, Julio Gaunard, and Lucilo de la Peña. See Hugh Thomas, *Cuba: The Pursuit of Freedom* (New York: Harper & Row, 1971), p. 593.

2. I wrote an article addressed to Chibás questioning his negative tactics and suggesting that he adopt a more constructive approach ("Recado crítico al Senador Chibás," *Bohemia*, 9 July 1950). Chibás responded with an article describing some newly appointed "technical commission" of the Ortodoxo party ("Teoría y práctica de un gobierno ortodoxo," *Bohemia*, 16 July 1950).

3. On 4 September 1933 a military coup overthrew the recently installed provisional government (after Machado's fall) headed by Carlos M. de Céspedes. The coup was supported by university students and some professors and by several revolutionary groups. As a result of various internal difficulties and, above all, U.S. opposition, Fulgencio Batista emerged as the figure of power. See Thomas, *Cuba*, chap. 54.

4. See Theodore Draper, *Castroism: Theory and Practice* (New York: Prager, 1965), p. 38.

5. Castro and some of his followers had prepared a proclamation to be announced on the radio if the attack on the Moncada police barracks on 26 July 1953 were successful. This proclamation, which did not become public at the time, stated, among other things, that "the Revolution . . . recognizes and bases itself on the ideals of Martí . . . and adopts as its own the revolutionary programs of Joven Cuba, ABC Radical, and the Ortodoxo party." See Thomas, *Cuba*, chap. 68.

6. It is a well-publicized fact that Castro was present at the cold-blooded assassination of Manolo Castro (no kin), the very popular president of the FEU, on 22 February 1948. See Alberto Baeza Flores, *Las cadenas vienen de lejos* (Mexico City: Editorial Letras, 1960), pp. 268–275.

7. Although the alliance between Castro and the Communists appears to have been formed early in 1958 (see Draper, *Castroism*, pp. 26–34), the Castro regime did not officially declare itself Marxist-Leninist until 1961. Unmistakable signs that the revolution had taken a radical course were apparent in 1960, however.

## 1. Two Wings for the Revolution

1. Most of my articles appeared in *Bohemia*, a weekly magazine of very wide circulation in Cuba in those years. My articles dealt mainly with political and cultural themes related to the development of Cuba.

2. Manolo Fernández was appointed minister of labor in the first revolutionary cabinet headed by President Manuel Urrutia in 1959.

3. Leví Marrero served as ambassador to the Organization of American States during the first years of the Castro regime.

4. For details about Castro's turbulent past, see Alberto Baeza Flores, *Las cadenas vienen de lejos* (Mexico City: Editorial Letras, 1960), pp. 168–181.

5. Fidel Castro, *La historia me absolverá* (New York: Club 26 de Julio de New York); Draper, *Castroism*, pp. 5–8.

6. Miró Cardona was appointed prime minister in the Urrutia cabinet in 1959. Later he presided over the Cuban Revolutionary Council, which was to have assumed power in Cuba if the 1961 Bay of Pigs invasion had been successful.

7. Delegates of the Grau San Martín branch of the Auténtico party (PRC) were in favor of a political formula. So was José Pardo Llada, a controversial radio commentator who represented the Movimiento de la Nación, a colorless and short-lived organization founded by the intellectual Jorge Mañach.

## 2. A Movement in Search of a Program

1. The Ortodoxo party split on the issue of revolution vs. politics. Carlos Márquez-Sterling, a distinguished intellectual and politician, became the leader of a conciliatory wing that advocated the acceptance of Batista's electoral plan.

2. See Hugh Thomas, *Cuba: The Pursuit of Freedom* (New York: Harper & Row, 1971), pp. 778–779, 884, 961; Alberto Baeza Flores, *Las cadenas vienen de lejos* (Mexico City: Editorial Letras, 1960), pp. 353–354.

3. In August 1955, for instance, several insurrectional groups connected with the Auténtico party were ready to start action in concert with the FEU. The final order was expected from Prío in Miami. It never came. Instead Prío announced a change to political plans "because conditions were not yet ripe for insurrection." See Baeza Flores, *Las cadenas*, p. 343.

4. Mario Llerena, "Queja contra la *intelligentzia* cubana," *Bohemia*, 1 June 1947 (my first contribution to *Bohemia*); Jorge Mañach, "Las cuentas que nos piden," *Bohemia*, 8 June 1947; Juan Marinello, "Del balcón a la nube," *Bohemia*, 15 June 1947 (Marinello intervened in the exchange, disputing both my views and Mañach's).

5. See Theodore Draper, *Castroism: Theory and Practice* (New York: Praeger, 1965), pp. 5–6.

6. I did write a proposal for educational reform in Cuba. The first part appeared in a review published by Cuban exiles in Mexico, one of whose editors was Teresa Casuso.

7. The title *Aldabonazo* (a knock at the door) was a reminder of the word used by Eddy Chibás in his last radio speech on 5 August 1951, just before he committed suicide. The official organ of the Castro regime also adopted the title *Revolución*, before switching to *Granma*.

## 3. Enter the American Press

1. See Teresa Casuso, *Cuba and Castro* (New York: Random House, 1961), p. 117.

2. See Nathaniel Weyl, *Red Star over Cuba* (New York: Devin-Adair, 1960), pp. 8–13.

3. See Hugh Thomas, *Cuba: The Pursuit of Freedom* (New York: Harper & Row, 1971), pp. 824–844.

4. Ibid., p. 868.

5. It has often been remarked that as a guerrilla Castro avoided exposing himself in direct combat, always using his telescopic rifle to shoot from a safe distance. See Weyl, *Red Star over Cuba*, pp. 151–154.

6. See Thomas, *Cuba*, pp. 917–918.

7. Castro's school-cities became reality soon after he came to power. "Many children . . . are taken away from home to go to the secondary boarding schools against their wills, and all teaching is carried out under the shadow of the regime's slogan for youth—*Estudio, Trabajo, Fusil* (Study, Work, the Rifle)" (ibid., pp. 1427–1428).

8. A revised version of the economic thesis appeared later in *Pensamiento político, económico y social de Fidel Castro* (Havana: Editorial Lex, 1959).

9. The Platt Amendment to the U.S. Army Appropriations Bill of 1901, giving the United States the right to intervene in Cuba's internal affairs, was forced into the Cuban constitution and became part of a permanent treaty between the United States and Cuba. The Platt Amendment was abrogated in 1934 as part of Franklin Roosevelt's Good Neighbor Policy.

10. Frank País, the son of a Baptist minister in Santiago, seems to have been a young patriot of genuinely democratic ideals.

11. The Civic Resistance Movement was a typical front organization under the direct control of the 26 of July Movement.

12. An assistant of Ruby Hart Phillips, who for many years was the *New York Times* correspondent in Havana, confided to a bookseller by the name of García that the NBC reporters were interested in having a secret interview with a leader of the opposition. Mr. García, with whom I was acquainted, suggested my name.

13. Robert Taber, as we shall see later, became deeply involved in the activities of the Castro movement and wrote a book about it, *M26: The Biography of a Revolution* (New York: Lyle Stuart, 1961).

14. Luis Amado-Blanco, a practicing dentist, was also for many years a theater and film critic for *Información*, a Havana daily. A close friend of Raúl Roa, he was named ambassador to Portugal by the revolutionary government, and was later transferred to the Vatican.

## 4. A Taste of the Underground

1. When the revolution came to power, Hernández, an auto mechanic with scarcely an elementary school education, ascended the bureaucratic ladder in the foreign service and for a few years was Cuban ambassador to Outer Mongolia. He appears to hold no important post now.

2. The "Manifiesto de la Sierra Maestra" may be found in Fidel Castro, *La Revolución cubana: Escritos y discursos*, ed. Gregorio Selser (Buenos Aires: Editorial Palestra, 1960), pp. 119–124 (cited in Theodore Draper, *Castroism: Theory and Practice* [New York: Praeger, 1965], p. 12n).

3. Raúl Castro's personal record was not necessarily unknown but, like so many other things, passed unnoticed until the radical course of the revolution and his own notoriety brought it into focus. Then it was remembered that, even before the Moncada episode in 1953, Raúl had been a communist sympathizer. In February 1953, for instance (just a few months before the Moncada assault), he had attended a Communist-front youth congress in Vienna, then traveled to Bucharest and Prague. On his way home he was accompanied by two Guatemalan Communists, and shortly after his arrival in Havana in June 1953 he sought membership in the Cuban Communist Youth. There is every probability, therefore, that five years later, as a major of the rebel forces in the Sierra Maestra and a member of the

Dirección Nacional of the 26 of July Movement, he was already a member of the Communist party, and that in this he was not alone.

4. Dr. Martínez Páez was named minister of health in the 1959 Urrutia cabinet. After holding the post for a brief period, he all but disappeared from the public scene.

5. See *Life,* 27 May 1957. A much more detailed version of the article appeared in the Spanish issue of *Life* a few days later. CBS aired a special program of Taber and Hoffmann's films titled "The Story of Cuba's Jungle Fighters."

6. At Franqui's request, I had written the editorial as well as several other articles for that issue of *Revolución.* None of them were signed.

7. After being in exile in Panama and Mexico, José (Pepe) Garcerán went clandestinely to Cuba with a small group that landed somewhere near Santiago in Oriente. They immediately clashed with government forces and Garcerán was killed.

8. Among my papers I have a copy of a communiqué from the Dirección Nacional of the 26 of July Movement, dated 3 November 1957 and received in New York, informing me of the expulsion of René Rodríguez from the movement "for acts of indiscipline and for having cashed a bad check for personal benefit using the credit of the Revolution." To the best of my knowledge, however, Rodríguez's expulsion was never actually made effective, and at this writing he is still in the high echelons of the revolutionary regime.

9. Heliodoro Martínez Junco, M.D., is at present minister of health in the Castro government.

10. Although the Ortodoxo party was rather conservative in general outlook, several well-known communist sympathizers served on its executive committee, among them Vicentina Antuña, professor of Latin at the University of Havana, who later occupied a high position in the Ministry of Education; Eduardo Corona, a lawyer, named ambassador to Ecuador by the revolutionary government; and Salvador Massip, a professor of geography at the university, who became ambassador to Mexico.

## 5. *The Manifesto That Was Not*

1. See Jaime Suchlicki, *University Students and Revolution in Cuba* (Coral Gables: University of Miami Press, 1969), pp. 67–98.

2. Miret confirmed this version to me in Mexico. See also Hugh Thomas, *Cuba: The Pursuit of Freedom* (New York: Harper & Row, 1971), p. 837.

3. Carleton Beals, "Rebels without a Cause," *Nation,* 184 (29 June 1957):560–568. A later issue of the same publication carried a letter from Beals to the editor. Its first paragraph said: "Since my article, The New Crime of Cuba [Part I], appeared in your issue of June 29, I have received via Mexico the text of a manifesto issued in the name of The 26 of July Movement, the largest of the groups backing Fidel Castro in Cuba. Entitled *Nuestra Razón* (Our Reason), the document supplies the ideological background to the Cuban revolt which I think it important for your readers to know. The following, then, is a summary of the text . . ." (*Nation,* 185 [21 September 1957]:140).

4. This was a private letter (not to be confused with the one cited in the preceding note) dated 20 July 1957 and addressed to Mr. Carey McWilliams, editor of *The Nation.*

5. Mañach had been one of the three members of the academic panel that examined my doctoral dissertation ("Jefferson and Religious Liberty in Virginia") at the University of Havana in 1947.

6. Among the organizations represented in the Civic Institutions were the medical and law schools, the National Council of Evangelical Churches, the Masons,

and the Lyceum. These civic groups played a prominent role in the opposition and thus attained marked political significance toward the end of the Batista regime.

7. I often heard it said that one of Castro's favorite books was *Mein Kampf.*

8. Che Guevara had not yet emerged as the important figure he later became in the movement.

9. See Enrique González Pedrero, *La revolución cubana* (Mexico City: Escuela Nacional de Ciencias Políticas, 1959), pp. 89–130.

## 6. Revolution vs. Politics

1. When Castro broke with the Junta de Liberación Cubana at Miami in December 1957, Chomón denounced him in the severest terms. A personal rival of Fidel for years, Chomón planned to launch a countercoup shortly after Castro entered Havana in January 1959 on the grounds that the DR had been ignored in the newly formed government. Soon, however, he became a Castro supporter and a member of the Communist party. He has held several positions in the revolutionary government and for some time was ambassador to Moscow.

2. Gutiérrez was one of the signers of an agreement between the Auténticos, under Prío, and the Ortodoxos, headed by Millo Ochoa, in Montreal in 1953. The so-called Pacto de Montreal between the two hitherto bitter political adversaries was aimed at forcing Batista to restore the political rights granted by the 1940 Constitution.

3. Both Nuiry and Fernández became Castro followers at the advent of the revolutionary government. While Nuiry took some minor post in the administration and soon faded into obscurity, as did Prendes, Omar Fernández ascended to important positions in the Communist regime, including minister of transport.

4. The expression "9 March" was often used to indicate the status quo before the Batista coup of 10 March 1952.

5. Yáñez Pelletier, a black, became one of Fidel's personal bodyguards in 1959. Having shown his dislike of communism, however, he was later arrested and tortured by the G-2, Castro's secret police. See Alberto Baeza Flores, *Las cadenas vienen de lejos* (Mexico City: Editorial Letras, 1960), p. 318. At this writing Yáñez is said to be near death in one of Cuba's political prisons.

6. Daniel was the nom de guerre of René Ramos Latour, a major of the rebel forces who had taken the place of Frank País after the latter was killed in Santiago on July 30. Ramos was also a member of the Dirección Nacional.

7. Chibás had been arrested as a result of his opposition activities. After his release he went into exile in the United States. See *New York Times,* 1 September 1957, p. 3; 1 November 1957, p. 7.

8. The others were Victor Buschman and Michael L. Garney. See Hugh Thomas, *Cuba: The Pursuit of Freedom* (New York: Harper & Row, 1971), p. 934.

9. In its proposition number 2 the Sierra Manifesto suggested the "designation of a person to head the provisional government whose election, as proof of the sincerity and impartiality of the opposition leaders as to who should be appointed, is to be left to the Civic Institutions."

10. The title of the *Cuba Libre* article was "Socioeconomic Objectives of the 26 of July." The same issue also carried a summary of *Nuestra Razón,* together with a facsimile of the booklet's conver.

## 7. The Turning Point

1. Castro frequently bypassed his organization's established channels and commissioned various individuals to carry out special assignments abroad. Since the

Committee in Exile was seldom advised about these special missions, the lines of authority frequently became confused.

2. Massip was for many years professor of geography at the University of Havana. Formerly a member of the Auténtico party (he was ambassador to Mexico during the Grau San Martín administration), he followed Eddy Chibás when the latter split from the Auténticos and formed the Ortodoxo party. Massip, who became a member of the Ortodoxo executive council, seems to have been the typical fellow traveler up to the time Castro came to power. He then embraced the Communist regime and was for some time Cuban ambassador to Poland.

3. Raúl Primelles, a distant cousin of Eddy Chibás, was a colorless Ortodoxo politician. At the beginning of the Castro government, Primelles was named to a secondary post with the Cuban UN delegation. Although apparently not originally a Communist, Primelles is said to have bowed to the Communists because, as he put it, "one has to eat."

4. At the triumph of the Castro revolution Bisbé became a follower of the new regime. He was named chief of the Cuban delegation to the United Nations, where he remained until his sudden death in 1966.

## 8. The Making of an Image

1. A rebel captain from Che Guevara's regiment by the name of Jorge Alvarez, who had been my pupil in our hometown elementary school, told me that he had taken part in a discussion with Castro in the city of Santa Clara when the rebel forces were on their way to Havana after Batista had fled the country. They were casually talking about the composition of the new government to be set up, suggesting names. Alvarez, unaware that I had left the organization, asked Castro, "*Comandante,* what about Llerena?" Castro replied contemptuously, "Nah . . . ese es un falsete" ("That's a false one").

2. U.S. House of Representatives, 85th Cong., 2d sess., 20 March 1958, *Congressional Record,* 104:4407–4408.

3. Ibid., 26 March 1958, pp. 4797–4799.

4. See *New York Times,* 28 March 1958, p. 1; 3 April, p. 1.

## 9. The Ideological Enigma

1. See Hugh Thomas, *Cuba: The Pursuit of Freedom* (New York: Harper & Row, 1971), p. 1005.

2. The strike was finally scheduled for April 9. It failed miserably. For details of this episode see Thomas, *Cuba,* chap. 81.

3. Congressman Manuel de Jesús León Ramírez of Manzanillo, a member of the Liberal party (not "liberal" in the American sense), one of the four groups in the government coalition.

4. In the late 1930s, for tactical purposes, the Communist party organized a front party called the Partido Unión Revolucionaria (PUR). They thus were able to campaign with two slates of candidates and win the votes of many people who would never have voted for a candidate labeled "Communist." See Thomas, *Cuba,* pp. 706–715.

5. See ibid., p. 1002.

6. Hugh Thomas (ibid., p. 822) finds in certain passages of Castro's 26 *cartas del presidio* (Havana, 1960) something "which recalls some of the better passages in the works of José Antonio Primo de Rivera [the Spanish Falange hero] . . ." Thomas adds: "At the rally on 28 January 1953 to commemorate the centenary of Martí's birth, Castro had led, he said, 'an erect group of ex-students and others in

military-style parade'—again an expression which perhaps owed something to José Antonio." Thomas includes a footnote that says: "For what it is worth, Pardo Llada [a controversial radio commentator turned politician and then Castroist] later said that he found Primo de Rivera's complete works in Castro's camp in the Sierra Maestra (*Bohemia Libre*, December 1961)." As mentioned elsewhere, Cubans who have known Castro since his student years have told me that he always took a marked copy of Hitler's *Mein Kampf* wherever he went.

7. See Thomas, *Cuba*, p. 812.

8. Theodore Draper, to me the most perceptive of the commentators on the essence of Castroism, has said: "Historically . . . Castroism is a leader in search of a movement, a movement in search of power, and power in search of an ideology. . . . Castro's ideology has never come out of himself. He has only produced a 'road to power,' which has attached itself to different ideologies. He won power with one ideology and has held it with another. . . . Castro did not have an ideological core of his own" (*Castroism: Theory and Practice* [New York: Praeger, 1965], pp. 44–48).

## 10. The Guevaras

1. After being Guevara's constant companion for several years, Hilda married him in Mexico in May 1955. They had at least one child, a girl.

2. I met Bayo during my brief visit to New York in February 1957 to make arrangements for the mailing to Cuba of offset copies of the Matthews articles on Castro and the Sierra Maestra guerrillas. Bayo maintained contact with some of the *fidelista* groups in the city. After I returned in October as an exile, Bayo, by now in Mexico, wrote hailing my appointment as public relations director and offering his cooperation.

3. See Teresa Casuso, *Cuba and Castro* (New York: Random House, 1961), p. 117.

4. The non-Marxist character of Apra's ideology is well recognized. Richard Lee Clinton, professor of political science at the University of North Carolina, writes in "Apra: An Appraisal," *Journal of Inter-American Studies and World Affairs*, 12 (April 1970): 284: "Having forsworn allegiance to pure Marxist doctrine, Apra was decidedly not a class-based party, as some have mistakenly asserted. . . ."

5. Jules Dubois, a long-time correspondent for the *Chicago Tribune*, established close contact with Cuban exiles in Miami in the late 1950s and for a time seemed to be sympathetic to the Castro movement. Later, however, Dubois wrote a book that reflected his disillusionment: *Fidel Castro: Rebel-Liberator or Dictator?* (Indianapolis: Bobbs-Merrill, 1959).

## 11. The Confrontation

1. Castro's deep resentment at the failure of the politicians, particularly Prío, to be more generous with their money surfaces again and again.

2. As a result of those contacts, Carlos Rafael Rodríguez, on behalf of the Central Committee of the Cuban Communist party, went up to the Sierra Cristal in Oriente early in July 1958 to see Raúl and then proceeded to the Sierra Maestra, where he held talks with Fidel and, presumably, Che Guevara. (The rebel advance westward started in August.)

3. In 1959 Sergio Rojas Santamarina was named ambassador to London by President Urrutia. Rojas soon broke with the Castro regime, however, when he realized the extreme radical nature of the revolution.

4. In November 1958 President Larrazábal sent an airplane with an arms ship-

ment directly to the Sierra Maestra. Luis Buch and Manuel Urrutia traveled on that plane.

## 12. Not on That Bandwagon

1. With Haydée Santamaría in Miami, she became the new logical channel for all communication, in both directions, between the Committee in Exile and the leaders in Cuba. I have long suspected that my correspondence with the Sierra Maestra at this stage was either deliberately delayed or retained altogether.

2. A copy of this release was sent to me by Representative Charles O. Porter, who at my request had written to the State Department concerning the arms shipments to Cuba.

3. Jay Mallin, *Strategy for Conquest* (Coral Gables, Fla.: University of Miami Press, 1970), p. 284.

4. See ibid., pp. 300–311.

5. My excessive sportsmanship was a foolish mistake. Having learned of my resignation, Llanusa and his friends attempted to make it appear that I had been expelled. They were unsuccessful.

6. Castro's own explanation, in a television speech nearly three years after he assumed power, was that he had been "an apprentice Marxist-Leninist since my student days" and that "having progressively become more experienced, I have become a better Marxist and shall remain so until the day of my death." See *Revolución* (Havana), 2 December 1961.

7. Interestingly enough, the same phenomenon is pointed out by a British author in reference to the state of mind of a segment of the Russian population during the days that preceded the fall of Tsar Nicholas in 1917. Edward Crankshaw describes those who served as steppingstones for the "cultivated Marxists and Socialist Revolutionaries grouped around Lenin" as an "anonymous and growing host of devoted, angry, gentle, confused, humanitarian idealists, many of them women, who wore out their lives and risked their freedom . . . in the name of a revolutionary movement from which they would have shrunk in horror had they been given an inkling of its future" (*The Shadow of the Winter Palace* [New York: Viking Press, 1976], p. 385).

## Appendix A

1. After he had been in power for some time, Castro revealed that his behavior had consistently been the exact opposite of that indicated by Martí. "On 2 December [1961]," says Hugh Thomas, "he explained to a somewhat surprised nation in a television speech that he had been for many years an apprentice Marxist-Leninist at least, even at the university, that he and his comrades had in the 1950s consciously disguised their radical views in order to gain power . . ." (*Cuba: The Pursuit of Freedom* [New York: Harper & Row, 1971], p. 1373).

2. Interestingly, Castro apparently felt no compunction about attacking "gangsterism" in a document addressed to people who were quite familiar with his own curriculum vitae.

3. Most revolutionary groups were thinking in terms not of popular revolt but of a countercoup—a tenth of March in reverse—aimed at the vital centers of government. Thus the attack of 13 March 1957 on the presidential palace. The idea was called *plan de ataque a la cabeza* (attack at the top) and essentially consisted of training select groups of men, storing large caches of arms in strategic places, and waiting for a propitious opportunity to start the action. So many details had to be at-

tended to, however, and so many circumstances were involved that the right moment very seldom presented itself. When it did, the authorities usually got wind of what was afoot, and the leaders were arrested and the arms confiscated.

4. Castro apparently wanted to give the impression of cooperation among a number of groups. Actually both the Civic Resistance Movement and the National Labor Front (FON) were deliberately created subdivisions—in short, front organizations—of the 26 of July Movement.

5. Castro alludes here to a provision of the 1940 Constitution which called for the oldest judge of the Supreme Court to assume the executive office in the event that the normal presidential succession was precluded by a grave national crisis.

6. This statement is untrue. The working class as such was never in sympathy with the Castro movement and did not respond to its invitations and propaganda, as witness the costly failure of the general strike called by the 26 of July Movement for April 1958. In fact, organized labor supported Batista to the end. For a documented and penetrating analysis of this and other aspects of the Cuban revolutionary process, see Theodore Draper, *Castroism: Theory and Practice* (New York: Praeger, 1965).

## Appendix B

1. In addition to the failure of the April general strike, there had been setbacks in the military field.

2. Raúl Chibás and Felipe Pazos spent some time with Castro during the summer of 1957. In July the three jointly signed the Sierra Manifesto.

3. The barb is primarily directed at former President Prío's Auténticos. Castro was perpetually resentful of millionaire Prío, who was not, in Castro's view, generous enough with his money.

4. Castro is probably alluding here to Léster Rodríguez, who was in frequent contact with Prío during the junta period (see chap. 6).

5. This was simply not true. It was an open secret that frequent arms shipments—usually, it is true, very small—were sent to the Castro forces in Cuba from several exile sources.

6. One more example of Castro's "special missions" outside the organization's regular channels.

7. Bebo Hidalgo was supposed to take Rodríguez's place in the Committee in Exile. He never had the slightest contact with the committee as such.

8. Although Castro is announcing the decision reached at the Sierra Maestra meeting the previous month in favor of a "revolutionary government," he still seems to be under the lingering influence of the traditional "provisional" concept.

9. Aware of the impending doom of the Batista regime, a few members of the judiciary, a class that traditionally sided with power, resigned early in 1958—a clear indication of how deeply demoralized the government already was.

10. Not until late May or early June 1958 did I learn that some Cubana de Aviación pilots who made the regular commercial flights between Havana and New York had been given a secret code and were serving as agents of the 26 of July Movement. Once I was called in cloak-and-dagger fashion to a New York hotel room to receive a message from Cuba for the Committee in Exile. It turned out to be something of minor importance.

# Index

## THE UNSUSPECTED REVOLUTION

Designed by R. E. Rosenbaum.

Composed by Vail-Ballou Press, Inc., in 10 point VIP Primer, 2 points leaded, with display lines in Helvetica Bold and Helvetica Black.

Printed offset by Vail-Ballou Press on Warren's Olde Style Wove, 60 pound basis.

Bound by Vail-Ballou Press in Joanna book cloth and stamped in All Purpose foil.

**Library of Congress Cataloging in Publication Data**
**(For library cataloging purposes only)**

Llerena, Mario.
    The unsuspected revolution.

    Includes bibliographical references and index.
    1. Cuba—History—1933–1959.  2. Cuba—History—1959–      3. Llerena,
    Mario.   4. Revolutionists—Cuba—Biography.   I. Title.
F1787.5.L55        972.91'063        77-3119
ISBN 0-8014-1094-0